Think Like a Tycoon

*Inflation Can Make You Rich
Through Taxes and Real Estate*

Bill "Tycoon" Greene

Cartoons by Edward Barker

Newly Revised and Updated Edition
Previously Titled *Two Years for Freedom*
in 5 Earlier Editions

FAWCETT COLUMBINE   •   NEW YORK

WARNING

As this book goes to press, some idiot who attended a free lecture is threatening to sue me. He quit his job to become an overnight real estate tycoon after hearing me on the radio. Without job, money, credit (and I might add, brains) no one has been willing to sell him his first property. In my Tycoon Class and here I say, **don't give up a regular job or income until your real estate empire has grown to sufficient size to supply the cash flow you need to live on and support your family. Your outside income provides stability and borrowing power needed at the early stages.**

All of the opinions given here and in my talks are based upon my personal experiences and research. When applied with common sense, I believe many of my ideas will be very helpful. **But the reader must necessarily proceed at his own risk.** Opinions expressed herein are often unconventional and controversial. It is recommended that **before making any deals or contracts involving legal or tax consequences, professional advice and counsel be obtained.** Don't sue me if they throw you out of the casino.

Sincerely,
Bill Greene

A Fawcett Columbine Book

Published by Ballantine Books

Copyright © 1980 by Bill "Tycoon" Greene. Previously published as TWO YEARS FOR FREEDOM. Preview edition, November 1978. First edition, May 1979. Second edition, June 1979. Third edition, October 1979. Fourth edition, January 1980. Fifth edition (revised), September 1981.

New material copyright © 1982 by Bill "Tycoon" Greene

ISBN 9780-449-90068-0
This edition published by arrangement with Harbor Publishing.

Manufactured in the United States of America

144915995

Contents

Introduction

If you enjoy dull, theory-filled books about real estate, Bill Greene's *Think Like a Tycoon* isn't for you. When I got my copy, I couldn't put it down until I finished it at 2 A.M. Its pages are filled with Greene's practical, profit-motivated, and realistic philosophy about real estate investing today.

This is a lively how-to-do-it book which explains in simple, easy-to-understand language, how real estate can be your vehicle to accomplish your financial goals. Whether you just want to buy your own home or become a real estate tycoon like Greene, you'll find this is a "fun book" which is deadly serious about what's involved— gaining your financial freedom in today's inflationary world.

Greene's story of how he started in real estate and acquired over $1,000,000 in property equities is outlined on the pages of this book. His style of telling how the reader can accomplish the same thing is unique. By use of funny cartoons and lively writing, Greene explains why real estate ownership is the best (and perhaps the only) way to (1) legally avoid paying income taxes and (2) build your estate and financial security at the same time.

This book is autobiographical. But it shows how the reader can apply the same principles that Greene used to acquire and profit from real estate. Greene's unusual personality comes through to the reader; by the time you finish the book you'll feel you've known him all your life. The important result, however, is the reader is made to feel that if Greene can accomplish real estate success, then anyone can.

While this book is entertaining, its main purpose is to give the reader a blueprint of the steps to acquire and profit from real estate today. Whether you're a real estate novice or a long-time professional property investor, you're going to enjoy and profit from this book.

Robert J. Bruss
Syndicated real estate columnist

CHAPTER 1
The Buck Starts Here

Getting rich is fun. More fun than being rich. That's why we'll start with a game.

Sit down in a comfortable place. Pretend that someone you know and love is giving you $200.00.

What will you do with it?
How will you enjoy it?
There is no right answer.
Just close your eyes. Take a while.
Do not turn the page until you have mentally spent that money.

Drift off . . . daydream . . .
Spend that money . . .

Have fun!

Is this what you did with $200?

A good drunk?

New camera, new watch,
weekend vacation?

Night on the town?

Get high?

Next, try it with $20,000.

Would you spend it on a terrific car and a trip around the world?

Now suppose that someone gave you

$2,000,000.00

Yes, TWO MILLION DOLLARS.

What would you do with it?

Think about it.

On the next page is the answer most of my students gave . . .

"Give it to the bank to manage!"

But if a trust officer is so good at investing,
how come he's a wage-slave?

Probably you were a dummy!

There are *right* answers!
All the answers you saw were wrong!
Daydreaming about how you will spend money will
assure that you stay on the
wage-slave treadmill all your life.

If you are not financially independent now, part of
the reason is that you squander seed money—
on trips, presents, consumer goods, trinkets and junk
you don't need.

**The first barrier between you and a net worth of
a million or more is the "consumer mentality."**

In the real world you can get $200 ahead with ease.
But if your first thought was how to "consume" your
first $200 you'll never be worth $20,000, or $2,000,000.

**Nevermore think of what you are going to spend money on!
Small sums are the seeds that grow into great fortunes.**

Concentrate on:

What useful products can you produce?

What services can you provide?

What needs can you fill?

These thoughts will help make you a millionaire.

CHAPTER 2
The Tycoon Mentality

If you sincerely want to become a Tycoon, you must **think like a Tycoon.** You can think like a Tycoon by reading this chapter very carefully. Though I will be talking mainly about real estate, the principles covered here apply to all forms of managing your money. Living a good life or being exceptionally successful in business requires more than a can of beer, a TV set, and thou.

Tycoon is a Japanese word meaning *ty*—great, and *coon*—shogun, a military leader. A Tycoon is someone with ambition and drive who has placed himself in a position of importance. In the case of a great general like Patton, or a great boxer like Muhammad Ali—or anyone great—one characteristic is universal:

Great people thoroughly enjoy what they do. To be great at what you do, you must believe that what you do is great fun.

An episode of the "Peanuts" cartoon strip once showed Charlie Brown playing with half a yo-yo. It was broken. But he was having a good time dangling it, bouncing it up and down the wall, and playing "fetch" with his dog Snoopy. Suddenly Charlie Brown's girlfriend Lucy comes along: "You stupid dummy," she says, "You can't have a good time with half a yo-yo. Everybody knows that." Poor, dejected Charlie Brown throws his toy on the ground. "I'm sorry," replies the little boy. "I didn't know I could not enjoy myself with a broken yo-yo."

The story has a moral for prospective Tycoons. Fuzzy-thinking leftists and other depressing types like Lucy have convinced many people

6

that making money these days is abnormal—or, at best, dull. They would like to make us capitalists feel guilty for becoming rich and—shudder—actually having fun making it.

Ignore these people. Fuzzy-thinking leftists fail to realize that capitalists don't just rake in money and count it—bank tellers do that. A Tycoon is involved in something creative and beautiful: He (or she) must invariably bring forth upon the world a product or service that people want. A "something" that people willingly part with their earnings or savings for. He's not ashamed to take their money because (unlike forcibly extracted tax money—which pays for dubious social services or more tax collectors that nobody wants) a capitalist exists for The People. He works for The People. He serves them only so long as his products or services meet their needs. A Tycoon needs The People as much as they need him. However, being creative—like an artist, musician, or new mother—a Tycoon has more fun at living than the wage-slave at his routine job. Tycoons enjoy doing what they can be great at—providing an abundance of goods and services that people want and can afford. Every Tycoon has an invisible directive flashing like a neon sign in his brain:

FIND A NEED AND FILL IT

A Tycoon doesn't count his money every day to measure his success. Dollars are just evidence of votes from the previous day, votes of confidence in the particular goods or services that the Tycoon is providing. But a Tycoon gets his confidence from within himself, not through these dollar votes. Any businessman who wants to keep on being successful, however, must continue to deliver needed goods and services, or the people will vote their dollars for a new Tycoon.

Some individuals, of course, can never become Tycoons. That's because they thwart themselves right from the beginning. They make excuses: "I'm not smart enough." "I don't have enough money to start." "I have no business sense." These are all cop-outs. With the right attitude, anyone, including you, can become a Tycoon. If you think you're dumb—relax. Most Tycoons have average IQ's. The straight-A students are too busy getting PhD's and looking for teaching jobs to make it in business. *You* can begin with little or no money, and become a multimillionaire. Most of today's industrialists were poor a few years ago. So not having any money, the second excuse, doesn't wash either. As for having no business sense—well, you're reading this book. That's pretty sensible. Whatever acumen you lacked before today, you'll have by tomorrow.

Other individuals wait until they are *already* Tycoons before they thwart themselves. All people should learn from their own mistakes, but you can benefit more cheaply from *other* people's mistakes. Look at what some successful Tycoons who *failed* have in common: Businessmen who have made it big once and then go downhill have frequently over-expanded. They got careless and didn't attend to emergencies or details. They didn't have *time* anymore. In contrast, a successful Tycoon leaves nothing to chance. He makes time to watch over his investments or hires competent help to do it for him. It's much easier to be extremely successful on a small scale when you're starting out in familiar territory than it is when you have the riches of a Howard Hughes or a J. Paul Getty. Does that surprise you? Allow me to illustrate: Once a real estate deal was proposed to me in Reno, Nevada. The big selling point was that one of the richest men in the world, J. Paul Getty (who made his fortune in oil), had taken 25% interest in it. Therefore (I was told) I should be willing to take 10% (ten "points" in Tycoon talk), because Getty was pretty smart and wouldn't have had a 25% interest in a deal if it wasn't any good. The deal went sour shortly after that. I should have known it would! Now when I hear that *extremely* rich people have an interest in a project, I run the other way.

That sort of deal usually is a tax shelter that won't make money for anyone but the promoters. Super-rich people seldom have time to investigate new ventures; they are too busy keeping what they have to be effective in fields outside their immediate area of expertise. I am sure that if J. Paul Getty had a good oil deal that he investigated and put together personally, he would have taken all of it for himself and not sold any points to outside investors. But the fact that Getty, a super-rich Texas oilman, living in London, was investing in a Nevada real estate deal, probably meant that he relied on someone else's judgment. That "someone else" would not have sought me out as an investor if it had been a super deal.

Tycoons who have been very successful *often* make bad investments. They don't attend to the details of investigating a situation as thoroughly as they would have done when they were starting out. The best deals are the deals that you go out and find yourself. Not prepackaged "no work, no worry" deals all wrapped up with a Red Ribbon. Where all you do is write a check, that Red Ribbon will only tie you in financial knots.

> **The Red Ribbon Rule:**
> If a deal sounds too good to be true,
> it *is* too good to be true!

Another common characteristic of a Tycoon destined to go downhill is that he feels "too important" to attend to humble work. He passes by one of his properties, for example. In the old days he would have taken time to pick up junk spilled by the trash collectors and put it in proper cans. At the very least he'd have given the janitor or the tenants a gentle reminder to clean up their act. But now, looking at the mess, he doesn't notice. He's too busy whizzing off to negotiate a pie-in-the-sky deal. A lack of pride in ownership means the start of decline—the beginning of the end. When you're no longer concerned with detail (and willing to see to it yourself), you're heading for trouble. If an owner doesn't care anymore, his business goes to pot.

Another characteristic of aging Tycoons is a sudden fear of competition. When new at the game, competition was a challenge. The embryo Tycoon stole his competitors' best ideas and avoided their mistakes. Determined to beat the competition one way or another, the upstart had to come up with innovative methods. He worked at it all day and Christmas too. However, once on top, some Tycoons start to worry about all the young upstarts moving into "their" backyards—as if it were an exclusive preserve. In the case of manufacturers it is "cheap foreign goods." "Why," they worry, "are those Sayonara Sleeping Pills becoming more popular than my Yankee Doodle Doze?"

Instead of trying to produce a new or better product, some old Tycoons retreat into deep leather chairs at the Union League Club. Old, has-been Tycoons never die, they just become ineffectual aristocrats. At worst, a formerly successful Tycoon these days becomes a "gold bug." A "gold bug" is someone who buries or stashes most of his assets in a Swiss bank in gold. Of course in a nation run by irresponsible politicians who print and spend money like toilet paper, building personal gold reserves, to a reasonable level, is only prudent. But when you start concentrating on reducing the size of your business operations and finding ways of becoming 100% liquid, then you can produce no products, no progress, and no profits. The entire French nation nearly collapsed economically in the pre–De Gaulle era because a large number of French people (perhaps for good reasons) chose to take their wealth, convert it into gold coins, and bury them in their gardens. Buried gold coins (while providing some degree of safety and security in times of political turmoil or revolution) will *not* make you rich. A business operation is like a vine. Once it stops growing, it dies.

What are characteristics that help a Tycoon succeed? A Tycoon on the way up is always able to motivate his staff, partners, and the people who work with him. When he is big, an enthusiastic, loyal staff will be needed more than ever. But sometimes a Tycoon forgets his staff. Don't forget—when you become valuable in terms of dollars, your staff becomes equally so in terms of support. Some employees respond best to praise and titles; others, to money. Imaginative gifts or bonuses can score you more points than money! How about a round-trip ticket to Hawaii for your secretary or property manager? The successful Tycoon always keeps thinking of ways to put a smile on the faces of his Team.

Some Tycoons believe that inspiring fear in their associates is an effective method of getting them to work. I strongly disagree. Fear is good only for incompetents, because only incompetents are afraid of getting fired. If an employee or business associate is good enough, he can always find work with the Tycoon down the road. Thus, if you can't make the work situation pleasant for those who contribute to it, something is wrong. You can never get the best out of employees through fear. Remember: Motivation is better accomplished by the carrot than the stick.

On the home front, the same rule applies. Keep the peace. Give recognition and daily compliments to the people around you—your children, your spouse, your friends. Make the people you know feel good about themselves. If they feel good about themselves, they'll work harder and feel better about you. If you're making a compliment, don't make the mistake of taking it back. I've heard people say things like, "Gee, you look younger. Are you dyeing your hair?" Say it and *feel* it. If you personally get a compliment, don't argue. Accept it graciously; a simple "thank you" will do. So make the people in your family and organization feel secure. If you feel it, say "I love you." Give praise and recognition generously! Tell them, "I really like being with you." Or, "I like working with you." Give the reasons. Your own life will be better if those you live and work with know that you like them. Tell them often. If you have to be critical, try to be positive in your criticism. When the toast is served burned to a crisp, say, "I really enjoyed the breakfast, honey, but next time around could you set the toaster a bit lighter?" For business associates just substitute different words. Try it—it works!

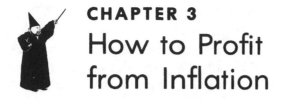

CHAPTER 3

How to Profit from Inflation

These are inflationary times, and the promise of having a million dollars twenty or thirty years from now should not dazzle you. It should not even be one of your goals, since you don't know exactly what a million dollars will be worth in terms of buying power in twenty or thirty years. If the present rates of inflation continue, by the year 2010, a million dollars will probably be one year's salary for a street-sweeper. Thus you don't really want *Money*. You want *Things*. Preferably things to own or to control that can be rented out and that will earn money while you own them. And preferably things that will not wear out, break up, or fall down too fast. In inflationary times it isn't money but wealth in other forms you want to accumulate. Anyone who keeps their money in money is getting poorer—at any interest rate they can hope to earn.

Therefore, you want plenty of debt. You want to *borrow* money to acquire *things* and also to acquire education in developing saleable skills. The fees and commissions earned as a doctor, lawyer, or plumber in your ordinary job and the rents received from your property should keep pace with inflation until the time comes when you're rich enough not to need an ordinary job. In the meantime, the money debts you have accumulated can be paid off with ever more worthless dollars. Let me explain more about debt.

Suppose you borrowed 100,000 eggs to buy an apartment building this year. With a typical loan you have thirty years to pay those eggs back. It's easy to see why real estate is such a good investment. You can estimate that thirty years hence the property may be worth a million eggs, but the debt used to finance the property will have been paid back with 20,000 eggs instead of the 100,000 eggs originally borrowed. Get the point? Borrow dollars today to buy an asset today: You pay back a lot less than you borrow in terms of real money.

Due to inflation, the quoted dollar value of all property will increase dramatically, yet you pay back debts with cheaper and cheaper dollars. With each passing year, all other things being equal, the debt you owe becomes less and less burdensome, while the property you bought becomes more and more valuable. Obviously the less money you put down to make a deal and the greater portion of the price borrowed, the more deals you will be able to make. The more buys you make, the wealthier you become. The nitty-gritty of my technique "how to buy property for little or no money down" is fully covered in the other chapters of this book.

So, in these inflationary times, a Tycoon must acquire as much property and as much debt as possible. Needless to say, there will be occasional disappointments. How can you deal with them effectively? If in real estate, you are trying to buy property, and a deal you've been negotiating falls through, there is a game or mental trick that you can play on yourself to feel better. Say this: "Had the deal closed it would have made me at least $20,000. But if ten of my no-money-down deals are rejected, I know that at least one out of twenty deals I negotiate will eventually work out. Thus, every failure, every deal that falls through, amounts to a $1,000 experience. And that's pretty good going for one morning's work." If you can think positively about what others might consider failures, the next failed deal will only encourage you to get on with it. Not dwelling on what you did wrong, but thinking about what you did *right* will soon have you scanning the classified ads again. There's an old Scottish proverb: "No man ever died from overwork." But people do die and certainly get sick from emotional problems such as anxiety or worry. These lead to ulcers and other diseases. So one of the best habits a Tycoon can develop is to laugh at his problems. Many times things will go wrong, but if you can manage to grow a funny bone, your body will never develop ulcers or high blood pressure. Take life easy. Remember, money should be thought of as gambling chips—and life as only a game.

Look back at the big tragedies of your preteenage life. Not winning the pitcher's position in the Little League—it was so important then. But does it matter now? You can laugh about it. When you were a teenager and got stood up by the Prom Queen, or were rejected as a Hamburger High cheerleader, you were miserable, right? But now it's funny. If you can cultivate the ability to laugh at your predicaments *at the time they occur,* you will be way ahead of other people who spend their time worrying, dwelling on their failures, and feeling sorry for themselves. Laugh a lot. Don't take yourself or your money too seriously!

My father knew an Italian gent named Joe Garibaldi (a fictitious name, but a real person). Joe had come to the states as an orphan, and worked at a Chicago newsstand when he was only eleven years old. In twenty years that first stand had grown into a chain. Joe, finding himself wealthy and lusty at age thirty-one, sent for a mail-order bride from his home town. She duly arrived and enjoyed living in America, being the wealthiest lady in her neighborhood. By 1929, Joe Garibaldi, like other newspaper dealers, tailors, and barbers of the era, fancied himself an expert in the stock market. He took the profits from his newspaper stands and everything else that he could borrow and invested in stocks.

We all know what happened in 1929. Joe Garibaldi went through the wringer, and by 1931 was back selling newspapers at good old newsstand number one. He took his losses like a Tycoon, realizing that it would be only a matter of time before he could repeat the wealth-building process and recoup his fortune. Yet all around him people were jumping out of windows. They didn't realize they should have thought of money only as gaming chips. If they lost their chips, the game wasn't over. Joe Garibaldi knew how to *think like a Tycoon.* To him, losing a hand meant accumulating more chips by selling papers again. He'd find another game to play someday. Not poor Mrs. Garibaldi. Joe's bride was unable to face the neighbors after having to sell the Cadillac and take in boarders. She went crazy, was put away, and to this day has never recovered from the fact that Joe lost their fortune in 1929. *She didn't know how to think like a Tycoon.*

Joe adjusted quickly. He merely reduced his expenses, got back to work and within half the amount of time it took him first time around Joe was once again prosperous. Like all Tycoons, Joe knew it's easier to make a million the second time around.

The Million-Dollar-a-Year Difference

Tycoons always have goals. Some weeks it's possible to make progress towards these goals, but some weeks, due to circumstances beyond your control, it isn't. Having no goals at all, however, is like starting in the middle of nowhere without a road map. It's impossible to know where you are or where you're going unless goals are selected, and a plan is established to give your life some positive direction. Any goal is preferable to just drifting. Selecting financial independence as a goal and thinking like a Tycoon will get you there. The first step of the Tycoon plan, then, is to decide that you want to be independently wealthy and that you'll *do* what it takes to achieve that goal. If that first decision is made, you will be independently wealthy in one to three years.

About a year ago, two people took my San Francisco *Tycoon Class.* One was Clara, a girl who sold soup wholesale to grocery stores. She did well in her job and was very effective at pushing clam chowder. Twenty-three years of age and she made $20,000 a year. A great start! At the same time, a boy we'll call Gunslinger took my class too. He got very enthusiastic about using the Tycoon techniques in real estate. He had no job, was a school drop-out, and had no real direction in life until he took the Bill Greene *Tycoon Class.* Clara was less enthusiastic about becoming a Tycoon. She continued to do well pushing fish stew, but she didn't do much about real estate. In a year, Clara looked at a total of three condominiums and eventually bought a pleasant middle-class condo apartment for $55,000. She moved into it. Period. Of course, the girl was better off than had she done nothing. But two years have now gone by. Clara still owns the one condominium she bought on a "20% down" standard deal. She now makes soup commissions of $22,000 per year, and saves little or nothing. She has an unrealized *profit* of $20,000 in the condo. Nothing wrong with that, but it's hardly spectacular.

Gunslinger, on the other hand, followed my program like a fanatic. Real estate seemed to become his reason for living. He looked at hundreds of properties and once he knew the market, began making ridiculously low or no-money-down offers on every deal he saw. Today he owns approximately eighty different buildings in central California. One year into the game, Gunslinger was a bona-fide twenty-two-year-old millionaire. One year it took him! Is that the American Dream or not?

Two people took the same class. They had the same information, the same level of intelligence. (Actually, Clara was a bit brighter.) The one you'd have expected to be more successful, a girl already earning $20,000 a year, now owns one property and has a net worth of $20,000. The boy who had no job and no assets became a millionaire in twelve months. What accounts for the difference between them?

Gunslinger got off his fanny, looked at many deals, and made lots of offers. He had motivation! Big but realistic plans! Gunslinger's goal was to be worth thirty million by the age of thirty. He acquired large amounts of property for little or no money down. A day did not go by during which he didn't make three or four offers on properties. Clara, in contrast, *already considered herself successful and didn't want to change her life drastically.* She made only one offer in an entire year, and only one deal. On that one investment she doubled her net worth. She made more than she'll save in ten years. She's very proud of her one real estate deal and is glad to have been inspired to "get into real estate" by the *Tycoon Class*. Compared to Gunslinger she's hardly a Tycoon. But who knows, maybe she'll become the first lady president of Campbell Soup some day.

If there's any moral to be drawn, it's that reading books like this and taking courses isn't going to make you a dime. But getting off your fanny, setting goals, and doing what has to be done to make it happen can result in a Million-Dollar difference. How much money you earn is solely up to *you*. Luck is for other people. When should you start this program of achieving the goals you set for yourself? I'll tell you when. Today! Every day is a new beginning, and once you have written goals, life has a purpose. Every day should be a pleasure and a challenge.

Do It Today!

As I said before, most people's problems come from "over-worry" and not over-work. They agonize about what happened in the past. But the past is over; it's finished. So forget about it and concentrate on what's happening *now*. Other people *worry* about the future. Equally unproductive! Get on with it. If worry can't be eliminated, try channeling it in constructive directions. Estimate what percentage chance there is that what you are worrying about will actually occur. For example, what is the percentage chance there will be a major earthquake in California? My research shows there has been a major earthquake about every sixty years. Therefore, viewing the situation optimistically, the possibility that it will happen next year is about one in sixty. If these odds are precarious enough to make you feel you should acquire earthquake insurance or should avoid brick properties likely to tumble down in an earthquake, then take action. Get insurance. Buy wooden houses. Taking sensible precautions in view of a reasonable estimation of risk makes sense. *Worrying about something uselessly is a waste of energy!* Worry and fear easily translate into paralysis and no action at all.

Don't Worry about It. Do Something!

Along with worry, another thing that will get in the way of success is fear of change. Change or innovation is always uncomfortable. Even going on vacation in some foreign country is a lot less comfortable than staying in Normal Town, Idaho. But if you want to grow intellectually and if you want your fortune to grow, you have not only to *accept* change, but to *seek it out*. Sure, the results are not definite. When you're a Tycoon there's no steady paycheck waiting for you at the end of each week. Tycoons must not be plagued with feelings of insecurity. If you feel secure only in a steady job that offers nothing in twenty years but a pension and a gold Timex, you are not thinking like a Tycoon. A Tycoon thrives on insecurity. He (or she) can achieve financial success in a few years far beyond what a wage-slave can expect in a lifetime.

Security is more feeling than reality, anyway. It's a state of mind. Don't forget, the pension a wage-slave earns won't support a decent standard of living at the time it becomes payable. Social Security is even worse. That's why I call it *Social Insecurity*. Subsistence isn't living. It isn't living or worth living for. Social Security provides for only a poverty-level existence. The Tycoon who acquires large amounts of income property or businesses will have the real thing: An income that keeps pace with inflation. Like love or happiness, security is a state of mind that nobody else can give you. It's a state of mind that only you can give yourself. Go out! Get a piece of the action going on all around you!

The feeling of being in a comfortable rut is not what a Tycoon wants. Naturally, there is always the problem of conflicting goals. A fat man might say, "I want a beautiful and healthy body, but I'm not going to give up eating bon-bons and potato chips. And I am not willing to exercise or diet." Obviously, if you're not going to do what is necessary to achieve a goal, you're not going to get it. It's that simple. If you can't give up a nice secure rut or a hobby that makes you feel good for a chance of making a million dollars, then you may never *get* the million dollars. You can't say, "I'd like to make a million, while keeping my present job, and still spend all my evenings and weekends sailing." If you're going to become independently wealthy within one to three years, your time must be allocated ruthlessly and you should expect to spend virtually *all* your spare hours on achieving financial independence.

Can you go halfway? Sure! It will just take longer. If, for instance, in real estate you decide to spend only Saturdays looking at new properties, it may take ten or fifteen years to get rich instead of one or two years. To my way of thinking, if a million dollars *can* be made in one or two years, it's worth spending all your spare time and energies on achieving that goal. The time to start acquiring is *now*. But *don't* quit your income-producing job until your real estate income is big enough to replace it.

A Tycoon always prepares written plans. He (or, as always, she) will schedule time, establish priorities and will stick to those objectives both long- and short-term. A Tycoon should have both a *Life Plan* and a series of five-year goals. The first five-year plan should outline what he hopes to achieve in half a decade and how he is going to do it. It should then break down into more detailed periods for the first year, namely, a monthly plan, a weekly plan, and a daily plan.

One man-with-a-plan was Frank Harris, who lived in the 19th century. One day at the age of fifteen, he sat down and mapped out his lifetime goals. He made a list of five hundred ridiculous things he wanted to do before he died. He set up his goal list in order of priority, and as the years passed he proceeded to work on them one by one. Sometimes they were prosaic goals like learning German. But other times they were glamorous or exotic things most people only dream about, like visiting every country in the world; becoming an internationally known journalist; seducing five thousand of the world's most beautiful women; becoming an American cowboy. At a ripe old age, Frank Harris died, having accomplished 90% of his five hundred objectives. His story is told in a spicy Victorian classic called *My Life, My Loves.* Good reading—even though Harris never was, nor wanted to be, a business success.

But Frank Harris was undoubtedly a success at knowing how to get the most out of life. How did he cram the adventures of five hundred men into one lifetime? By setting *goals!* By planning ahead! By plotting and working steadily to achieve those goals.

Now maybe travel bores you. Or you're allergic to horses. All you want is to be the richest man in Duluth, Minnesota. To do it, all you need is a reasonable plan. To achieve that goal your daily activities should always be related to achieving your objectives. Eventually you'll make it. If you schedule time, establish priorities, and stick to plans, there is no way you can not achieve your goals. To think like a Tycoon, however, once your plan is in effect, you must *stick to it.* You must acquire the patience to see it through, plus the flexibility to alter it if the original premise on which the plan was based changes.

There always have been, and always will be, negative people who say, "These things can't be done." Or, "You're doing it the wrong way." What you want is too "abnormal" or whatever. Remember Charlie Brown and Lucy? You must not drift, deviate, or be discouraged, regardless of what others say, do, or think about you and your goals. *You* know best. Success speaks for itself. Remember, Tycoons like us are the "doers" of the world, the caretakers of life's abundance.

Capitalists do a lot of good too. We create jobs for people less creative or dynamic than we; we produce better products, better places to live. We achieve more good than "social" engineers, academics, theorists, do-gooder social workers, or fuzzy-thinking leftists. Any, or all of whom, by the way, will criticize our actions.

The communists should only know how much they would benefit from Tycoons. If ever you visit the Soviet Union, that neon light in your head will start flashing overtime; the needs are shocking. Most apartment buildings are in the same bad shape as our worst public housing projects. Driving between Moscow and Leningrad there are no decent places to eat even borscht, much less get a cheeseburger. Oh, for one McDonald's. Functioning gas stations are hundreds of miles apart on even the most-traveled roads. Consumer goods of all types are in dreadfully short supply. If you're looking to buy chewing gum, ballpoint pens, an alarm clock, or 99% of the consumer goods we all take for granted—forget it!

Of course, while I have few kind words for the communist governments, which are the most oppressive and meet the fewest needs of their citizens, I don't have too many kind words for our own government. At this point, government officials are confiscating a big percentage of our gross national product in the form of taxes. And the things taxes pay for are almost always pure waste. What could be more useless than the billions we spent in Viet Nam? The equipment abandoned there and now owned by North Viet Nam represents the third largest arsenal in the world. If some Tycoon could arrange to buy all this army surplus back from Viet Nam and resell it to the U.S.A. (as some Tycoon eventually will do), he could make several billion on the deal. Then the U.S.A. could give it away again!

Get a Little Help from Your Friends

Have you ever heard of Reverend Ike? Reverend Ike is a black preacher who operates mostly out of New York City and talks to his congregation about material success, prosperity, and making money. One of the things he says is that you should go out of your way to cultivate successful, powerful, intelligent people. People who are the way *you'd* like to be. The Bible according to Reverend Ike says: "If you hang around street-corners with losers, you *are* a loser." You are judged by the company you keep and you'll end up with values of your peer group.

Where can you get role models if your friends are all deadbeats or jailbirds?

Interestingly enough, I found that most successful people have avidly read the biographies of other well-known people in the fields in which they are interested. One example was the late Mr. Gus Levy, an almost legendary figure on Wall Street. I was privileged to be his house guest many times and to get to know him fairly well, because his son Peter was my college roommate. While at his house one day I was surprised to see that his personal library consisted almost exclusively of the biographies of men and women who had made a success of themselves in finance, on Wall Street or in Europe. No trashy novels for him.

When I asked Mr. Levy about his choice of reading matter, the man replied, "Many of my best ideas were variations on deals I read about in historical biographies of Tycoons." Mr. Levy also told me that he learned something special from these biographies: "Virtually everyone who made a big success of themselves had been the protégé of a winner!" In his own case Gus Levy made an effort to become the protégé of the senior partner of a big respected Wall Street firm. Mr. Levy came up with some good ideas in the field of arbitrage—that is, buying and selling the same stock or commodity in two different places at the same time to take advantage of international price differences. He made the firm big trading profits by borrowing an idea from the biography of Bernard Baruch who'd made similar deals thirty years earlier. Soon Gus Levy became a senior partner of the most prestigious firm on Wall Street. He later became chairman of the Board of Governors of the New York Stock Exchange.

Mr. Levy owed a lot to the Tycoons he met only in books. Maybe you will too if you read some of the selections on my book list. Reading a selection of these books is recommended for important reasons. Potential Tycoons can not only apply the same principles these people did to make the *right* deals, but also, with the benefit of hindsight, profit from where these Tycoons went *wrong*.

In reading biographies, you should gain greater understanding of economic history and the role of the Tycoon in history. You'll learn that the possibility of acquiring great wealth in this country has been around only for the last hundred years. Before then, you had to be born with a silver spoon, or you ended up in a poverty trap. Virtually all fortunes today are made from scratch—the aristocracy's dwindling contributions to the economy consist of donating funds to the Daughters of the American Revolution. Prior to the Civil War, then, there were only about five or ten self-made millionaires in the entire U.S.A. They made their money shipping, whaling, or slave trading. Perhaps the first national property Tycoon in America was Hetty Greene (no relation to the author). She invested her small whaling fortune in industrial slums all over the U.S.A. Her real estate was low-grade, low-rent tenements. Hetty was such a tough negotiator and tightwad that she earned the nickname *The Witch of Wall Street*—the title of her biography.

Another early real estate developer was Vincent Astor, who got his grubstake together as a fur trapper. His motto was "Never Sell the

Land." He bought only first-class property in busy business locations. Both Hetty and Vincent made a hundred million dollars, when a million was really worth something.

The Civil War caused great industrial expansion in the North. Building boomed in the cities. It was a period of rapid social and economic change. The stagecoach was replaced by the iron horse as railways crisscrossed the United States. But money was made mainly by people "out of railroads" (like stock promoters) rather than by people "in" them (like investors). Bankruptcies and lawsuits were common, and wealth changed hands rapidly.

Land up until this time, don't forget, was incredibly cheap by today's standards. Roads were poor and there was so much property around that the government gave away millions of acres to homesteaders. To buy several thousand acres near a city was no big deal. But railroads meant mobility and changed the nature of the real estate market. Urban land prices soared as people moved out of the country into sooty American cities where good-paying jobs were available in steel mills and other new industries. Cornelius Vanderbilt made his first million transporting these newly mobile masses. He sent his "clipper" sailboats from Europe to New York City and from New York to California via Nicaragua. The discovery of gold near Sacramento caused the California Gold Rush, a stampede the likes of which America never saw again. Vanderbilt found a need and filled it! He made a deal with the locals in Panama to allow his passengers to cross overland on his trains and transfer to another Vanderbilt clipper waiting on the other side. The Vanderbilt clipper was faster and cheaper than going overland, and much safer than going by covered wagon. Vanderbilt made it easy for would-be Bonanza Kings to get from the East Coast to California.

Now we come to my favorite book, *The Robber Barons*. The most colorful robber baron of the 19th century was Big Jim Fisk. He was a complete opportunist. Dumb. Crude. No special talent except for making money. Jim eventually took over the Erie Railroad, and being especially fond of lady singers, built the opera house in New York City so he could become its "casting director." Unfortunately for poor Fisk, one day he got it on with a cute soprano, and ended up murdered by the lady's lover. Moral: Tycoons should steer clear of sopranos. Or anyone else with jealous lovers.

In this same era, another robber baron, John Rockefeller, made half a million in the leather business. Like all great Tycoons he then diversified. He bought oil wells and started selling kerosene, which was used for lamps. Those were the days before cars. Finding he wasn't making enough profit from kerosene—did Rocky give up? Of course not. He put his brains to work and came up with a deal that thousands have been copying ever since. What was he trying to sell? Kerosene. What uses kerosene? Lamps. So Rockefeller gave away the lamps. All over the world. The customers were so delighted with their free gift that they bought their fuel from—you guessed it— Rockefeller's Standard Oil Company. Gillette did the same thing with razor holders. And then sold his blades by the millions.

This is a valuable lesson for all modern Tycoons. Both Rockefeller and Gillette saw a need. How to fill it? By giving away another product, which depended on refills that only they sold.

This technique is still used today. Melitta coffee pots were originally designed to use no other filter papers than their own brand. So anybody using the cheap Melitta coffee pot has to buy their filters from—Melitta. The same with Hoover and their vacuum cleaner bags. Have you made your fortune today? Get your free ideas from people who have!

Biographies exist of hundreds of great Tycoons, and I highly recommend you read some of them. These men and a few women had several characteristics in common. They stole the ideas from each other. All found a need and filled it. In the case of some cosmetics magnates, they created needs. Most started from scratch. Historical biographies of Tycoons who made it are inspirational. Practical. Fun. They're also free if you go to the public library.

Besides cultivating and studying people who can do them good, another admirable characteristic of many Tycoons is that they speak well of other people. There is an old saying: "If you can't say anything good about someone—keep quiet." I've found that to minimize the number of enemies and keep friends to a maximum, it's a good idea to praise people wherever possible. If you can give someone a sincere compliment, give it! If talking about ex-lovers, ex-employers, or ex-business associates, try to be positive about them, not negative. Even if the experience you had with a particular person was unpleasant, if you speak well of them, it might get back to the person in question. They will then be more likely to speak well of you. To paraphrase the Golden Rule: Speak about others as you would have them speak about you.

Tycoons must be optimistic—about friends, about finance, about the future. That does not mean that you should ignore obvious risks, but given a choice between visualizing a future of rosy progress and one of gloomy fiascos, you will be better off viewing the future positively, and acting accordingly. The most visible business pessimists, led by Harry Browne and other predictors of disaster, are the "gold bugs." Remember them? Usually right-wing lunatic fringe types who think that the world-as-we-know-it is about to come to a grinding halt. The way to survive into the future, say the most fanatic "gold bugs," is to leave the country now or take to the hills. Bury stashes of gold coins and an arsenal or two of automatic weapons.

In my opinion, there may be a time for all that someday, but these guys are missing the biggest real estate boom in the history of the United States Sun Belt. Since the odds of a 1980–1990 economic collapse are, in my view, about 10%, I would spend only a very small portion of my energies on disaster preparation. I'd much rather believe that over the next five years things are going to get better—that profits will continue to be made in the free enterprise system and that the *taxpayers' revolt* that we see taking place in the United States today will actually lead to a new era of prosperity. A trend away from the welfare state we've been drifting into during the last fifty years.

Most folks stand around watching other people acquire wealth. They'd be amazed at what they could get by making an offer!

How about a "1031 Exchange" tonight, baby?

Do It, Don't Talk about It

Another thing you will notice about the way Tycoons think and act is that they avoid unnecessary conversation. Some time-wasters merely sit and shoot the breeze for hours on end. They discuss the weather. The state of Coors beer. "And hey—did you hear that Mabel went home with Henry last night? Robin was so upset she took downers and then Blanche came in . . ." Tycoons don't gossip. They don't "make conversation." Silence gives the impression of strength and knowledge. But when they do speak, they have something important to say. A Tycoon does not brag about himself, either. He doesn't have to toot his own horn. Success speaks loud and clear.

The Tycoon's Morality

Much of the business inspirational material I've read has made a great deal of "morality." Many people feel that being a "womanizer," a drinker, or a dope-smoker are pit-stops on the road to failure. But, based on the Tycoons that I have known, the fact that they indulged in occasional immoral delights has had no effect on their financial success. Of course the key here is moderation. If entire energies are devoted to close encounters of a physical kind, then obviously there isn't enough time in the day to be successful in business. But spending a moderate amount of time on "vices" or other interests won't, I think, affect the outcome of your future. Of course, a "vice" can be viewed in many ways—and when people talk about drinking too much, I always remember the story about the Temperance League.

Once, in an antidrinking demonstration, the Temperance League lady took a can of worms and put half the worms in one glass and poured water on them. Then she took the other half of the worms and poured ninety-proof vodka on them. The worms in water wriggled around, but the worms in vodka curled up and died instantly. The prohibitionists ended the demonstration by asking the question, "Now what did that tell you about drinking?" Someone stood up in the audience and shouted, "If you drink a lot, you'll never have worms."

You can see that what is considered a vice by some may be considered beneficial by others. So try to be tolerant. Remember: As a real estate Tycoon you might one day find yourself buying a house from somebody who drinks too much. Lecture to them about the evils of drink and you'll blow the deal. A *reasonable* amount of missionary zeal for your favorite cause outside of business hours, however, should not inhibit your business success. Who knows—it might even add to it. Take religion for instance . . . .

Become a Transcendental Tycoon

Don't laugh. A few words on meditation isn't as out of place in a real estate book as you might imagine. Some years ago the Harvard Business School recommended it for relieving stress in executives. And who can argue with the "B" school? You don't have to wear white robes or chant exotic mantras; you can meditate effectively right now. Here's the secret.

Whenever you have a problem or just lack a sense of well-being, place yourself in a horizontal position in a darkened room. Get comfortable. Eliminate distractions, and banish all thoughts. Breathe in a regular manner. Concentrate on relaxing each part of your body, from toes to ankles to calves and so forth, until you have consciously relaxed *all* your body. At the same time concentrate on breathing. Silently repeat a meaningless word. It should be a word that has no particular association, such as "abracadabra" or "Sears and Roebuck." Softly, silently chant this word over and over. Do it in rhythm with your breathing. For instance, breathe in—*abra,* breathe out—*cadabra, abra, cadabra* . . . If you can do this successfully in a quiet place, with near total relaxation, you will achieve a particularly satisfying state of mind. Some would call it a religious experience.

Meditation can be utilized a number of ways. Use it simply to get to sleep. Or practice it in the middle of the day instead of a cat nap. It'll clear the mind and you might even find solutions to many of the troublesome problems of the day. A "natural high," some call it. But whatever it is, it's an altered state of consciousness that is invariably beneficial. It's cheaper than alcohol or dope, and like I said, it's recommended not just by me, but by Harvard Business School.

In case you're now too relaxed to remember, here's a quick summary: Persistence and enthusiasm are a Tycoon's most important tools. You learn how to do something right only by doing it wrong first, so view all mistakes with a sense of humor as experiences that will do you some good. Every mistake, every "failure" is a valuable experience. Problems are just exciting challenges. *Laugh a lot.*

Pay no attention to negative people. Ruthlessly cull the people who tell you "it can't be done" from your address book. When you're really depressed, don't dwell on failures. Think about what you did right, not what you did wrong. Never worry! If you use meditation to clear your mind, you will often find that your subconscious will work out creative solutions that will magically surface when you come out of your higher consciousness.

No one ever made a big success of themselves without failures. Winston Churchill, in World War I, was the instigator of a disastrous plan to invade Turkey at Gallipoli. It was such a massive failure that Churchill was forced to retire from public life in disgrace. He wrote, studied, and made no attempt to come back for many years. But he was preparing to be a leader again. He did not give up. Remember your biggest successes will come after your biggest failures. A Tycoon is never a quitter!

A Tycoon is always alert for changes in the economy. He always asks, how can I profit from the coming events? A real estate example: If you see for one reason or another a major employer in your area is having problems, like Boeing did in Seattle, that means the layoff of a lot of people. That could cause a temporary depression in the market. It might be the time to sell or trade property while prices are still up and to build up cash reserves to acquire property when everyone is depressed. Property sells below replacement costs during depressions. The Tycoon knows it pays to buy when everyone else is panicking. In San Francisco and Los Angeles during 1977–1978, prices got a little crazy, went up too much too fast, and intelligent investors reduced their holdings to look at better deals available in other parts of the country.

A Tycoon always has historical perspective, you see. He knows that a big boom is almost always followed by a bust. After a very healthy rise in the stock market or the real estate market there's a period of leveling off or even declining prices which is called a "correction." During that "correction" (a bad one is called a depression), the Tycoon must be ready to move on to more lucrative areas. Even different countries, if necessary. When the stock market died in the United States around 1968, people who stayed with it wasted ten years of their lives. They didn't know what you know: A Tycoon is ready to go where the action is.

Avoid Being a Consumer

Finally, I must outline the most important rule for a Tycoon, and that is: **Don't be a consumer.** If your mind is always focused on how to blow the next few hundred dollars, you'll never accumulate the capital you need to be successful.

These are my three rules to avoid being a consumer. If you see **it** in a store and are about to buy **it,** ask yourself:

1. Can I live without **it**?

2. Is there something I can trade for it?

3. Can I get it cheaper somewhere else?

Hopefully the mental process you go through with those three questions will make you forget about it, and cause you to look for more productive uses for your money. Like where to invest a dollar and get back two. Not where to spend a dollar and get back nothing except an expensive memory. Whenever possible, don't even think about consumer goods like cars, vacations, pet rocks, or any sports requiring expensive trappings. You're independently wealthy *only* when you've enough money coming in from your investments to enable you to quit working. *Then,* the surplus left over from paying for basic necessities can be spent on consumer goods.

Not only does a Tycoon not consume, he generally pays little or no taxes. The government under our confiscatory tax schemes is theoretically our 50 to 70% partner. All Tycoons (and I personally) don't pay any income taxes because we spend (far too much) time figuring out how to legally shelter income. I do this by making business deals that bring me tax losses (on paper) in excess of the money I put into the deal.

Corporations avoid taxes by simply charging more for their product. The fuzzy-thinking leftists of the world don't realize that General Motors, although it seems to pay about 50% corporate income tax, really passes its taxes along to the consumer.

Take the Chevrolet, for instance. It could sell for $3,000. But does it? Of course not. "Consumers" shell out $8,000. Why? Because $5,000 is needed for taxes, and corporations must always raise the price of their product to cover all costs. This way they get the needed return on their investment. Corporations don't pay taxes, *people* pay taxes. In reality, taxes are always just another add-on cost for the consumer. If the Feds cut out real estate tax incentives, rents would merely go up 50% to pay the new taxes.

If you are in real estate, at least for now you can set up deals in such a way that income is sheltered and taxes are deferred into the distant future. The average middle-class wage-slave has no way of avoiding taxes relatively legally. If he makes $30,000 a year he'll pay about a third in taxes. He could avoid the whole thing if he took the time to read my chapter "Pay No Taxes Ever Again—Legally!" If you're going to be a Tycoon, you will have to keep clear not only of taxes, but of flakes, frauds, and Red Ribbon deals. The Red Ribbon Rule is to avoid a deal presented to you all wrapped in a Red Ribbon, your only requirement being to write out a check, sit back, and watch the profits flow in. Don't do it. The deal will never happen. *Avoid sucker investments.*

The best business deals are the ones you create, where *you* personally see a need and are willing and able to do what it takes to fill it.

Double ESSers

No matter how good a deal sounds or what guarantees you're offered, never get involved with a person of bad reputation. That person will find a way to do a "double S" on you. Screw and Sue, in other words. "Double eSSers" are people who want to get something they are not entitled to. They get you into lawsuits which are a waste of much money and valuable energy. Always find a way to settle quickly with a double eSSer, then never have anything more to do with him. Go on to something more productive.

Women in a divorce situation are often double eSSers. One lady I knew, let's call her Sue Screw to make the point, was married to a wealthy fellow named Sam. The marriage fell apart and Sue hit Sam with a vengeance. She contacted famous divorce lawyer "S. S. Castrator" who wanted a court order for Sam to pay alimony of $1,000 a month. Sam refused such a high sum. He offered $600 per month as an out of court settlement. Was Sue Screw satisfied? No. She would rather fight! Things dragged on for years, with Sam refusing and Sue screwing, but Sue fought on. Sue didn't realize that 80% of all alimony orders are in default anyway within two years after the alimony award. Eventually the case was decided, five years and $20,000 in court costs later. Sue Screw was awarded her $1,000 a month alimony. Sam moved to Israel and became a kibbutznik. She never got a dime. If only she had accepted Sam's original offer. Sue could have bought real estate and been a lot richer both financially and emotionally. So: the Bill Greene Rule on double eSSers is: Forget it. Stay out of court—settle quickly. Do something productive instead. The only one who wins in a lawsuit is the lawyer. Double eSSers exist in business too and they come in all three sexes. So always be sure the people you rely on in a deal are dependable and of super reputation. The same rule applies to you:

Don't be a double eSSer!

From time to time for very good reasons, you may have to be technically a "lawbreaker." But never take what isn't yours. It's just that sometimes the laws of the country or a community make no sense. Number one priority has to be "look to your own survival." When a place like Rhodesia prevents Rhodesians from simply picking up their chips and moving to safety, it may be necessary to circumvent the law. Governments are immoral, cynical, and inhumanly interested in their own self-perpetuation. Always at the expense of their citizens—sometimes at the expense of their citizens' lives.

On a less dramatic level, if the building code in Atlanta, Georgia, makes it impossible for me to complete a necessary repair or alteration on one of my buildings, I may find it necessary to make that repair anyway and take my chances of getting caught. Economic survival on a day-to-day level is as important as my personal survival. My feeling is that you should respect the laws of your country or community where you can, but when they get ridiculous, follow your own conscience.

On that score, every Tycoon reading this book should realize that the free enterprise or capitalistic system is fighting a losing battle for survival all over the world. Only political involvement by us may preserve it for our children. Consider joining all local property owners' groups. Consider the Libertarians. It's a new political party in America, dedicated to fiscal conservatism in government, plus maximized individual freedom. The interesting and usually wealthy people who've joined this party feel there are just too many laws and too much taxes for anybody's good. They feel that the public sector—namely government—has overexpanded and has become dangerously all-powerful. The Libertarian Party, which is a behind-the-scenes mover in the current taxpayers' rebellion, is a group you should consider getting behind. Membership is about $20 per year and their number should be in your telephone book. If not, write to Libertarian National Headquarters, 1516 P Street, N.W., Washington, DC 20005. They will forward your letter and get you on the mailing list. At the very least you'll make some interesting contacts.

I remind you again that every Tycoon, certainly when he starts out, should prepare written plans. Set forth your goals and what it is you want to accomplish. The world steps aside for a man (or woman) with a plan.

Have complete confidence in yourself in whatever you're doing. Recognize that if you're well prepared, well educated, well organized, and have a plan, you will not fail to achieve your goals.

After you become a Tycoon and are financially independent, ask the question: What would I do if I had only six months to live? Then do it. With financial independence, you finally have the power to do whatever you want. Real power, i.e., the freedom to determine your own destiny. While on one level I talk about how to make money, at a deeper and more philosophical level, I'm talking about this freedom.

You get freedom only when you don't have to work at a job you hate or live with a spouse just because he/she is paying the rent.

When you have no money problems, you can enjoy life infinitely more. Enjoying your family more might be one of the unexpected benefits, because the reason you will be with them is that you want to enjoy them, not that you have to.

Once you've made a lot of money, look around and think about protecting your fortune by diversification. Remember, real estate in the sun belt, that whole southern area between San Francisco and Atlanta, Georgia, has been booming for some time now. It will probably continue, but you must be ready at any time to transport yourself or your business into other areas, even other countries. It never hurts to start your diversification of investments program from a position of success.

Don't wait for the boom to bust: While still doing well in real estate, set aside funds to establish reserves or, even better, look for different business ventures. Anyone who can relate to what I've discussed in these pages has the capacity to become financially independent in one to three years. And to keep it, you don't need luck. Luck always comes to those who think like a Tycoon. At my *Tycoon Class,* which has now been attended by over 16,000 graduates, I often end my lectures by telling my students, "Look to the right of you and look to the left of you. Including yourself there are three people. In a few years one of you is going to be in essentially the same economic position you're in today. And the reason will be that you did not set goals and get off your fanny. Another one of you will be much improved and will probably own a couple of properties. You'll have doubled your present income. The third person will be a millionaire, and a real Tycoon."

The choice of whether you do nothing, apply yourself moderately, or make it big is yours! America with all its defects is still the land of opportunity! "Life is a banquet," said Auntie Mame, "but most people never get near the table."

The choice is up to you. Are you ready? Let's take Step One of the Tycoon Plan: Tomorrow morning, at 9 A.M., go to see a banker.

CHAPTER 4

Acquiring Financial Independence

What is financial independence? To me it's the wonderful feeling of getting up in the morning without having to go to a job I hate. It's living *where* I want to live—not where I can afford. It's living *with* people I love—not someone I'm stuck with because they are supporting me. Financial independence is never worrying about rent money, grocery money, or doctor bills. It's going out and having steak or lobster once in a while. It's having basic needs and even a few luxuries, without being a wage-slave or doing prostitute work. It is, in a word, **freedom!**

Some would equate financial independence with servants, a summer home in Monte Carlo, a Rolls Royce. But to me that is *show*—not freedom. Financial independence *will* buy freedom from a boring job. It will buy time to pursue your own interests: freedom to travel, to read, to write, to create, to play, or to do your life work whatever it may be. Not necessary to be fashionable, chic, or Jet Set. A mansion, poodles, servants, and a Rolls Royce only tie you down. I know. I've tried that lifestyle.

The *political* freedom we have (to a limited extent) is nice. It's wonderful to be able to write your congressman. You can even climb on a soapbox and call the president names. You can complain. I wouldn't want to take away that sort of freedom. But what value is freedom to exercise your vocal chords or pen if you are stuck in a daily inescapable rut of earning a subsistence living? The only worthwhile freedom we, as individuals, can hope to achieve in America is **financial independence.**

I am going to tell you how to get this freedom in less than three years. It will take all your spare time and energy. I will show you how to use your energies to effectively accumulate wealth. I'll show you how to work for maximum results. With a hell of a lot of effort you can make your first good deal. And one good deal can make you thirty thousand bucks. In a few months you may be able to do that once or twice a week. If you are willing to work very hard you could be a millionaire in a year. Using my methods you should be able to make *your* million in less than three years.

After you have your first million, then you've got freedom. It won't be exactly what you imagined, because a million dollars isn't what it used to be. Being a millionaire today is about the same as being worth $100,000 after World War Two. But a million still spells financial freedom for a small family.

With a million invested very conservatively to yield 10% or $100,000 per year, there may be only about $20,000 spending money left after federal and state income taxes. Rent of $1,000 per month hardly buys the sort of apartment that one associates with millionaire status, and rent alone can take more than half a millionaire's income. About $8,000 per year is left for food, entertainment, medical bills and supporting the family. Since a first class maid or butler commands a salary of $20,000 per year, obviously there are going to be no servants, Rolls Royces, or summer homes in Monaco even if you have a million.

But if you've got a million dollars, you do have freedom. You don't need an expensive apartment and you don't need to put on a show for anyone else. But you can afford to live where you want. Not regally, perhaps, but comfortably. I think I will convince you, if you are not already convinced, that buying real estate—primarily investment (or rental) property, is a policy of **minimum risk, maximum return.** It's the best thing you can do with your time and **small amounts** of money. It can make you a million dollars in less than three years. You can never hope to save anywhere near a million (in today's dollars) working for someone else.

Most of my disciples start out being what I call wage-slaves. They work at a 9 to 5 job. If you are a wage-slave maybe you don't understand why it seems impossible to save and harder and harder to get by on what you earn. Each year, though you *may* work harder, and even though you get decent raises, your standard of living seems to be going down. Fact is, it doesn't only seem that way. It's true. **The American standard of living is dropping!** At the same time the real standard of living in places like inflation-free Switzerland is going up drastically. Here in America,

The wage-slave mentality

after fifty years of having the highest per capita income in the world, we have dropped to a miserable tenth place. By the time you read this even the average Chinese communist may be able to afford more goods and services than you can! Right now workers in Germany, Switzerland, Arabia, Japan, and even in Sweden, Denmark, and Norway do better than Americans. Why? Our inflation-eroded, highly taxed dollar simply buys fewer and fewer good things than it used to.

Let's assume you are lucky enough to make $20,000 a year. The tax bite on $20,000 at a 34% effective tax rate for a single tax-payer is about $6,800. That leaves you with $13,200 to spend. Now, let's assume in the following year you don't get a raise. You still make $20,000 a year, but inflation has pushed up prices of normal things you buy at a minimum of 10% a year. I'm talking about rent, coffee, sugar, bread, and just about everything else. Since prices are going up a minimum of 10%, in year 2 you end up with the same $13,200, but with a 10% inflation rate *you* are left with only about $11,880 in purchasing power. So, if you made $20,000 last year you had roughly $13,000 in purchasing power. But if you made the same amount of money this year, your purchasing power went down to below $12,000. This little mathematical exercise explains why your real standard of living *is* dropping drastically every year.

Now, suppose for a second example you are lucky enough to have received a 10% cost-of-living raise. Next year, your salary is $22,000.

But guess what? The government raises your tax bracket from 34% to 36%. Remember, every time you get a raise your tax bracket gets a little higher. So therefore, when you deduct the new higher taxes from your $22,000 salary, you are left with a net of around $14,000, because your tax is now about $7,920. Giving effect to the 10% inflation, you take off $1,408 to arrive at your real purchasing power, a net of $12,680.

Remember, in year 1 you earned $20,000 and your net purchasing power after taxes was $13,200. But with a $2,000 raise in year 2, your purchasing power is down to $12,680. So you have taken a loss of over $500 in your purchasing power even with a $2,000 wage increase.

Why is that? Because your tax bracket went up at the same time the dollar went down in value. And that doesn't even include the extra 10% bite that's going to be taken out of your wages for new social security taxes. Nor do we consider state and local taxes that have been rising at an average rate of 15% per year. State income taxes usually take another 10% of your income.

In view of this situation, many people want to find a scapegoat. Some say (with a degree of accuracy) it's the "politicians" that are just taxing us to death. Therefore, the answer of some irate citizens is to become Tax Resisters: Break the law! Don't pay any taxes! Go to jail. I don't like this "solution," because if *you* go to jail, the government will just raise the taxes of the rest of us to keep you there.

Some others would say (also with accuracy) that America has a terrible socialistic government and that what we ought to do is emigrate to a real free, good country like Switzerland where they don't have such a big, bad government and such terrible inflation. Well, I'm an American, you're an American, and unfortunately we are stuck here because "real good countries" like Switzerland generally don't want us. We have to make the best of a bad situation right here.

From my point of view, the best thing an American can do is to invest in well selected, income-producing real estate. Done right, a real estate investment program will make you a millionaire in a few years. With real estate, the government's inflationary and unfair tax policies can actually help you—probably because a lot of congressmen and senators own real estate. Since politicians seldom pay any taxes, partly because of their real estate holdings, they haven't gotten around to taxing real estate incomes. It would hurt most politicians too much.

If real estate is so sure fire, why isn't everyone into it? Virtually all rich Americans *are* into it. But what about the nonrich? Let's look at how the great unwashed masses spend their time and view their future.

Most people, and that may be you, have a 9 to 5 job. You *may* feel pretty secure while you are in the job. It's not *too* bad a job. And after a day at the salt mines, sitting down to dinner and watching tv is about all you have energy for. The weekend with the spouse (and more tv?) goes by so fast you don't have time to think about any financial plan, much less have time to do anything constructive. Besides, the average Joe feels reasonably secure in his rut of a wage-slave job. He feels secure for up to twenty or thirty years. Right until the day the pink slip comes and he's fired, he feels secure. It's a false security: The vast majority of retired or laid-off older workers are destitute.

It's not uncommon to see people fired after thirty years. And when they look into the pension plan that was going to take care of them in their old age, there is a loophole: If fired before retired, they don't get anything. So, don't *you* be misled into feeling that there is any security in a job working for someone else. You can be laid off at any time, unless you're the one who owns the company. And as far as pensions and Social Security are concerned, I'd call most people's retirement plans *Social Insecurity*.

Though government and your pension fund take more and more out of your income, they give you back less and less. You get back inflation-eroded dollars when it comes time to retire. Social Security allowances or pensions won't give you enough to live on with any style or even dignity. But if you wait until you're sixty-five to retire, statistically you'll

Inflation chews up your lunch money.

What Things May Cost

	1962	1980	Compound Annual Rate of Increase 1962–80	What It Would Cost Assuming Same Rate of Increase as '62–'80		Assume 15% Rate of Increase	
				1987	1997	1987	1997
One-family home	$17,600	$68,000	7.8	$149,288	$301,134	$288,800	$1,227,000
35-foot cabin cruiser	21,500	62,375	5.5	106,545	181,995	264,950	1,125,509
Annual college costs	2,650	8,825	6.8	17,241	30,643	37,480	159,240
Chevrolet-four-door	2,529	6,100	4.5	9,473	14,711	25,911	110,000
Social Security deduction	150	1,200	13.2	4,233	13,577	5,593	26,000
Two-week London vacation	893	1,235	1.7	1,468	1,747	—	—
Auto insurance premium	87	305	7.1	632	1,217	1,295	5,503
Man's wool suit	130	270	3.4	401	546	1,146	4,871
Monthly electric bill	8	35	8.2	79	168	148	631
Prime-rib dinner	4.65	12.25	5.1	21.30	33.99	52	221
Haircut	1.00	3.75	7.6	21.30	15.70	16	68
Paperback novel	.95	2.95	5.9	5.28	9.46	13	53
Hamburger	.60	1.50	4.7	2.33	3.62	6	27
Pizza (slice)	.15	.70	9.0	1.68	4.07	3	13
Gasoline (gallon)	.31	1.30	5.0	2.11	3.45	6	23
Chocolate bar	.05	.25	9	.60	1.45	1	5
Daily newspaper	.05	.25	9	.60	1.45	1	5
First-class postage stamp	.04	.20	9	.48	1.16	1	4

Sources: Bureau of the Census, Chris-Craft, Harvard University, General Motors, State Farm Insurance, Hart Schaffner & Marx, Edison Electric Institute, Howard Johnson.

What You May Earn

	1962	1977	Compound Annual Rate of Increase 1962-1977	What You Would Earn Assuming Same Rate of Increase as '62-'77	
				1987	1997
Corporate attorney					
Gross earnings	$16,440	$38,828	5.9%	$68,881	$122,196
Aftertax earnings*	12,872	27,459	5.2	40,153	63,851
Constant $—1977	25,829	27,459	0.4	22,634	20,289
Aftertax earnings as percent of gross	78	71		58	52
Production Worker					
Gross earnings	5,021	11,740	5.8	20,631	36,255
Aftertax earnings	4,420	10,137	5.7	16,012	24,787
Constant $—1977	8,869	10,137	0.9	9,112	8,027
Aftertax earnings as percent of gross	88	86		78	68

*Assumptions: Married taxpayer, joint return, two dependent children, standard deduction, no change in 1977 tax structure for subsequent years; gross earnings less net tax liability, state and local income taxes (assuming the same proportion of state and local income taxes to federal income taxes); Social Security tax for 1987 estimated from pending legislation.

be dead within two years anyway. In my view two years of doddering retirement when you're too old to enjoy many things is no decent reward for forty-five years of work.

Let's suppose that *you* want to provide for your "golden years." You hope to live in a reasonably comfortable manner. The most common choice is a savings account. Banks and savings and loan associations are now paying about 6 to 8% interest. This is only 2 to 4% after taxes. But we're averaging well over a 10% annual inflation figure. That simply means that with the value of the dollar going down at least 10% a year, you *lose* 6% or more per year on money left in savings accounts.

Many economists predict that we will be faced with triple the present rate of inflation in the next few years. Well, I don't have a perfect crystal ball for predicting the future. I couldn't give you a definite figure but can observe the inflation rate going up at an ever increasing rate. I would guess that in the next few years 10 to 15% annual inflation is the *minimum* we can look forward to. Keeping money in dollars has to be nothing less than economic imbecility.

Another "investment" mistake is putting money in stock. Did you realize that during the last fifteen years, the quoted value of the average stock has gone down around 20%? Many individual stocks are down 70%. Now this 20 to 70% decline is not adjusted for inflation. We are talking about dollar figures. If you adjust for inflation, the stock market performance has been abysmal! Virtually every stock is down 50% with many down over 95% in real or constant dollars.

Next is insurance. Buying insurance is the absolute worst thing you can do with your money. Insurance gives you about a 2% after-tax return on the "investment" feature. That translates into an 8% annual capital loss after inflation. So, unless you need some term insurance to take care of youngsters who are unable to support themselves in case you die in the first year of your investment program, stay away from insurance entirely. If you need insurance to provide for dependents, stick with term life insurance. This has no "investment" feature, but it will pay back substantial sums if you die unexpectedly at an early age.

Then there are "tax shelter" syndicates. These are package investment deals that stockbrokers, real estate brokers, and promoters put out for the unwary, wrapped in a red ribbon, complete with printed brochure and smooth salesmen. In general, they stink! My own personal survey of real estate syndicate and other tax shelter deals indicates that *only 1 or 2% of those deals ever return the investment, much less any profits.*

There are, of course, a few worthwhile promoters and syndicators who have good long-term records. Almost everything they touch makes

10 to 30% a year for their investors. But an ordinary real estate deal that you can make yourself should return over 300% a year tax free on your investment. The best syndicators won't be advertising or going to look for you with a smooth sales pitch. They won't be advertising because they have their own following and don't need or want your business. There is a lot of money around, but few good Red Ribbon deals. And only if you know where to find them. You don't. You can only buy turkeys.

With everything else so bad, what has done very well for the long-term investor almost uninterruptedly from 1776 to now? I'll tell you what: homes and moderate- to low-rent income property. Even during the most inflationary times in Germany, when money was worthless and rent controls went into effect, real estate worked out well for people who owned a home they turned into a rooming house. Equally good was a two- or three-unit, low-rent apartment building.

Suppose you had $100,000 ten years ago. Instead of investing in the stock market or a savings account to lose most of your capital you might have bought four ordinary three-bedroom, two-bath homes in any desirable major city of California. In those days a nice, above-average tract house cost $25,000. Now, ten years later, that same home will be worth a *minimum* of $100,000. You could have bought four homes then for $100,000, but today you could get only one. The future probably will produce similar or greater price increases.

But what if we have a depression? In the worst depression the United States ever had, 1929 to 1935, this is what happened to real estate: In those days, when a low-rent apartment went for $10 a month, those low rents went up to $14 per month. Why? Because people moved out of their expensive $40 apartments and doubled up in the cheaper places. Low-rent housing did *very well* as an investment during the last depression.

Now of course some people in those days, like today, bought expensive, high-rent properties with negative cash flows. They went bankrupt. Some people *do* lose money in real estate. I will talk at length about the *no-money-down deal*. It should be obvious that if you put little or no money of your own into a real estate deal, there isn't much to lose.

Some uninformed people would say that if you have big mortgage debts and you owe money to a lot of people, then those lenders can come after your other assets if you default. In California and many other Western states that just isn't true. There is *no personal liability* on purchase-money mortgages on one to four units.* If a real estate deal

*See C.C.P 580b and related California statutes.

goes sour, the buyer can just walk away from it and tell the lender to take the property. That's all they get. They can't come after you for the money. So, in a no-money-down deal, which I'll show you how to do, there's absolutely no downside risk.

For all practical purposes there is no personal liability on any real estate loan in California* because a lender has two choices:

a. In the event of default he can take back or sell the property in 110 days at a trustee's sale, but only if he lets the debtor off the personal liability hook.

b. If a lender wants to enforce personal liability he must go through a complex, expensive, and impractical *judicial foreclosure*. There the deadbeat debtor must be left in possession for a year, and then for another year the deadbeat can still *redeem* the property for the amount of the loan balance.

Let me show you how to buy your first investment property. Every journey starts with a first step. But before you take your first steps to financial independence, let us look at one detour you *shouldn't* take: the stock market.

---

*State laws vary widely, but in every state and in Canada, experienced brokers and real estate lawyers have devised ways to avoid personal liability on real estate loans. Land trusts, straw men, and forming a corporation to take title are the most common. I advise you to stay away from personal liability whenever possible.

CHAPTER 5
The Stock Market— A Game for Fools

Most people feel that the stock market is a bad bet just because historically, over the past ten years, it has been so lousy. Money put into an above-average portfolio of stocks ten years ago is worth slightly less than if it had been kept in cash. That means that (after adjusting for inflation) an investor who put $10,000 into *reasonably good* stocks ten years ago has purchasing power of about half of what he started out with. But to make a judgment about the future *only* from looking at the past can be a shallow and misleading analysis. When "most people" feel that a particular investment is good and shows great promise, that is usually the signal for the astute—for the Tycoons—to sell out. But when everyone is depressed and articles in the media bear pessimistic titles like my chapter heading, the smart money can move in and pick up bargains.

With that said, you might expect me to reverse the thought of the title and tell you that *now,* while the stock market is still depressed, is the time to plunge. I can't do that. At almost any price level the stock market as an investment is a worse bet than putting your money "on the line" in a gambling casino. My thoughts may be easier to understand if we compare a $10,000 cash investment in stocks with a similar investment in real estate.

Let's assume that you buy 1,000 shares of Growth, Inc., a company that in its way is one of the best prospects in the market. Its sales and earnings growth are far better than the national average. Its particular business prospects are good, and best of all the price of the stock is depressed. On today's market it may be one-third or more below what it was selling for ten years ago. We can assume that just as you would go out of your way to find a really good four-unit apartment building, you did the research necessary to find an extra-ordinary growth stock. And we will further assume that the income, market value, and all other aspects of your stock investment perform at least as well as an assumed real estate investment of the same dollar amount.

All other things being equal, the stock in our theoretical example should perform exactly as well as the real estate investment. Naturally, in a stock you don't have the element of control that has made real estate so profitable for diligent property owners. But we won't consider that. We will assume that the strangers running the corporation are just as competent as you would be yourself. It quickly becomes clear from the comparisons below that the *tax policies* of federal and state government have made the stock market a "no-win" investment. And it is those policies combined with the effects of over-regulation, government inspired inflation, and labor problems that make investment in securities strictly a fool's game.

Real Estate Investment	Stock Market Investment
Earns $1,000 (rents less expenses). Investor keeps $1,000, totally tax sheltered by depreciation allowances.	Earns $1,000 in net profits. Average corporate tax (state and federal): $600. Maximum possible dividend to a typical professional person is taxed as unearned income at 85% combined state and federal rate, or a tax of $340.
Net Cash to the Investor	Net Cash to the Investor
$1,000	$60

The above illustrates that the net cash return to the investor in the stock market is only 6% of the amount returned to the real estate investor in a similar investment.

It requires over fourteen times as much money invested in the stock market to produce the same return available from real estate!

In view of the foregoing, it is extremely unlikely that 100 shares of Growth, Inc., will ever go up in value at all—because who would want to invest in a deal that is fourteen times worse than what you can get elsewhere?

But for the sake of this example, let's assume that a few years later the market price or value of both the stock and the real estate has exactly doubled.

Real Estate	Stock
Assume investment in "average" four-plex with "average" leverage.	Assume investment in stock with maximum permitted leverage during "average" period.

Real Estate		Stock	
Cost	$100,000	Cost	$20,000
Loan	90,000	Loan	10,000
Equity or starting investment	$ 10,000	Equity or starting investment	$10,000

We assume that ten years later, both investments appreciated 100% in dollars with no adjustment for inflation.

Real Estate		Stock	
Selling price	$200,000	Selling price	$40,000
Less loan	90,000	Less loan	10,000
Profit before taxes	$110,000	Profit before taxes	$30,000

The above illustrates that because of tradition and legally imposed restrictions on the amount of money that can be borrowed, much higher leverage is available in real estate than in stock market investments. Also, the interest rates for real estate loans tend to be lower than for stock market margin loans.

Taxes on Real Estate Profits (assuming reinvestment in real estate)		Taxes on Stock Market Profits (assuming reinvestment in stocks)	
Profit	$110,000	Profit	$30,000
Taxes	–0–	Taxes (at highest combined California and federal rates, approximately 45%)	13,500
Net profit	$110,000	Net profit	$16,500

The preceding illustrates that with a profitable investment, it would take ten times the initial cash investment in stocks to produce the same after-tax capital gain available in real estate, or, looked at another way, a stock would have to increase in value ten times the amount that a building would have to go up to yield the same net return after taxes.

To visualize something overlooked by analysts, let's assume that the stock of Growth, Inc., *did* go up ten times as much as comparable real estate.

Cost	$ 20,000
Selling price	$200,000
Less loan	20,000
Pretax profit	$180,000
Less 45% capital gains tax	84,000
Net after tax (cash)	$ 96,000

or 100% per year increase for ten years

Because of the tax bite, it is apparent that to equal the net-after-tax performance of real estate, a stock market investment must do *considerably better* than 1,000% of what the real estate does in order to yield the same after-tax return.

What general rule could be a guide to when real estate prices have gone so high, and stock market prices have gone so low that switching from real estate into stocks would be a good bet?

Due to the fact that real estate investors *will* have to pay capital gains taxes on the sale of real estate in order to get into stocks, the strategy indicated would seem to be this:

1. No matter how great the disparity, *never* sell real estate to purchase stocks—rather *borrow* against the real estate to invest in stocks.

2. The signal to begin shifting assets from real estate cash into stocks will come only when securities can be purchased for approximately 1/20 of the value of real estate earnings. In down-to-earth terms, if a property, after paying all expenses exclusive of loan amortization yields $1,000 per year, you would be wiser to invest in a corporation owning similar property only if it were paying a dividend of $20,000 per year.

   On a pure numbers investment basis, one would shift from real estate into stocks if there were a ratio of only $1 to $14, on pretax earnings, but the greater regulation of companies, the greater possibilities of lawsuits, labor disputes, higher business taxes, and the general outlook for private enterprises cause me to look at stock only if it earns twenty times better than real estate.

These recommendations apply only if real estate retains its current favored status, being both relatively unregulated and effectively tax exempt. If rent controls or tinkering with the existing tax incentives becomes a possibility, I would borrow heavily against real estate, invest in hard assets like gold, silver, antiques, or art works, and make plans to abandon properties. This was the only path open to thousands of investment property owners in New York City or London when rent controls inflicted terminal cancer on the real estate markets there.

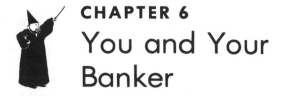

CHAPTER 6

You and Your Banker

Bankers must all go to a class where they learn the basic rule of *their* trade: *Never lend to anyone who needs money.* In the old days before I learned the secret, I walked into a bank cold and asked to borrow. They requested collateral in the form of some asset worth *more* than I was asking to borrow. They asked me to pledge bank accounts or marketable stock worth double the amount I needed.

In those old days I tried to explain that if I *had* a savings account for more than I wanted to borrow I could use my own money and would not have to borrow. If I had stock of double the value of the hoped-for loan, I could sell half my stock to get the money I needed. Several times my unsecured loan requests were refused, and I was left frustrated. But that was a long time ago, before I learned how to get unlimited money—whatever I wanted, from any bank.

Let me share the unbelievably simple secret that will get you a million or more in unsecured credit, whenever you need it.

Before I learned how to do it myself, I made some wrong assumptions about how unsecured loans were made. I figured that family ties, school contacts, or some clubby-social considerations made the difference between outsiders like me and the favored few who were extended unsecured credit. I was very wrong. Banks are interested in making loans to almost anyone. The only reason they refuse to make a loan is they are worried about getting the loan paid back. If you can convince a banker there is no risk, you will get the money. If your ability to repay is an unknown or in doubt, you get the cold shoulder. Here is how you can establish credit.

First, open a checking account at a large commercial bank—not a savings and loan association, which, by law, cannot make unsecured loans. Put enough money in your checking account so there will be no service charges. Be sure your new checking account is classified as a business or *commercial account*. Do that by calling yourself "John Your-name and Associates."

Once your account has been opened wander over to *the platform*—that section where the bank officers sit. You'll notice the two flashing neon signs that say **Smartie Desk** and **Idiots Report Here**. You may have trouble seeing these signs because they are invisible to the unedu-cated eye. But if you ask "Who handles consumer loans?" and "Who handles commercial loans?" someone at the bank will tell you.

Consumer loans are used to buy consumer goods, like vacations or a new car that will be a worthless, rusted hulk in five years. The interest rate for foolish pleasure loans on disposable consumer products is usual-ly much more than the interest rate on commercial loans. **Idiots Report There.** Commercial loans are used, or at least *should* be used, to invest in deals that will bring you back $2 for every $1 that you borrow. Now do you begin to see the flashing lights?

Walk over to the **Smartie Desk,** the chap or lady who makes commercial loans, and say something cute, like, "Hi there, I'd like to have a relationship with you." After their initial puzzlement subsides, you explain that you are starting the *Joan Yourname Business.* While you do not want a loan immediately, you want to establish rapport today. You want to know their commercial credit requirements. Explain further that you want your potential banker to know you and to be aware of your needs for credit.

Establishing rapport with an intelligent and reasonable bank officer *on your wavelength* is of the utmost importance. If you are an attractive young lady-tycoon-to-be, perhaps your best banker will be an old fuddy-duddy. You can flatter him with your attention and charm. Fuddy-duddy might turn a wheeler-dealer like me down in an instant, but the attractive Miss Leggs could do very well with him. A young and aggressive black man might do better by seeking out a female loan officer with an Afro than Mr. Fudd.

Unfortunately some prejudices both positive and negative do exist. It is up to you to exploit them to your own advantage. A Chinese vice-president, for instance, might be more understanding to a Chinese customer than a closet neo-nazi who feels non-Germans are inferior beings. But racially prejudiced bank loan officers are relatively rare in my experience. The old school ties, family connections—all these things may *help* but are by no means a major factor. It is important that the bank officer starts out liking you. As I said, try to get one on your wavelength.

It may appear that I am telling you, "Forget your principles and pander to the base instincts of dirty old men" (in the case of Miss Leggs), or, "Give up your legal rights to equal treatment" (in the case of Mr. Afro). That is one way of looking at it. You could, as a female or black, seek out a bank officer who instinctively dislikes you and vice versa. Then when he refused to make a loan, you could sue. Ten or fifteen years later, your civil rights case might be decided. You might win. You might lose. But many years would have gone by, and your program of becoming a millionaire would have long been sidetracked.

This book is about the world as it *is,* or at least how I perceive it. It's not a fairy story of how it *should be.* Getting ahead will definitely involve being agreeable, even charming, to people that socially you might have no use for. It will involve going around obstacles rather than fighting staunchly for "your rights" and thereby spending your life waiting for your case to be decided in courts of law. More than anything else, it involves the constant application of common sense. If your goal was to be a great medical doctor, kissing the fanny of a hospital administrator who is balky about signing your certification may be *necessary* if you don't want to go back to driving a cab. Once you have the certification you have the freedom to proceed according to your own values.

This book is about *freedom,* and a net worth of a million dollars buys *freedom.* Making a million in a few years is not easy. It may involve compromises and sacrifices you don't feel should be necessary. It will involve dealing with people you would rather not deal with. It will involve exploiting every talent you have and every opportunity you come across. Thus, the example of a black friend of mine who refused an executive partnership because it seemed his potential partners wanted him as their *token Negro.* He was a fool! You must get the job, deal, or loan first. Then you prove how good you are. The boss, partners, or bankers will soon become color-blind. If you have the tycoon mentality, you will exploit all your assets to the fullest.

Getting back to the narrower issue of loans. Whatever your financial needs are, do not be afraid to shop banks and loan officers until you find one or more you can relate to. Bankers are just employees trying to do their job. That job is to make solid loans to reliable people; to get the loans paid back as agreed: on time, with interest.

A bank couldn't stay in business for a month if it was not able to lend out its capital and deposits. That's their business. They *need* borrowers. They *want* you to succeed. But no matter how charming you are, and how much your new banker likes you, their job is to keep alert for telltale signs that will indicate how reliable you are likely to be. Do you bounce checks? If you do, forget about ever borrowing a dime—or change your habits. A person sloppy enough to be writing overdrafts frequently is automatically labeled *irresponsible* and a poor loan risk.

Do you make regular deposits to your account that indicate a steady source of income? Do you make occasional larger deposits indicating that you are a successful *wheeler dealer?* You should. If you appear to have a regular income or are a successful person with a cash flow, this establishes credibility. The record established at your neighborhood branch bank with the bank manager, and ultimately with the big shots at "head office," is what gets you a million dollars, unsecured. If you think it can be done in a week, forget it. This is a one to three year program. Patience and the approach outlined here will get you all the credit you need. But it could take a couple of years.

After establishing rapport you are ready to apply for your first loan. Remember the bankers' rule on first loans is that *you will not get it if you need it.* Thus, your first small loan of say $500 is only to establish credibility. You want to establish a record that you pay back on time or, better yet, *early.* If you do not have any good deals to invest in, *create* a not too fanciful story about ten cases of rare wine you can purchase at a bargain price in a nearby town and sell to local wine connoisseurs at a 100% profit. Or perhaps you can invent a deal involving an antique dining room set that you can buy for $500, refinish in your basement, and resell for $1,000.

When applying for your first loan, offer to transfer $500 from your checking account to a savings account to stand as security for the $500 you want to borrow. Or be ready to put up some shares of stock.

Remember, even when you borrow 100% secured, the loan is still to *you* and if the loan officer suspects he will have to grab the security, he would rather not make the loan. Bad loans are a headache, cause public relations problems, and if you do not service your first loan as agreed, you might as well move your account somewhere else and start all over again. You also might just as well forget about being a Tycoon without the backing of a banking community that perceives you as a responsible and worthy customer.

Rule: During your first year of borrowing, pay off every loan early! Assuming you have made that all important first bank loan for a term of three months, go in and pay it off in three weeks.

The Small Gift Rule. A small or token gift can be given *after* some service has been rendered. It is not a bribe. You already got your loan. You go into the bank on payoff day with your check. You effusively thank the banker for his help and tell him about all the money you made on the Chair Deal or the Wine Deal. You happen to have with you a sample chair or bottle, which you give the banker to show him the product you were trading or producing. You say, "By the way, that's an extra (or factory second). Why don't you keep it?"

Once I (really) invested in a soap factory. When the loan was paid off everybody in the bank got a bar of cucumber-flavor glycerine soap. To this day, the tellers, clerks, and loan officers remember me as the "soap guy." I get super service at that branch. The most important thing about the small gift rule is that your banker will remember you. You stand out among the sea of supplicants he must listen to every day. Effusive thanks or buying your banker lunch is a variant on the small gift rule. It psychologically conditions your banker to expect a goodie or some strokes for himself at the same time he collects for his employer. Verbal praise can mean as much as a material thing to some individuals.

For your second loan, which should be requested soon after the first has been paid, ask for at least double the amount of money of the first loan. Have another "good deal story" ready. You may have to do the "savings account as security" bit again, but it's likely that if your checking account balance is for more than the amount borrowed, you can, for loan number two, merely informally promise your banker that you will keep your checking account balance over the amount of the loan.

Before the loan is due, handle the payback, small gift, and effusive thank you scene as before. The third, fourth, and each succeeding loan should be for more money, longer terms, and with less security than previous loans. You may have to provide financial statements, copies of income tax returns, and so on once you get over $5,000: But by then the banker with whom you have established rapport will *help* you prepare statements and documentation that will look good to higher-ups.

Your loan officer should be a firm ally within six months. You can even confide in him that your first loan was not really used for a wine deal, but you were just establishing credit and your relationship with him. He will confide in you that he, too, read this book and knew what you were up to all the time. Needless to say, by your third loan, you should have found some uses for borrowed money. The whole purpose of this exercise is to establish a credit line so that you can pick up bargain deals, products or businesses for cash when opportunities present themselves.

Around the time of your third or fourth loan, consider going through the whole process of establishing rapport with another banker at one or more different banks. You should not tell the first banker about bank number two and three unless he asks. Bankers do not like what they call *double borrowing.* But here is how it works.

Assume you went through the same process of building confidence with a series of secured, then unsecured, loans of increasingly large sums at a second bank. While you will have to meet interest payments out of personal funds, you can borrow $10,000 from bank number one. When it is due, you repay it with $10,000 from bank number two. When that comes due, pay it off with a new loan from bank number one. If you want to get complicated, pay that loan off with a loan from number three.

The result is that your $10,000 is always *rolling over* between banks. The full $10,000 can be in deals out there working for you—hopefully earning 100% per year or more while your loan interest is only 15% or so per year. As mentioned, banks do not particularly like this double or triple borrowing mode of operation. Yet all big companies and all Tycoons operate on borrowed money from multiple lenders in much the same way. This handbook is just making you *aware*, as a future Tycoon, of what is going on in the *Real World*. Once you make your first deals with borrowed money, refinements in your system of paying back loans will come from your own experiences. Your borrowings will be scheduled in accord with your own needs and in line with the requirements of your banks or other financial backers.

Words of Caution: Always try to be liquid enough to clear up all your short-term loans at least once every year or two. If your double or triple borrowing *is* discovered, admit what you are doing honestly and candidly. You may be surprised, as I was, when banker number one said to me: "You don't have to go through all that nonsense with three banks; we will give you whatever you need, up to a million, if you just clear the decks every now and then and continue to show us that you have the ability to pay off *all* your short-term loans from time to time."

After that, for several years, I did all my short-term commercial borrowing with one bank, and they did indeed give me whatever I wanted. It took me three years, but by paying my debts on time, taking my banker to lunch, and establishing social and personal contacts with higher-level bankers in the same bank, I eventually got carte blanche. If I could do it, so can you.

Bankers now invite me to lunch and ply *me* with small gifts. If times get tough and it's impossible for you to repay a loan on time, don't be afraid to ask for an extension of the payback time. If this happens on your first, second, or third loan, it will be harmful to your credit. But after a dozen loans or a year of dealing with the same banker, you will have established enough credit and credibility to call your banker and say things like, "I have written a check for $50,000 to acquire a property worth $100,000. In line with our previous agreement, will you cover it with an unsecured loan until I line up a long-term loan? I'll have you paid back in three months." With established credit, you can make a partial payment in three months and get the loan extended for another three months if necessary.

The most common way of handling a cash flow or bouncing check problem is the worst. At the first sign of trouble the deadbeat puts a pillow over his head and does nothing. Even worse, he disappears. Goes fishing. His phone is disconnected for nonpayment of bills, and mail is returned to creditors unopened. As a result any normal banker gets all upset, makes a bad debt report to the higher-ups and the borrower has zero credit. Even if at a future time the borrower belatedly pays back the loan, the sour taste of irresponsibility remains. How much better and simpler it would have been if the embryo Tycoon went to his banker, explained the problem, received the standard permission to extend the loan, and then made token payments until conditions improved.

If you can not meet a loan payment, or cannot resist an opportunity to make a deal with what would otherwise be a bouncing check, you *must* always call or stop in at the bank and explain quite truthfully what has happened. More importantly, you must tell your lender what you are going to do about it. If over a period of years a businessman never had any temporary cash binds he'd be a most unusual character indeed. You become an even better risk if you show skill at extricating yourself from occasionally difficult positions. Obtaining a long-term savings and loan secured mortgage (due in twenty or thirty years) is my favorite way of paying off short-term debt. If you own real estate or a business, getting a mortgage or doing a sale-leaseback can usually raise needed cash.

Bankers hate lawsuits and foreclosures and would much rather give you a chance to settle up on terms you can live with. They do not want to terminate a good relationship with a bad lawsuit. To sum up, this is how to borrow a million unsecured:

1. Always borrow from the commercial loan department. Never have anything to do with consumer credit.
2. Establish a relationship at one bank.
3. Borrow money you don't really need on a secured basis to establish credit and credibility.
4. Establish credit at more than one bank.
5. Always borrow more than you need.
6. Always pay back your first loans early.
7. Each time you apply for a loan borrow more than your previous loans, even if you don't need it.
8. Deposit unused funds in another bank, as reserves.
9. Always keep cash reserves of at least 25% of your loans.
10. Establish bank friendships on levels that are appropriate for your level of operations. You should aim to be on a first name basis with the bank president within one year.
11. Meet your obligations punctually. Remember the *small gift rule*.

12. In times of difficulty, after you have established credibility, never appear irresponsible. Never disappear. Always stay in contact. Prepare and show them your plans for solving any problems. If you are reasonable, a bank will always grant extensions. Occasional financial difficulties are an expected part of all business operations.

High Finance Is Not a Mystery. It involves the steady build-up of unsecured credit for the apparently credit-worthy person. You, as a Tycoon, can use other people's money in many ways, as explained in other chapters. With a good line of unsecured credit you can take advantage of special situations that less credit-worthy individuals can't handle. Cash is king, and when a financially troubled company or disgusted property owner wants to sell in a hurry, you will be able to pick up bargains. You cannot be a Tycoon without a substantial line of unsecured credit. Take Step One. Visit the **Smartie Desk** today.

CHAPTER 7

Fuzzy-Thinking Leftists

The first fuzzy-thinking leftist I recall in my life was Mr. Stanley, a very brilliant high school social studies teacher. He had reputedly inherited a small fortune from his wealthy Eastern family, and he imbued us all with the desire to make the world a better place in which to live. At the time—1955—this meant joining the United World Federalists and wearing a green feather to symbolize opposition to Republicans, Joseph McCarthy, and the military-industrial-corporate conspiracy.

Mr. Stanley's parents had placed his inheritance with the trust department of a major New York bank. This gave him a monthly check. He had the disdain for private property that seems to come only with a regular welfare or trust-fund check. His parents were wise because Mr. Stanley would have given it all away to worthy causes had he been able to.

He mobilized many generations of privileged upper-middle-class kids to support all the favorite leftist-liberal causes, from civil rights in Georgia to ecology. As far as we were concerned Mr. Stanley was as right as anyone could be. He was clearly a good man: a Quaker, a pacifist, and a man who got behind all benevolent causes—sometimes even before they became fashionable.

I remember him telling us in class, "There's nothing more stupid than nations going to war over how to distribute God's bounty—and how to distribute it—that's the only argument between the capitalist and communist world."

He influenced us all. No one in the class considered going into business as a career. We all hoped to go into teaching, government service, or the professions. We were determined to "help people." It never occurred to us that the production of goods and services for profit might be of more help to the world than becoming a political scientist or social worker.

Our Mr. Stanley was multiplied by fifty when I got to college. Even at the Wharton School, supposedly a bastion of capitalistic education, I never received an hour's positive exposure to Libertarian thought. Laissez-faire was presented all right, but as a long-dead, no longer applicable 19th century philosophy. On our first day of orientation at Wharton, one of the many fuzzy-thinking leftist academics I was to come into contact with there announced the purpose of our education: "We are going to turn you into good administrators, so that when the revolution is over, they'll still need you to run the business, whether or not you control the stock."

In the 1950's there was a lot of talk about "people's capitalism" and how our form of government was becoming more Sovietized, just as the communists were discovering the "profit motive" and becoming more Americanized. It was predicted that within a decade or two we'd truly become "one world." None of the academics mourned the passing of the free enterprise system. I didn't know there was a choice or that there *was* any wave of the future outside of socialism.

It took me another twenty years of dealing with the real world and real people to look at things differently. I still feel that the Mr. Stanleys had OK moral positions in matters of individual liberties, civil rights, and such—but they were dead wrong in their antibusiness attitude. The fuzzy-thinking leftists made us all believe there was something wrong with owning property and producing goods and services for profit. As a result, government was allowed to erode the economic freedom of the individual with progressive confiscatory taxes and incredible regulatory burdens. The result was a shift of interest and employment away from the private productive sector into "public service." Today nearly two out of every four people are, directly or indirectly, government employees. Of the remaining two, one spends full time coping with red tape and tax planning required by the public sector. That leaves one person to support three drones and their dependents.

Thus has the fuzzy-thinking leftist vision of utopia been fully implemented by total government control over almost all segments of the economy. Real estate is the last bastion of capitalism and free enterprise. That's why Americans are the best-housed people in the world. Despite the great job private real estate owners are doing, it could be the next to go. Trouble is, socialism doesn't work economically, and as the result of our "welfare state" there is far less individual freedom in the United States now than there has been (in any peaceful era) since 1776. (As of 1981, to restore freedom and reduce taxes, Bill Greene formed the non-profit *Free Enterprise Society*. To subscribe to its "Tycoon Newsletter" send $2 to Greene at Box 810, Mill Valley, CA 94942.)

Not all fuzzy-thinking leftists look like this.
They just think the same.

CHAPTER 8
Your First Investment Property

Let's go to kindergarten! The first thing you must do is to toddle out into the real world and see what's on the market. There is a lot of property out there. Much of it is for sale, at a price. The prices or availability of only a tiny fraction is known to your potential competitors—other buyers. What's "advertised" or openly listed with brokers is like the tip of an iceberg. Most people in real estate never get below the tip. You'll soon learn about the vast untapped market below the surface in "Finding Super Deals"—but for now just buy a magic marker and your local weekend newspapers. The tip of the iceberg will be quite enough to keep you busy for the next four weeks.

Once you've bought the papers don't waste time with the sports pages or news. Throw out everything but the classified section. Turn to the property ads. Circle every ad for investment property located within half an hour's drive from your home. Look at them carefully. Go over expense and income figures with sellers or their agents. For at least a month, look at a minimum of twenty-five offerings every weekend. Spend weekday time after work looking at more deals if you can. This first exposure to the conventional market is your kindergarten. Don't get carried away. Don't buy anything. You are not educated yet—not until you have seen one hundred properties. Just look! Ask questions.

Assume that sellers and their agents are lying to you. They are! Values and rental incomes will be exaggerated. Expenses will be grossly understated. But you can ferret out real figures. Check everything.

Don't be afraid to call up the county tax assessor for actual taxes. Go over to the garbage people for debris collection rates. Review tenant's leases. Follow up "for rent" ads. Pretend to be a prospective tenant to discover true rent levels in your chosen area. Make no serious offers until you have looked at at least *one hundred* properties! **Then make a low offer or a no-money-down offer on every deal you look at!** After looking at one hundred properties you will then recognize an outstanding deal when you see it.

Until you become an expert, here's one rule of thumb to tell what property is worth if you are going to hold it for income. Take the monthly gross rent you expect to get (not necessarily existing rent). Multiply by eighty to get "the value." For example, let's talk about a duplex that rents for $200 per month for each unit. That's a total of $400 per month. Now to apply my rule of thumb, take those monthly rentals of $400 per month and multiply by eighty. That will give you $32,000; $400 times eighty is $32,000. In many areas, if you shop you can buy a two-unit property earning $400 per month for $32,000 in an average neighborhood in average condition. That may seem like an incredibly low price to those who have been looking at property in Beverly Hills, but in many parts of California and certainly in much of the sun belt, six and one-half times the gross annual rent or eighty times the gross monthly rent is the going value. It is necessary to pay a premium for apartment buildings with condo-conversion potential or in areas perceived as more desirable than average. In places where landlords pay high fuel bills, like Boston or Chicago, paying eighty times the gross monthly income for apartments would be too high.

If you expect to make an income from any property, you should *never* pay more than one hundred times the gross monthly rental. The $32,000 property we are talking about must be purchased for under $40,000. If bought for more than $40,000 it would be a bad deal and it would need cash from your pocket each month to meet expenses and mortgage obligations unless you could raise the rents quickly and substantially.

Naturally, the rental figures that you use in this rule of thumb should be realistic rents you can expect to collect—not actual rent. Actual rents could be too high or too low for the existing market.

Many investors use a multiple of the annual gross rents as their rule of thumb. You can earn a positive cash flow with a price of from five to seven times the annual gross rents. At prices above eight times the expected annual gross—unless the property is in a spectacular location—*pass the deal!* There are still many properties available at bargain prices if you know how to find them. In my "heyday" in Marin County, I was making about three deals a week. Most required little or no cash investment. All were scheduled to break even or produce a small cash flow within a few months.

If you want to judge your own performance, if you are closing less than one deal every six months, you are not operating anywhere near Tycoon levels. It may take six months for you to get rolling in the business. One deal a month should be your initial goal. One deal a month will make you a millionaire in two to five years.

Now concerning the no-money-down deal, some real estate brokers will say, "I've been in the business twenty years and I never saw a deal like you want." The unfortunate fact is that most real estate agents would not know how to make a no-money-down deal if it fell on them. Agents seldom know how to create anything but very standard financing arrangements: 20% down payment and 80% financing from a savings and loan association. In my opinion, most real estate agents won't be much help because they just aren't very creative at their trade. Probably 5% of the real estate agents in any locality make 90% of the local commissions.

Until you've become a serious buyer the best ones, who have all the good deals and could arrange no-money-down purchases, won't want anything to do with you. So before I tell you how to select a good broker and get them to feed you their secret listings and super terms, let me tell you how to make good deals *without* the help of a real estate agent.

Besides following all the for-sale-by-owner ads, simply walk around a neighborhood you feel comfortable in. Particularly in spring-time. You'll see people working, painting houses, planting in yards. You can be sure they are not tenants! Tenants never work in their houses or gardens. Anyone doing beautification is probably an owner. Ask a person working in his yard about his place. Particularly if he's older and near retirement, once you start talking you may find that he has some interest in selling and moving. Don't be too disappointed if in your first few conversations no deals materialize. It could take six months until you get rolling. But if in six months you haven't bought anything, you are doing something wrong.

Expect to make one hundred cold contacts to get five hot prospects. Five prospects may yield only two deals. To make your first super real estate deal will take much effort and persistence. Getting acquainted with older people in your neighborhood is another good way to spend part of those first months. If they like you, you will make many useful contacts. Eventually you'll get several direct (no broker) deals at reasonable prices with good terms.

During your educational or looking phase, don't neglect to prepare yourself intellectually. Finish reading this book. Take an elementary federal tax course and also basic accounting. Consider going to a community college for an evening real estate course. Be extroverted and expand your contacts. You might also consider good real estate seminars like my *Tycoon Class*. It's one of the best. I cram into one weekend all the basic information you'll need. But similar information is available in books like this, or in my cassette lectures.* As mentioned, you can get courses at local colleges. They are not expensive. The problem is, many college instructors go by the books. They learned from the books and have never been out in the real world. I know of few teachers who make big money wheeling and dealing. That's why after you've learned the basics the best ideas will come not from books or courses but from looking at many properties and negotiating in the field. Very much secondary are the courses. To repeat, suggested college courses in the order of importance are accounting, real estate, and federal tax. Courses will do you more good and give you more usable ideas *after* you have educated yourself in the field and understand what opportunities are on the market.

Now let's talk about no-money-down deals. Why would a seller ever want to take a no-money-down deal? I'll tell you why. Because what is a no-money-down deal to you as buyer will not necessarily be a no-money-received deal to the seller. Say a seller owns a $100,000 property with no mortgages on it. If you bought it from him subject to obtaining an 80% first loan, then he gets $80,000 cash when the deal closes (from the new financing). If you owe him $20,000 that's only a small 20% of the sales price not in cash.

You, as a buyer, might make a no-money-down deal if a second mortgage lender agreed to lend the $20,000 down payment. Thus, what is a no-money-down deal to you may yield the seller 100% of his sales price in cash. But many sellers, particularly older people, like to hold high-interest-yielding mortgages.

Typical real estate agents or brokers do not like a no-money-down deal. They expect a 6% commission in cash. Look at a $100,000 deal. A broker wants a $6,000 cash commission when the deal closes. And of course, the extra $6,000 has to be generated somewhere. So, usually, it's

---

*See order form at back of this book for "home study course" or the "Tycoon Newsletter," which lists upcoming seminars.

harder to make a no-money-down deal with a hungry broker in the picture than if you are dealing directly with the seller.

For the moment assume that we found a good property and a willing seller (a little old lady with a nice four-plex in a neighborhood you have decided is convenient and desirable). You negotiate a price with her: $100,000. The terms are no money down: an 80% bank loan with the seller carrying $20,000 at 10% interest for ten years. Many older owners of real estate live in a world of 6% interest, and 10% seems "high" for them.

Sometimes a seller or lender will give you the argument that if you don't have any money in a deal, you are likely to walk away if times get tough. Supposedly you have "nothing to lose." It may take a little convincing to overcome that fear on the part of the seller. You have to show the seller, the little old lady in our case, that perhaps you have had the same job for quite a long time and you are a steady person; a family man. Whatever works! After twenty visits, a few small gifts, and a lot of conversation, hopefully you can convince the seller that your motive is not to get her property and then walk away from it but rather to keep it and improve it. Of course, that truly *should* be your motive. You must convince the seller you will provide the dependable monthly checks she needs.

Of course, if you do not pay the $20,000 debt back, she can always take back her property and sell it to someone else. That is what a second mortgage is all about. It is not as if the seller is getting "nothing." She is getting $80,000 cash from the proceeds of the first mortgage and an additional $20,000 note from you. The note itself has a cash value and could be resold at a discount by the seller. Discounts on second mortgages typically range from 20 to 40% of the face value. So there's only a limited risk in making a no-money-down deal with you. Still you always have to convince sellers and lenders that you are reliable.

Now let's analyze a typical deal. We'll take the $100,000 four-plex and assume the fair rents are $300 a month each on the four units that you just bought. An income of $300 for four units is a total of $1,200 per month. Eighty times that is $96,000. So $100,000 fits my rule of thumb as the fair market value of that particular property. I told you that the gross rents per month for all the units combined is $1,200. If you multiply that times twelve, you will get an annual gross rental income of $14,400 per year. Six and one-half times the annual gross is about $99,000.

Your payments on the first mortgage would be at least $10,000 per year. Your real estate taxes in that deal in most states would be under $2,000 while your upkeep and maintenance would be another

$2,000 per year. The reason I'm throwing these figures out now is that there are certain rules of thumb that you should know.

Figure real estate taxes in most Western states are going to be just about 20% of your gross rent.* Other expenses in round numbers will be about 20% depending on the age and condition of the building. The rest of the rental income will go to the amortization of the loan. And that figure of course will be different in every case depending upon what arrangement you made for financing. But in the case we are talking about, the loan amortization payments would be over $10,000 per year. The expenses and taxes altogether would be about $4,000 a year; total $14,000. With a gross rental income of $14,400, the net cash flow would be only $400 per year at best.

Seeing this small figure you might ask what's so terrific about spending a lot of time negotiating a deal, running the property, putting out a lot of work and effort, improving the property, collecting rent. Maybe if you are lucky and have no vacancies or major repairs you take out $400 a year. You say to yourself, "I didn't put up any money but what's so terrific? $400 a year? That's peanuts. How is that kind of deal ever going to get me financially independent? I can see that it might possibly make me a millionaire in three thousand years—but what's with this two years Greene talks about?" Well, the cash flow in real estate, so long as you break even, is the least important consideration. Let's talk about what's really important. How do you make money? The first invisible profit is the benefit you get from depreciation. Depreciation is an artificial bookkeeping or accounting figure that the Internal Revenue Service with its Alice-in-Wonderland rule book says you are allowed to offset against your other income when you own real estate. The government assumes that when you buy a $100,000 property, the land will not depreciate. The land in our example may be worth $20,000. They will let you assume that the structure is worth $70,000. Now you see, the land value of $20,000 and the structure value of $70,000 make up a total value of $90,000 in all. What happened to the other $10,000? The other $10,000 can be allocated to personal property. That's stuff like carpets, drapes, refrigerators, and so on. Who allocates? You do.

You can depreciate a building and its contents but not the land on which it stands. You are allowed to depreciate a structure in as little as

*Under the recent Jarvis-Gann Amendment in California, real estate taxes should be about 1% of what you pay for the building, or $1,000 per year in our example. In Nevada, taxes are also about 1% of value. Check actual figures by merely calling your friendly county tax assessor.

ten years if that building is old, decrepit, falling apart and wood frame. That type of building is my favorite investment because it can always be assigned a relatively short remaining life for IRS purposes.

Who sets that life? You as the taxpayer are responsible for estimating that remaining useful life of any building you buy. If you said to yourself in good faith, "This building would need a major remodeling after ten years to stay competitive and rentable," you would be entitled to use a ten-year life and a ten-year depreciation schedule in computing your income tax. That ten years would be divided into the price of the property; ten into $70,000 equals $7,000. You would then get an "artificial loss," a depreciation figure of $7,000 per year. That is the depreciation on the structure, $70,000 spread over ten years. That figure alone would go a long way to save and possibly eliminate your federal and state income tax.

The main benefit of buying real estate is not the cash flow. (Cash flow is what you have left from your rents after you pay the mortgage, taxes, and operating expense.) The main benefit you are going to reap during your first year is a tremendous tax refund windfall.

Here is a bird's-eye view of how you get the tax refund. You bought that $100,000 building. You start year one taking straight-line depreciation over a ten-year life, meaning $7,000 per year. As explained, depreciation is an artificial loss. In the real world your property can double or triple in value. Still, for *tax purposes* it is treated as if you really lost money. Remember, depreciation occurs only for tax purposes and for accounting purposes. There is no real loss. But for IRS purposes it's *as if* you had a business loss of $7,000 out of pocket.

So you start out with that benefit of $7,000 a year loss, being the depreciation on the *structure*. There was also $10,000 worth of carpets, drapes, stoves, fixtures, refrigerators—that sort of *removable* or detachable category of thing the IRS calls personal property. Personal property can be depreciated over a much shorter life than the structure itself. The IRS says a three- to six-year useful life would be reasonable for old appliances, carpets, drapes. That would give you up to $3,333 worth of depreciation on the personal property the first year that you own the building. But the IRS says, "Take another 20% on top of that for your depreciation of personal property in your first year."*Why? That's the rule. With a six-year life and accelerated depreciation you get an extra 20%

---

*Of course, under the 1981 ERTA, depreciation has been replaced by the Accelerated Cost Recovery System explained elsewhere in this book.

first year depreciation on furnishings and fixtures. Why? That's the law. Don't question a gift from the IRS!

So, when you add that to your depreciation of the building, you are taking $7,000 depreciation on the structure and a total of over $5,000 first-year depreciation on the personal property. That is over $12,000 deductible from your other taxable wage-slave income.* Large "paper losses" are typical in low-down-payment deals where the rental income and operating expenses are about equal.

If you have another job and you happen to be making wages of $10,000 a year, this depreciation of $12,000 resulting from your first real estate deal will result for federal and state income tax purposes in your reporting a net income of less than zero. That will translate into at least a $3,000 a year tax savings.

For a plumber or brain surgeon with $250,000 of earned income and $250,000 of unearned income, the first-year tax savings resulting from the purchase of larger amounts of property could be well in excess of a quarter million dollars per year.

Clearly, the main benefit of buying a few run down buildings for little or no money down will be a magic wand to eliminate current and future taxes for ever and absolutely! Equally amazing: You will become entitled to a refund of taxes you have paid during the prior three years—plus interest.

Yes, best of all, you can carry these artificial real estate losses back three years and get a refund of every bit of income tax you have paid in the last three years. Not only that, you get interest ranging from 6 to 12% per year on the amounts refunded from the government.

The U.S. government will subsidize your entry into the real estate game to an almost incredible degree. The income tax refund check you get from the treasury could be $10,000, $500,000, or more, depending on how much you paid in taxes during the past three or four years. The more you paid, the more you get back.

The next benefit you get from owning real estate is the dollar appreciation resulting from inflation. We talked previously about the negative effects of a 10% inflation rate on the worker, saver, or rich person with money in the bank. The same 10% decline in value of money or a wage-slave's purchasing power will make the buildings that you bought for $100,000 worth at least $10,000 more paper dollars a year later. The real value of the property may be the same—but because of your high indebt-

---

*The mechanics of how to figure depreciation are explained in detail in our companion volume, *Landlording*. See order form in back of this book.

edness you make out like a bandit. When you bought a building for no money down in year 1, in year 2 with 10% inflation you would be able to sell that building for a $10,000 real money cash profit. Since that $10,000 would be taxable you'd no doubt prefer to refinance the property and pull out $10,000 in tax-free cash by borrowing, yet keeping the property.

Let's consider the tax-free borrowing power that will be yours once you own property. You bought a $100,000 duplex a few years back. It's gone up in value to $150,000 just as a result of inflation. It was a very average deal. Nothing special. You did no work—made no physical improvements. Because it has gone up in dollar value from $100,000 to $150,000 you will be able to borrow around $40,000 more against the property. That maneuver is called "refinancing."

How does refinancing work? Once you borrow that money, the bank isn't concerned with what you do with it. You can spend it on a lover or give it to the Red Cross. You can fly around the world, buy yourself a yacht, or do whatever turns you on. Refinancing proceeds are *like income* because you can spend the money any way you want. But because it is borrowed, the IRS *doesn't consider it taxable income.* **Borrowed money is never taxable income!** So one of the best things about real estate is that it gives you more and more borrowing power as the years pass. The more inflation we have, the better it is for the real estate owner.

The next logical question is, if you borrow money, don't you have to pay it back? The answer is *you* don't have to pay it back because *your tenants will pay it back.* What's more, under your expert management and continuous upgrading rents can be increased at the rate of 10 to 20% a year. Inflation will in a few years time make your loan payments insignificant.

After inflation the next thing to consider is your due reward for creativity and good management, initiative, and skillful negotiating. Many times, a property you buy will be run down and painted an ugly color. You may choose to paint it with super-graphics or give it charm by adding geranium window boxes and bright shutters. Cosmetic improvements, tastefully executed, can make your property worth infinitely more than it was when you bought it. Then too, the fact that you looked at considerable amounts of property before you committed yourself to any particular one means that you probably bought "right," or slightly below market value. If you also negotiated hard and received good financing terms, a good long-term loan in and of itself makes the property worth more: most buyers do not expect to get a no-money-down deal, and if you got 100% financing, other buyers will beat your door down to take the deal off your hands for a premium or profit to you above the loans. If you did not get better than average terms, you should have been able to negotiate the seller down to a price of at least 10% below market.

As you can see, the real benefit on our $100,000 deal is not the pitiful $400 cash flow you might have available to spend, but will be the invisible benefits:

Depreciation—The magic wand that eliminates present and future taxes and gets you a *refund* of whatever you have paid during the past three years. Projected value on your first deal: $10,000.

Creativity and Management—The reward you have earned by carefully improving your property and managing it well. Possible resulting improvement in value on your first property: $10,000.

Initiative and Negotiation—Real estate is an "imperfect market" say the economists. As a result, if you search carefully and negotiate hard, it is to be expected that properties you acquire will be bargains worth $10,000 more than what you paid.

Inflationary Price Increase—In a highly leveraged real estate deal, because of the decline in the purchasing power of the dollar, the fixed-debt amortization payments become less of a burden because they are made with upward rising rents. The underlying market values of income properties increase at something more than the inflation rate. Assumed one-year gain on first deal: $10,000.

Total up those four factors and you will see a possible increase in your net worth—one year after your very first deal—of $40,000! While this figure is arbitrary, it represents a composite—and a very conservative composite—of typical results. Total idiots—people who can't chew gum and drive a car at the same time—achieved similar results over and over again.

If you could make $40,000 on one no-money-down deal, what would you make on fifty or one hundred deals? Get used to multiplying and having your results come out in million dollar plus figures—because you'd make between one and two *million.*

Can *you* do it? The answer is unquestionably, *yes!* You don't have to do it in one year by making two deals a month. Take it easy. Just do one a month. You'll be a millionaire in two years.

Now skeptics will say, "You can't do that. It's not that easy." But if you own an ordinary home or if you know anyone who has bought an ordinary home in the last few years, just ask them. Ask *any* homeowner! A place I bought about five years ago when the price of a home was $25,000 required a down payment of $2,500. The average loan was for $22,500 at 7% interest. Just look at it today. The average selling price of that same property is close to $100,000. But the loan I took out five years ago is now paid down to $18,000.

What is the equity in such a home? Equity is the market value less the loan balance or the anticipated net cash receivable if you sold. In this average deal, the equity is $82,000. Thus, $2,500 invested five years ago in a very average home has turned into an $82,000 equity. And it's the easiest money that I or all those other homeowners who bought five years ago made in their lives. If they had bought a dozen homes five years ago, all you'd have to do is multiply $82,000 by twelve. Owning a dozen dinky homes makes you a millionaire.

Will it happen again in the next five years? If inflation keeps increasing at its present rate of increase, instead of looking at $82,000 in equity you'd probably be talking about much more appreciation in similar properties bought today. But if inflation does not continue at the same rate and drops to half, you'll make only $33,000. That would not be too bad a return on a $2,500 investment without a risk.

As you can guess, most people who invested $2,500 in a home purchased five years ago probably did not shop too hard. They didn't know the secrets or tricks of the trade explained here: How to eliminate closing costs for instance. They were not good negotiators. They had low ambitions. They had no motivation to make a fortune in real estate. They just wanted a place to live! They didn't have the drive to look at one hundred deals a weekend and pick out only the three best ones. Still, the average homeowner picked up from $70,000 to $80,000.

What did that same guy save at his wage-slave job? What did *you* save while working at your eight-hour-a-day job? The average guy was lucky to save $1,000 a year! In five years that totals $5,000. Five years ago that could have bought a new Cadillac. Today you don't even get a used Volkswagen for $5,000.

The moral should be clear. In an inflationary era, you can't get ahead working for a wage or salary. But you can make a great deal of money using borrowed funds to buy real estate. I've done it; my associates are doing it all over the United States and you can certainly do it. If this sounds inspirational, like a pep talk, that's what it's meant to be. Because negativism is sure defeat. If you feel you can't make it, that attitude will bog you down and prevent you from taking the first step.

You *can* make big money in real estate without quitting your present job and without risking anything except time you would be wasting anyway. If you go into the real estate marketplace with a positive attitude and if you make enough offers, you'll be surprised at the exceptional opportunities just waiting like ripe fruit on trees. But you must get out there and circulate. You must get out there today and start looking at properties. There's no way that you can fail! There's no risk!

If you put little or no down payment on properties, the most you can lose is your time. If you put 10% down you will soon get your money out in the form of tax savings or refinancing. Of course, if you put no money down in the first place, there's no risk at all. In California, lenders, for technical reasons, cannot go after your personal assets if you default on a purchase-money real estate loan used to buy four units or less. Now I'm not telling you to default. But *if* the world turns to ashes and we have a quake, or the worst depression we've ever had hits, it's comforting to know you *can* walk away. You can walk away and still hold on to whatever else you may own.

Can you make a lot of money in real estate today? Probably, yes. Not everybody can do it. If you are very rich, you may have problems. Rich folks are usually not hungry enough to get out in the rough-and-tumble market and make deals. Rich people always seem anxious to make a big down payment. Or maybe to pay all cash. They are conservative. In inflationary times that is not the way to do it. If you bought a $100,000 property for all cash and it went up in value 10% a year, all you get is a 10% profit on your money. But if you buy ten $100,000 properties for 10% down and they each go up 10%, you make $100,000. Over 100% on your money. Rich people do not seem to understand that using leverage or debt is how you make money from inflation. Creditors lose their shirts. Rich people are usually of the creditor class. They are wiped out by inflation. To make big money you can't be too smart or too intellectual. If one thinks too much about the pros and cons, and intellectualizes endlessly over "to buy or not to buy" a particular property, someone else will turn the deal before you even make a decision. Action, not thoughts, makes Tycoons.

You cannot be lazy. If you have a problem with a stopped-up drain, or some tenant complaint, you have to get out there and snake it. If you don't keep your tenant happy, it's "curtains." If you just sit back and pay no attention to your properties; if you let the rents get behind; if you don't stay on top of the collections—real estate will not work out for you. Keeping up with properties, getting along with your tenants and doing simple repairs promptly is very simple. Very necessary!

Real estate is not a lazy person's business. Sure, after you've been in it a few years you can hire managers, bookkeepers, handymen. They will be your buffers. But for the first few years you will have to work like you have never worked before. If you are too lazy to get off your fanny and look at properties and keep them up once you own them, you won't make it.

Quit watching soap operas on television. Take that TV set, put it in the closet. Leave it there for three years. Get out, start looking at property this weekend. The first step is to get out into the real world. Inertia is the greatest problem. Get off the time-wasting TV–*Time* magazine treadmill. Quit wasting time. This month look at one hundred properties! All your spare time should be devoted to looking at properties, starting now. After you've looked at one hundred properties, then make a low-down or no-money-down offer on every single property that you look at. You can make low offers and know that you are doing right because once you have looked at a hundred deals you will know what every property is worth. Being successful in real estate is like being an athlete. The more you work at it, the better you get. If you get out there and you look you'll get an education and many contacts. If you make a lot of offers you'll own property. Once you become a landlord, if you make the effort to effectively manage your property, you will get very rich, very soon.

The heart of this little pep talk—to repeat for the tenth time—is that you should *get out there*. Now! Live, sleep, think, and eat real estate and talk to everybody you run into about their real estate. Talk to everybody that knows anything about real estate. That way you will be getting a very good education. After looking at all the property on the market in your community, you will be as good an appraiser as anyone else. And once you've looked at one hundred deals, you'll develop a very good sense of what things should sell for. When a bargain comes up, you'll be able to recognize it. That's probably something you can't do right now.

I want to end this section by actually writing up a deal with you. Let's use a form I recently put together. Since every state has slightly different laws, it's a good idea to have a local lawyer who specializes in real estate check over the form you expect to use. This *Offer to Purchase Real Estate* can be used when you attempt to buy any type of real property. If you don't like my form, or on general principles, you should write for sample forms to: **Professional Publishing Company**, P.O. Box 4187, San Rafael, CA 94903. They have agreed to supply my "Tycoons" with a thick sample pad of all their real estate forms for $2. I'm sure these forms will give you many good ideas! You should never be afraid to modify a printed form to fit your needs—by changing the language, crossing out paragraphs you don't like, or by cutting and pasting. It's *your* contract and must be tailored to fit *your* needs.

Offer to Purchase Real Estate

RECEIVED FROM: *Bob Buyer, Yourtown, Yourstate*

TELEPHONE: *(333) 444-5555* or his assignee, hereafter "Buyer," THIS SUM RE-
CEIVED AS A DEPOSIT: *$1,000* ( ) Personal Check, ( ) Cash, ( ) Cashier's
Check, ( ) Deposit to Escrow, ( ) Other: *Note* ON A TOTAL PURCHASE PRICE
OF: *One Hundred Thousand Dollars*

For real property situated in the city of _____*Bigtown*_____ county of _____*Globe*_____
state of *California* ADDRESS: *1 Bargain Ave., a duplex with 3 garages,*
assessor's parcel #12345

SUBJECT TO THE FOLLOWING TERMS AND CONDITIONS: *Buyer to assume*
existing $70,000 loan from XYZ Savings & Loan Association. Seller to carry back
$30,000 second loan at 10% interest only for 10 years. Escrow to be at Founder's Title
Company, Yourtown Office.

Note: Buyer is acquiring property for long-term investment purposes, not for resale.

ADDENDA: *The attached "Exhibit A" is part of this agreement.*

PERSONAL PROPERTY INCLUDED WITH THIS REAL ESTATE: *Drapes & wall-*
to-wall carpeting in living room, 2 gas stoves, 2 GE refrigerators, washer & dryer,
assorted garden tools, 6 potted cactus plants on front deck.

ENCUMBRANCES: All liens against property including bonds or assessments are to be
paid by the seller. Taxes to be prorated to date of sale. Clear title to be provided by
seller.

CLOSING COSTS: Escrow charges and "points" to be paid by the seller.

DEPOSIT INCREASE: Not applicable.

TITLE INSURANCE POLICY TO BE PAID FOR BY: (*X*) THE SELLER (Binder Rate)
( ) THE BUYER.

OCCUPANCY DATE: ( ) _____ (*X*) UPON RECORDATION OF DEED.

The date of closing shall be *Feb. 2, 1981* . If seller remains in possession after the closing and buyer has performed fully, seller shall pay buyer
$ *30.00* per day from date of recording to date possession is delivered.

Seller shall leave in escrow **$** *750.00* as a security deposit for cleaning,
damage, and rent payment in the event possession is not delivered at closing.

RISK OF LOSS: Shall be Seller's until date of closing.

PRORATIONS: Shall be made as of date of closing as per custom in the area.

MAINTENANCE AND CONDITION: Seller agrees to maintain and deliver all heating,
sewer, electrical, plumbing appliances and equipment in good working order, to maintain and deliver the grounds and property in clean condition with no broken or cracked
glass and all debris and personal property removed.

CODE VIOLATION: The seller warrants that he has neither created nor has any knowledge of legal violations relating to this property.

PEST CONTROL: Inspection report to be obtained at expense of: 1. (*X*) Seller; 2. ( )
Buyer; 3. ( ) Seller agrees to have all needed pest control work done at his expense and
to deliver to buyer a termite-cleared property; 4. (*X*) Property is to be taken in its present
condition subject to buyer's approval of termite report.

TIME IS OF THE ESSENCE IN THIS CONTRACT.

Bob Buyer
_____

Barbara Buyer
_____
BUYERS

DATED: *Jan. 1, 1981* TIME: *9 A.M.*

ACCEPTANCE

The seller accepts the above offer. At the closing, seller agrees to pay a real estate broker's commission of _____*none*_____ for services rendered. In the event legal action is instituted to enforce this contract, the prevailing party is to receive attorney's fees. The seller acknowledges receiving a copy of this contract.

I acknowledge that the buyer and
seller signed this document in my   *Sam Seller* _____
presence and in the presence of   *Sally Seller* _____
each other: **SELLERS**

*Norah Notary*_____ DATED: *Jan. 1, 1981*   DATED: *Jan. 1, 1981* TIME: _9 A.M._
NOTARY PUBLIC

Now there are timid souls out there reading this book and they think that if you offer $100,000 on a property and things do not work out you will have big problems. By not working out I mean you've changed your mind and don't want to buy. The timid souls think you could lose "everything" just by making an offer. "They" would come and "they" would take home, bank accounts, and car.

Nothing could be further from the truth. When you make an offer on this form (and you make it right) and the seller accepts it, guess what? The seller must sell to you. But if you do not want the property before the deal closes you can walk away from the deal with no loss, no penalties, and no cost whatsoever. In most real estate deals, done my way, even after the deal *closes* you can walk away from it with no loss whatsoever. So let's get into a sample offer right now. Let me show you how to fill out a standard purchase agreement. You can do it in a way to tie up the property so the seller can't get out of the deal. *But you can.*

First of all, fill in the line *Received From* with your name (Bob Buyer in our example), your address, your town, and your phone number. In every real estate deal there is a lot of communication that has to go on, and if the seller does not have your address and does not know how to get in touch with you, all sorts of things can go wrong. It can blow a deal out of the water. These days everybody thinks they are a celebrity and has unlisted phone numbers. If you can't get in touch to arrange for the lender to get in to appraise, it's very frustrating indeed. Naturally you want the seller and any real estate agents involved to have your name and number just as you need the seller's and his agent's names, addresses, and phone numbers. The best way to keep that information handy, right at the start of negotiations, is to put everybody's

name, address, home and office phone number on the offer and acceptance form.

The next thing for you to fill in is where it says *Sum Received as a
Deposit.* You do not want to give the seller any deposit if you don't
want to tie up $1,000 of real money just because a broker says it is
"customary." Not at all. So where the box that says personal check or
cash or cashier's check appears, you mark the place that says "Other."
You write in "Note."

A note is something you can make up or get at any stationery store.
This is what your note might look like:

Straight Note

$ _1,000.00_ _Modesto_ , California, _January 1_ , 19 _81_
Upon closing of deal on 1 Bargain Avenue after date, for value received,
I promise to pay to _Sam Seller, only if needed to close this real estate deal_
 , or order, at
the sellerstown office of St. Paul Title Company as escrow agent
the sum of _one thousand_ **DOLLARS.**
with no interest from _date_ , until paid at the
rate of _-0-_ per cent per annum, payable _in full at the closing, if_
required under terms of attached purchase agreement and deposit receipt dated
January 1, 1981

Principal and interest payable in lawful money of the United States of America.
Should default be made in payment of interest when due the whole sum of principal and interest shall become immediately due at the option of the holder of this
note. If action be instituted on this note I promise to pay such sum as the court may
fix as Attorney's fees.

Bob Buyer

As you see, you will be able to make a dozen offers a day without
putting up one dime. And there is no reason the seller should not accept
a note instead of real money. The real money in most deals is going to be
held by a broker or escrow company anyway. The seller doesn't get it. In
those rare deals where you are forced to put up some real money, keep
the deposit as low as possible. Like $100. I seldom make a deposit of
more than $500 no matter how big the deal is.

This is what a California Trust Deed looks like:

Recording requested by

Bob Buyer

And when recorded mail to

Name	*1 Bargain Avenue Partnership*
Street Address	*Your P.O. Box*
City & State	*Yourtown and State*

_____ SPACE ABOVE THIS LINE FOR RECORDER'S USE _____

SHORT FORM DEED OF TRUST AND ASSIGNMENT OF RENTS   A.P.N.

This Deed of Trust, made this <u>*1st*</u> day of <u>*January, 1981,*</u> _____ between <u>*the 1 Bargain Avenue Partnership,*</u> _____ herein called *Trustor,* whose address is <u>*yourbox, yourtown*</u> St. Paul Title Company, a California corporation, herein called *Trustee,* and <u>*Sam Seller*</u> , herein called *Beneficiary,* Witnesseth: That Trustor irrevocably grants, transfers and assigns to Trustee in trust, with power of sale, that property in _____ County, California, described as:

Insert legal description of
1 Bargain Avenue

Together with the rents, issues and profits thereof. *Subject, However,* to the right, power and authority given to and conferred upon Beneficiary by paragraph (10) of the provisions incorporated herein by reference to collect and apply such rents, issues and profits.

For the Purpose of Securing: 1. Performance of each agreement of Trustor incorporated by reference or contained herein. 2. Payment of the indebtedness evidenced by one promissory note of even date herewith, and any extension or renewal thereof, in the principal sum of **$** <u>*30,000*</u> executed by Trustor in favor of Beneficiary or order. 3. Payment of such further sums as the then record owner of said property hereafter may borrow from Beneficiary, when evidenced by another note (or notes) reciting it is so secured.

To Protect the Security of This Deed of Trust, Trustor Agrees: By the execution and delivery of this Deed of Trust and the note secured hereby, that provisions (1) to (14) inclusive of the fictitious deed of trust recorded in Santa Barbara County and Sonoma County October 18, 1961, and in all other counties October 23, 1961, in the book and at the page of Official Records in the office of the county recorder of the county where said property is located, noted below opposite the name of such county, viz.:

COUNTY	BOOK	PAGE	COUNTY	BOOK	PAGE	COUNTY	BOOK	PAGE
Alameda	435	684	Marin	1508	339	Santa Barbara	1878	860
Alpine	1	250	Mariposa	77	292	Santa Clara	5336	341
Amador	104	348	Mendocino	579	530	Santa Cruz	1431	494
Butte	1145	1	Merced	1547	538	Shasta	684	528
Calaveras	145	152	Modoc	184	851	San Diego	Series 2	
Colusa	296	617	Mono	52	429		Book 1961	
Contra Costa	3978	47	Monterey	2194	538		Page 183887	
Del Norte	78	414	Napa	639	86	Sierra	29	335
El Dorado	568	456	Nevada	305	320	Siskiyou	468	181
Fresno	4626	572	Orange	5889	611	Solano	1105	182
Glenn	422	184	Placer	895	301	Sonoma	1851	689
Humboldt	657	527	Plumas	151	5	Stanislaus	1715	456
Imperial	1091	501	Riverside	3005	523	Sutter	572	297
Inyo	147	598	Sacramento	4331	62	Tehama	401	289
Kern	3427	60	San Benito	271	383	Trinity	93	366
Kings	792	833	San Bernardino	5567	61	Tulare	2294	275
Lake	362	39	San Francisco	A332	905	Tuolumne	135	47
Lassen	171	471	San Joaquin	2470	311	Ventura	2062	386
Los Angeles	12055	899	San Luis Obispo	1151	12	Yolo	653	245
Madera	810	170	San Mateo	4078	420	Yuba	334	486

74

California Trust Deed, *continued*

(which provisions, identical in all counties, are printed on the reverse hereof) hereby are adopted and incorporated herein and made a part hereof as fully as though set forth herein at length; that he will observe and perform said provisions; and that the references to property, obligations, and parties in said provisions shall be construed to refer to the property, obligations, and parties set forth in this Deed of Trust.

The undersigned Trustor requests that a copy of any Notice of Default and of any Notice of Sale hereunder be mailed to him at his address hereinbefore set forth.

STATE OF CALIFORNIA,   Signature of Trustor

                                    SS.

County of *Placer*

On *1 Jan. 1981* before me, the under-   *Bob Buyer, Partner*
signed, a Notary Public in and for said   *1 Bargain Avenue*
State, personally appeared _____   *Partnership*
Bob Buyer, partner of the 1 Bargain
Avenue partnership   ,
known to me to be the person whose
name *is* subscribed to the within instrument and acknowledged that *he*
executed the same.

WITNESS my hand and official seal.

Signature *Norah Notary* _____   *(Seal)*

Title Order No. _____

Escrow or Loan No. _____   (This area for official notarial seal)

DO NOT RECORD

The following is a copy of provisions (1) to (14), inclusive, of the fictitious deed of trust, recorded in each county in California, as stated in the foregoing Deed of Trust and incorporated by reference in said Deed of Trust as being a part thereof as if set forth at length therein.

To Protect the Security of This Deed of Trust, Trustor Agrees:

(1) To keep said property in good condition and repair; not to remove or demolish any building thereon; to complete or restore promptly and in good and workmanlike manner any building which may be constructed, damaged or destroyed thereon and to pay when due all claims for labor performed and materials furnished therefor; to comply with all laws affecting said property or requiring any alterations or improvements, to be made thereon; not to commit or permit waste thereof; not to commit, suffer or permit any act upon said property in violation of law; to cultivate, irrigate, fertilize, fumigate, prune and do all other acts which from the character or use of said property may be reasonably necessary, the specific enumerations herein not excluding the general.

(2) To provide, maintain and deliver to Beneficiary fire insurance satisfactory to and with loss payable to Beneficiary, the amount collected under any fire or other insurance policy may be applied by Beneficiary upon indebtedness secured hereby and in such order as Beneficiary may determine, or at option of Beneficiary the entire amount so collected or any part thereof may be released to Trustor. Such application or release shall not cure or waive any default or notice of default hereunder or invalidate any act done pursuant to such notice.

(3) To appear in and defend any action or proceeding purporting to affect the security hereof or the rights or powers of Beneficiary or Trustee; and to pay all costs and expenses, including cost of evidence of title and attorney's fees in a reasonable sum, in any such action or proceeding in which Beneficiary or Trustee may appear, and in any suit brought by Beneficiary to foreclose this Deed.

(4) To pay: at least ten days before delinquency all taxes and assessments affecting said property, including assessments on appurtenant water stock; when due, all incum-

California Trust Deed, *continued*

brances, charges and liens, with interest, on said property or any part thereof, which appear to be prior or superior hereto; all costs, fees and expenses of this Trust.

Should Trustor fail to make any payment or to do any act as herein provided, then Beneficiary or Trustee, but without obligation so to do and without notice to or demand upon Trustor and without releasing Trustor from any obligation hereof, may: make or do the same in such manner and to such extent as either may deem necessary to protect the security hereof, Beneficiary or Trustee being authorized to enter upon said property for such purposes; appear in and defend any action or proceeding purporting to affect the security hereof or the rights or powers of Beneficiary or Trustee; pay, purchase, contest or compromise any incumbrance, charge or lien which in the judgment of either appears to be prior or superior herein; and, in exercising any such powers, pay necessary expenses, employ counsel and pay his reasonable fees.

(5) To pay immediately and without demand all sums so expended by Beneficiary or Trustee, with interest from date of expenditure of the amount allowed by law in effect at the date hereof, and to pay for any statement provided for by law in effect of the date hereof regarding the obligation secured hereby any amount demanded by the Beneficiary not to exceed the maximum allowed by law at the time when said statement is demanded.

(6) That any award of damages in connection with any condemnation for public use of or injury to said property or any part thereof is hereby assigned and shall be paid to Beneficiary who may apply or release such moneys received by him in the same manner and with the same effect as above provided for disposition of proceeds of fire or other insurance.

(7) That by accepting payment of any sum secured hereby after its due date, Beneficiary does not waive his right to require prompt payment when due of all other sums so secured or to declare default for failure so to pay.

(8) That at any time or from time to time, without liability therefor and without notice, upon written request of Beneficiary and presentation of this Deed and said note for endorsement, and without affecting the personal liability of any person for payment of the indebtedness secured hereby, Trustee may: reconvey any part of said property; consent to the making of any map or plat thereof; join in granting any easement thereon; or join in any extension agreement or any agreement subordinating the lien or charge hereof.

(9) That upon written request of Beneficiary stating that all sums secured hereby have been paid, and upon surrender of this Deed and said note to Trustee for cancellation and retention and upon payment of its fees, Trustee shall reconvey, without warranty, the property then held hereunder. The recitals in such reconveyance of any matters or facts shall be conclusive proof of the truthfulness thereof. The grantee in such reconveyance may be described as "the person or persons legally entitled thereto." Five years after issuance of such full reconveyance, Trustee may destroy said note and this Deed (unless directed in such request to retain them).

(10) That as additional security, Trustor hereby gives to and confers upon Beneficiary the right, power and authority, during the continuance of these Trusts, to collect the rents, issues and profits of said property, reserving unto Trustor the right, prior to any default by Trustor in payment of any indebtedness secured hereby or in performance of any agreement hereunder, to collect and retain such rents, issues and profits as they become due and payable. Upon any such default, Beneficiary may at any time without notice, either in person, by agent, or by a receiver to be appointed by a court, and without regard to the adequacy of any security for the indebtedness hereby secured, enter upon and take possession of said property or any part thereof, in his own name sue for or otherwise collect such rents, issues and profits, including those past due and unpaid, and apply the same, less costs and expenses of operation and collection, including reasonable attorney's fees, upon any indebtedness secured hereby, and in such order as Beneficiary may determine. The entering upon and taking possession of said property, the collection of such rents, issues and profits and the application thereof as aforesaid,

California Trust Deed, *continued*

shall not cure or waive any default or notice of default hereunder or invalidate any act done pursuant to such notice.

(11) That upon default by Trustor in payment of any indebtedness secured hereby or in performance of any agreement hereunder, Beneficiary may declare all sums secured hereby immediately due and payable by delivery to Trustee of written declaration of default and demand for sale and of written notice of default and of election to cause to be sold said property, which notice Trustee shall cause to be filed for record. Beneficiary also shall deposit with Trustee this Deed, said note and all documents evidencing expenditures secured hereby.

After the lapse of such time as may then be required by law following the recordation of said notice of default, and notice of sale having been given as then required by law, Trustee, without demand on Trustor, shall sell said property at the time and place fixed by it in said notice of sale, either as a whole or in separate parcels, and in such order as it may determine, at public auction to the highest bidder for cash in lawful money of the United States, payable at time of sale. Trustee may postpone sale of all or any portion of said property by public announcement at such time and place of sale, and from time to time thereafter may postpone such sale by public announcement of the time fixed by the preceding postponement. Trustee shall deliver to such purchaser its deed conveying the property as sold, but without any covenant or warranty, express or implied. The recitals in such deed of any matters or facts shall be conclusive proof of the truthfulness thereof. Any person, including Trustor, Trustee, or Beneficiary as hereinafter defined, may purchase at such sale.

After deducting all costs, fees and expenses of Trustee and of this Trust, including cost of evidence of title in connection with sale, Trustee shall apply the proceeds of sale to payment of: all sums expended under the terms hereof, not then repaid, with accrued interest at the amount allowed by law in effect at the date hereof; all other sums then secured hereby; and the remainder, if any, to the person or persons legally entitled thereto.

(12) Beneficiary, or any successor in ownership of any indebtedness secured hereby, may from time to time, by instrument in writing, substitute a successor or successors to any Trustee named herein or acting hereunder, which instrument, executed by the Beneficiary and duly acknowledged and recorded in the office of the recorder of the county or counties where said property is situated, shall be conclusive proof of proper substitution of such successor Trustee or Trustees, who shall, without conveyance from the Trustee predecessor, succeed to all its title, estate, rights, powers, and duties. Said instrument must contain the name of the original Trustor, Trustee and Beneficiary hereunder, the book and page where this Deed is recorded and the name and address of the new Trustee.

(13) That this Deed applies to, inures to the benefit of, and binds all parties hereto, their heirs, legatees, devisees, administrators, executors, successors and assigns. The term Beneficiary shall mean the owner and holder, including pledgees, of the note secured hereby, whether or not named as Beneficiary herein. In this Deed, whenever the context so requires, the masculine gender includes the feminine and/or neuter, and the singular number includes the plural.

(14) That Trustee accepts this Trust when this Deed, duly executed and acknowledged, is made a public record as provided by law. Trustee is not obligated to notify any party hereto of pending sale under any other Deed of Trust or of any action or proceeding in which Trustor, Beneficiary or Trustee shall be a party unless brought by Trustee.

DO NOT RECORD

REQUEST FOR FULL RECONVEYANCE
To be used only when note has been paid.

To St. Paul Title Company, Trustee: Dated _____

The undersigned is the legal owner and holder of all indebtedness secured by the within Deed of Trust. All sums secured by said Deed of Trust have been fully paid and

California Trust Deed, *continued*

satisfied; and you are hereby requested and directed, on payment to you of any sums owing to you under the terms of said Deed of Trust, to cancel all evidences of indebtedness, secured by said Deed of Trust, delivered to you herewith together with said Deed of Trust, and to reconvey, without warranty, to the parties designated by the terms of said Deed of Trust, the estate now held by you under the same.

Mail Reconveyance To:

_____   _____
_____   _____
_____   By   _____
_____   By   _____

Do not lose or destroy this Deed of Trust OR THE NOTE which it secures. Both must be delivered to the Trustee for cancellation before reconveyance will be made.

Short Form
Deed of Trust
With Power of Sale
As Trustee

ST. PAUL TITLE
Company

Affiliate of the
St. Paul Companies, Inc.

**COMPLETE STATEWIDE
TITLE SERVICE**

*Used with permission of St. Paul Title Company

Next: *Real Properties Situated in.* Just fill in the address, city, town, county, and state. For example, *10 Bargain Avenue, Your Town, Your County, Your State.* Then always describe the property, write down what it is. For instance, "single-family home," "duplex," "ten apartments," or whatever. Why? To guard against buying "illegal" units that were built without proper permits.

The next empty lines are for the terms and conditions. Of course, the best terms or conditions for a buyer are an "interest-only loan" at as low an interest rate as possible with no payments at all for as long as possible. The principal should be due in as far a distant future as the seller will consider. The terms are simply the best that you can negotiate. As a reasonable example: The seller will carry a $100,000 deed of trust for ten years at 10% interest, payable interest only. If you think it is unusual to buy a $100,000 property with no money down and an interest-only loan, be informed it is not unusual at all.

Brokers representing sellers do not like no-money-down deals but I have done it many times, even with agents in the deal. In fact, I bought one property recently for interest only, ten years, 6% interest. Why? Because I gave the seller a higher price than he was asking for. As a result the seller was absolutely delighted to give me an interest rate well below the going market rate. Taxwise the deal worked out better for both of us. A high price and low interest rate gave me maximum depreciation. The seller had a tax-deferred installment-sale capital gain. He paid no tax at all on the sale. He'll get less ordinary income and more capital gain in later years.

Now, for *Addenda.* That space gives you a chance to get a rebate for repairs. For instance, if you had obtained a commitment for an 80% institutional loan, you might want to have an addendum letter to promise that you will get a rebate to cover $10,000 in repairs needed on the property. Do you follow that? If you want a no-money-down deal, many times the lender—that is the institution willing to give you a first mortgage on the property—will lend you as much as 95% of the purchase price. But unless it's a government-backed loan like FHA or VA, the lender generally will not want to give you a 100% loan. They want you to pay at least some down payment out of your own pocket. As a result you might not want to advertise the fact that the source of your $10,000 down payment is a repair allowance you're getting from the seller.

What about personal property? You always have to be careful. When you tour a property you're going to buy, there may be plants, chandeliers, carpets, or nice drapes that you hope to get as part of a package deal. But the seller doesn't feel they should be included. To avoid disputes, anything in the way of a fixture or movable object that you think should go with the property should be listed and attached to your offer in the form of an inventory. Then if the seller does not want to throw it in as part of the deal, argue and settle before rather than after the deal closes. There are often lawsuits or hard feelings on the subject of what was and what wasn't included. The general rule is that if personal property is not specifically mentioned in writing, it does *not* go with the deal. Rule? Settle what is included and what is not before the property changes hands. After property changes hands, possession is 99% of the law. Remember, refrigerators, appliances, drapes, furniture, and detachable fixtures are typically removed by the seller and taken with him. Plants or bushes in the ground should stay, but potted plants or movable window boxes can be taken out by the seller.

When you come to the next line about *Encumbrances,* they are talking about mortgages or liens on the property—like unpaid plumbing bills. All encumbrances should be paid by the seller, unless you plan to assume them and deduct the amounts due from the price.

Closing costs should also be paid for by the seller as far as I'm concerned (if you can get away with it as a buyer).

Once again, forget that the seller's broker tells you it's the "custom in the area" that buyers pay for certain things like title insurance. Just put in "to be paid by seller." If the seller accepts, you are home free. If the seller balks, it gives you something to negotiate about. Title insurance in northern California is generally paid for by the buyer. But that doesn't mean that you can't put in an *X* in the right place to suggest that it's going to be paid for by the seller. Not only that, if you check "to be paid for by the seller" and also insert the words "binder rate," then you can sell or trade the property within two years and get that title insurance premium back. Yes, you get the whole title insurance premium the prior seller paid even though it did not cost you a dime. We're talking about a tidy sum too. Title insurance costs around 1% of the property value. On a $100,000 property title insurance might be nearly $1,000.

Let me give you another little hint about the date chosen for closing. The closing date should be the day *after* rent is due. Let us say that you are talking about a building that is bringing in $1,200 a month. And you are doing a no money down deal. By closing the day after rent is scheduled to be collected you will actually get an extra $1,200 in cash at the closing. That's not only a no-money-down deal, but a way to take out cash at the close. The reason it works out this way is that rent is typically paid a month in advance, but loan payments are paid a month late, i.e., rent for January is due January 1st; the January loan payment is due February 1st.

Now what is the blank for *Deposit Increase?* Some sellers like to get their deposit increased after the happening of certain contingencies such as when the loan is approved. If you are a seller, a substantial deposit assures that your buyer is serious and that he is not stringing you along. But as a buyer I always write in there, "not applicable." I've given the seller a $1,000 note, and I do not want to come up with anything more until the deal closes. And as you saw in this particular deal, I'll probably get money back at the closing.

As to occupancy, check: *Upon Recordation of the Deed.* This doesn't mean you're personally going to occupy (for example) all four units of a rental property. It just means you are going to get the keys.

On the closing date you are going to be entitled to take control and collect future rents, you'll also be responsible for repairs, taxes, etc. from the date of possession as stated on this agreement.

Last but not least, the most important thing on this form is what I call the *Escape Clause*. If you look over the provisions on the reverse side of the standard offer form, you will see several clauses about pest control. Who pays for the so-called termite report? Generally, the buyer. But I always check off *Pest control inspection to be paid for by the seller*. And then I check off number 4, which means the building is taken "as is," subject to my approving the termite report. This is innocuous looking but it is the most important clause in your whole purchase offer. It's your escape clause. You've agreed to buy the property "as is" but only after you've read the termite report. **The termite report should always be subject to your approval.** Even if there is no termite damage at all (and that hardly ever happens), you can still say, "I don't *approve* the termite report." Perhaps you *like* termites. And you'd hoped there might be a few in the building. The fact that you don't approve the report lets you out of the deal completely. That's why this standard deposit agreement —the same one that every knowledgeable buyer in the business uses—is a one-way street for the buyer. Once the seller accepts, the seller cannot get out of it. But for you it's just a piece of paper.

The seller has to sell you his property at the agreed upon price. But you can get out of buying it by simply not approving the termite report. How do you *not approve* a report? Well, you just attach it to a letter and you send it back to the seller (or his agent). In the letter you say, "The deal is off. I do not approve this termite report." That lets you out of the deal. So that's it. You are out of the deal. It's dead. Nothing else is going to happen.

Naturally, you will neither get rich nor make too many friends if you abort all your deals. But isn't it comforting to know how to draw up an offer so that you can't possibly lose anything? When you make a Bill Greene–style offer in a typical real estate deal, there's *no risk*. The point is you can't get hurt financially by simultaneously making a lot of low offers. There's no money of yours at risk. There's nothing valuable of yours that the seller could keep. You've given him a note that's payable only if you close the deal. If a seller accepts your offer, you get what amounts to a free option on the property for the closing period which is whatever is stated in your offer. It's usually thirty, sixty, or ninety days. If you were going to buy an option on $100,000 worth of stock for ninety days, you'd have to pay big money for it. But when you make an offer on $100,000 worth of real property you've got thirty to ninety days to re-sell your contract for $110,000 to someone else. The "option" you obtained was free of cost.

You could make $10,000 or more by merely assigning the deal to someone else. In stocks, you can never guarantee yourself against loss. But in a no-money-down real estate deal or during the period from acceptance of your offer until the close, as I've shown you, there's no possibility you'd lose anything. In the real estate business we call that "no downside risk and unlimited upside potential."

A very good thing that happens once you start owning real estate is that you'll never have to pay federal or state income taxes again. You'll never pay income taxes! Once you have acquired a substantial amount of real estate, overflow depreciation and creative accounting will not only shelter all your future income but you'll be able to get a loss carry back for the last three years. Your depreciation losses will so far exceed your income that you can think about how to earn money in other ways. Some marginal projects might look better to you because you won't have to pay any taxes on the additional income or profits. By refinancing your properties every year you'll wallow in unlimited tax-free cash to spend.

The big question that people who think they're smart always ask me is "If it's so good, why doesn't everybody do it?" The fact of the matter is that about 60% of the population of the United States does do it. And although 60% of U.S. families own real estate, most heads of households are timid souls. Property owners in general usually own only the home they live in and maybe one other property. A mere 5%—that's of course over ten million people—own several investment properties. Wouldn't you like to be a member of that 5% group that owns several properties? It's a big club. There are ten million bigtime property owners out there. You *should* be one of them! Or perhaps you'd rather be a member of the 35% of the United States population which doesn't own any real estate at all and are for all practical purposes economically unfree. They are wage-slaves or welfare cases. For the most part, they choose to be "victims" of the system rather than masters. For them, things are going to get worse in the coming years. The taxpayers' rebellion will reduce the dole to less than subsistence. Workers will have to work more hours or become minor league capitalists to preserve their present standard of living.

I think making the choice to be rich is pretty easy. Getting started in real estate involves nothing more than getting off your fanny and beginning to look at properties. Once you feel comfortable, start to make offers. Get an education. Don't be afraid to take good courses like the Bill Greene *Tycoon Class*. Investment seminars and all related expenses (getting there, meals, etc.) are tax deductible. Learn how to make offers, how to negotiate, how to look at properties. Learn everything you'll need to know about real estate. But even if you do nothing more than read this book you'll have learned the most important secret. *You have to get out there and hustle.* There never was and never will be a shortage of promising deals. If you know that basic secret, you are in a position to start your own program today.

There are no convenient excuses for a real estate Tycoon's failures. The nature of the business makes it impossible to blame anything but your own laziness for lack of financial success. No one discriminates against property owners on account of sex, color, social class, educational background, religion, or handicaps. Some sellers may not like you. But if I sense that someone does not want to deal with me for reasons of personal prejudice, I simply send in a friendly ringer: If a black seller does not want to deal with me because I'm white, you can be sure I'm not going to court and wait five years till my civil rights case comes up. I simply send in a black friend to negotiate on my behalf. He closes the deal for me, transfers title to me, and I owe him one.

In getting loans, minority group members and females actually have a slight edge over garden-variety white protestant males. The reason is that the Feds have launched a program to make lenders give preference to borrowers in these heretofore disadvantaged groups. The main problem for the lender is *finding* qualified minority or female borrowers.

The only way to be a loser in real estate is to think of yourself as a loser and to sit at home doing nothing but watching the boob-tube. If you get out there and use the tricks of the trade in this book you'll make your million in one, two, or possibly three years. If you do everything wrong, you'll still make it in five years.

There is more to learn—the fine points—tricks of the trade. They can make or save you an *extra* million or three during the next few years. It's cheaper to learn about mistakes to avoid from someone like me than to make my most costly mistakes all over again yourself. Finish this book, look at properties, read the recommended books in my list. Take good courses and seminars—particularly the Bill Greene *Tycoon Class*.*

If you could read and relate to this chapter, you've got what it takes to be a Tycoon.

---

* My non-profit "Tycoon Newsletter" always contains a current schedule of weekend seminars and free lectures. See last page of this book.

You mean that with this book and nothing else
I could own that building, for no money down?

> *Bill Greene:* **Yes! Yes! Yes!**

Depreciation

Question: **Will You Please Explain** *Depreciation?*

Depreciation is an abstract concept that can put you in a position where
you never have to pay another cent in income taxes. You might even be
able to get a refund of taxes you have paid for the past three years. This
is how it works.

The IRS allows you to deduct a portion of the value of a building,
car, or other property owned and *used* by you *in business* over what they
call its "useful life." What the IRS feels is the useful life, and what, in
reality, is the actual useful life may be totally different. But you have to
play by their rules. Any IRS office will give you suggested depreciation
schedules on items of interest to real estate Tycoons. Drapes, carpets,
and furniture in rental units would have a useful life of about three
years. A brand new "tilt-up" concrete-wall warehouse would be assigned
by the IRS a useful life of as much as fifty years. Everything else is in between. Depreciation on property is determined largely by the type of
building materials used, and the type of use anticipated. Thus, assuming a warehouse building cost $50,000 you could deduct from your in-
come $1,000 per year for fifty years as a "reserve for depreciation."

Even though you did not lose or spend $1,000, if you claim the
$1,000 depreciation for accounting purposes in figuring your income
tax, you would be treated exactly as if you spent $1,000 cash per year on

repairs, or any other expense that could be deducted from income. If your warehouse was subjected to unusual wear and tear, you could claim a shorter useful life. The IRS ignores the reality that inflation is probably increasing the value of your warehouse by at least 10–20% per year.

For a different example, assume that you were able to buy a wooden *rental** house and rent it out. Say you assign $25,000 of the price to the land and $50,000 to the building. Further assume you were able to borrow $75,000 to make the purchase. An older wooden house would have a useful life of say ten years and this useful life of ten years divided into the structure's cost of $50,000 would allow you to get a depreciation deduction of $5,000 per year, even though you didn't put up a dime of your own money for the purchase of the property. Assuming you earned $5,000 per year at your regular job for the next ten years, you'd pay no income tax because each year you would have a $5,000 depreciation "loss" to offset against your $5,000 of earned income. *You are never allowed to depreciate land* because the IRS feels its useful life is infinite.

There are lots of technical variations, but I hope this explains basic depreciation. Under the 1981 Economic Recovery Tax Act, "depreciation" got a new name and is now called "Accelerated Cost Recovery System." This is even better than depreciation because it permits you to write off (or depreciate) any structure over a 15 year life. At the owner's option an even faster accelerated write-off of 175% of the 15 year life is allowed. If you take the 175% you don't get capital gains treatment upon sale.

---

*You can't take depreciation on a home used solely as a personal residence. But if you have roommates who pay rent, or if you use your home for business purposes, you can depreciate that portion of your residence used "solely" for business purposes or for the production of income.

CHAPTER 9

Get Yourself Organized

If your goal was not to make a million, but to climb Mount Everest, your preparations would not be limited to putting on tennis shoes and buying an Air India ticket to the base camp, would it? You would prepare carefully. You would learn all about climbing, and Everest in particular. You'd get your personal affairs in order, make sure of your financing, spend a few years on smaller peaks, getting yourself into shape mentally and physically. After all that, with tried and tested gear, you'd make the climb. Mountain climbers tell me that when you make it to the top, the feeling of exhilaration and freedom is unequalled by anything. Maybe that's true, but to me, once you get to the top of a mountain there is nothing to do but come down again.

The freedom that means something to me is financial freedom—and attaining it is a lot easier and less risky than climbing mountains. Don't get me wrong: this exhilarating financial freedom requires the same planning and preliminary testing as climbing Mount Everest.

America today is "Answerland." Everybody has answers to what we want in life. Encounter group! Primal Scream! The spiritual path of Yoga and Brown Bread . . . but to me, working on my inner life was not an answer. I wanted to be financially independent, and two years after starting my real estate career, I made it to the top.

I don't have The Answer, but one thing is certain—this book is not designed to make you feel better between your two ears. This is no head trip. I'm telling you how to get out in the real world and work effectively.

If you follow my program, the rewards are great. You can make $30,000 or more, on one deal! With a lot of effort you might be able to do it once or twice a week. And if you can do that for a year or two, outmaneuvering petty bureaucrats and outwitting the tax man, you will be a millionaire. Within two years! Now, that may not be The Answer. But being rich is a comfy solution to a lot of problems.

Making a million, getting ahead, achieving independence—whatever you call it—can be done by anyone. Sometimes people create their own mental barriers that make success harder to achieve.

Some barriers are more binding. Like being married, for instance. I've found that making money is easier if you are *single* and can move with opportunities. That goes for men and women. Getting tied down, particularly if your spouse doesn't share your vision, gets in the way. Children can absorb money like a sponge and make it even harder. If you have ever marvelled at those terrific success stories of the penniless immigrants—like Onassis—who made it big in a foreign land without even knowing the lingo, and you wondered what they had going for them, well, they had one big advantage: they were *single*. Don't be in any rush to get hitched.

Now if you've already got a spouse and hungry kids, that doesn't mean you have to give up. Certainly not. The fact is that most Tycoons do make it while being married. Some even had their kids early in life. Of course because there are more married people than singles, it is likely that you'll have more married Tycoons than single ones.

So hold off on having those kids until your Tycoon career begins to blossom. If you already have children, don't despair. Let them earn their keep as soon as possible. Even a three-year-old can put on postage stamps, seal envelopes, sharpen pencils, and help around the office. What's more, they love it. Had your daddy put you to work when you were three, you wouldn't have to be reading this book now. You'd have had your million and your financial freedom by the time you were twenty-one.

However, if you are planning to tie the knot, here are a few things to look for. Get a spouse who has a career and will be busy pursuing his or her interests while you go about yours.

Second choice is a spouse who leaves you alone during working hours, doesn't give you any opposition, and who will not be a consumer and spend all your capital—the quiet, traditional-type mafia spouse who doesn't get in the way or ask too many questions. The worst spouse is a neurotic nut who keeps you worrying all the time, can do nothing but spend your money, and disparages every project you work on. The one-word solution to that type of marriage is— *divorce!*

In some communities local prejudices can be a real barrier to financial success. If you have unusual sexual preferences, skin color, religion or politics not acceptable in your community, I have another one-word solution for that—*move!*

Frank the Family Man

Years ago when I started my first business tracking down missing heirs to estates, most of the people I hired were duds. But a year or so into the business, Frank answered an ad and started working for me. He was intelligent, motivated, and hard working. He made about $10,000 a year before he met me and this rapidly doubled. I suggested he invest his $20,000-a-year income in real estate to build up a nest egg. But Frank had nine kids and even when he doubled his income once again (which he did the following year), orthodontists, music lessons, athletic gear, and other family expenses absorbed all his extra income like a sponge.

Now, I'm sure Frank enjoys his family. He spends all his money and spare time with them. But Frank's timing was off. In my opinion, he should have made his million first and had his nine kids later. A big family may be fun, but it certainly limits your freedom of choice.

If you want to be rich—
Don't get married! Don't have kids!

Overcoming Hang-ups

Many people create barriers to success with imaginary handicaps. They blame their loser-status in life on irrelevant things. My friend Anna, for instance, felt she was unattractive. Before becoming successful or even trying, she just had to have a nose job. If the nose job did her any good, it was 99% psychological. A big nose won't have any effect on your business effectiveness.

One of the world's greatest orators, Winston Churchill, couldn't speak very well when he was a boy. He lisped. Another person with a similar affliction was Demosthenes the Greek, who practiced speaking with stones in his mouth until he overcame his handicap and who, like Winston Churchill, became one of the greatest orators of his age. My personal acquaintances include a friend from high school who had polio. Yet he went on to become a great American golfer. I myself was never a very good student in high school. I barely passed English composition in college. But you're reading my book, aren't you?

Instead of dwelling on faults or defects, just get on with your plans. Don't cop out. You'll find over and over again that people who had more serious problems than yours were able to overcome them. If you have something wrong with you don't use it as an excuse. *Act*—do something about it. Or do something *in spite* of it.

Psychologically Incapable of Success

My high school friend Cory was good looking, talented in sports and music, and was voted "Most Likely to Succeed." He had the sort of personality that everyone likes. Women were crazy about him even in high school. I cultivated him because he was everything I was not. He was far more popular and talented. At parties he was the best dancer. He had a smooth line for the ladies and a snappy retort to make everyone laugh.

He was always the colorful one, while in a social situation I was nervous and never had much to say. We started out in the army together. He came out tops on the leadership tests and was soon an officer. I stayed at the lowest possible level and was never considered a very good soldier. After the army, he moved in with a stunning New York fashion model and together they moved out west, where he built magnificent houseboats. *Life* magazine even did a picture story on his creations. But Cory never cared about money. He spent it as fast as he made it—one of his endearing qualities, people said.

During all these years, however, I was living a nonflamboyant life. When I started to get rich I tried to do business with my old friend Cory.

At one point he invented a process for making artistic stained-glass windows out of plastic resin. I found a builder who placed a big order with Cory. But Cory failed to deliver. Another time we were in a real estate deal together. But when the time came to sign the papers, Cory was off waterskiing and he never showed up. Cory had talent, people liked him, but he never followed through on a deal. Eventually creditors were following him. I invited Cory and his lady friend over to my place for an occasional free meal. I knew times were rough for him. Once, a few sterling silver knickknacks were missing. I found them in a pawn shop and learned that Cory had pledged them. By that time we were in our late thirties. Not kids anymore. Cory was still charming and a good talker. But for reasons I will never understand, Cory seemed intent on putting barriers between himself and success. Even from me, his only substantial friend in the business community, Cory cut himself off by stealing a few dollars worth of nothings. Last year Cory took a dry dive from a local office building.

Maybe Cory had it too easy. Maybe the girls who aren't so pretty or the guys with crooked buck teeth are the ones who will make it as Tycoons. They have to show a world that does not accept them just how good they are. Maybe that's why top capitalists are often members of minority groups, or are seldom selected in school as "Most Likely to Succeed." That's my theory anyway.

The Mañana Syndrome

What is the main reason that enthusiastic, healthy, capable men and women never make it? **They never start.** Or, having prepared Step One of a plan, they piddle away time until the "long run" arrives. And in the "long run" we are all dead. Making money is like being an athlete. You have to organize and develop good habits and keep at it. Once you start to become a champion, work even harder! Have you ever known exactly what you had to do, but just couldn't bring yourself to do it? You did something else to waste time, like cleaning up the house, going to a movie, or sleeping. You just didn't feel like working because you weren't properly inspired. So you procrastinated.

Then, first thing you know other things came up—busy work, social obligations, a TV program you couldn't miss. The mañana syndrome has hit you. Without something to snap you out of it, it could be terminal. You suddenly realize that there are so many other things to do that you dread even starting the main project.

So you waste time with trivia. You begin to feel "too tired" to do anything. You wake up feeling guilty. You finally decide that you have to get organized, but first you must buy some vitamin pills and have a few drinks. Finally after piddling away the day "getting in the mood," you belatedly start your project. But within a few hours you find yourself back in the old mañana rut.

Well, you are not alone. We all have the mañana syndrome—this mental and physical paralysis that starts when we are in school and gets worse until we apply the following simple cure. Here's my secret:

Remember the Popeye cartoons when you were little? Popeye the Sailor Man always got himself into bad trouble, but one way or another, at the very high point of the story, he'd open a can of spinach. He munched. Then swallowed. And then the musical theme signaling the victory of spinach over the mañana syndrome came on loud and clear. Ra, tah, ra ta ra tah. Ra ta ta ta ra ta TAH. By the last ra ta, Popeye could do anything. His muscles swelled. He bent iron bars. And his enemies fell before his mighty onslaught.

Think of the Popeye song whenever you are procrastinating. Have a drink of carrot juice, a candy bar, or your own spinach substitute.* Hum the theme song. After that, there is no excuse. Go to your list (of what you have to do) and do the first thing on it. Schedule exactly how much time you will need, but if you run over the time, keep at it until you are finished. If you are in the middle of a real estate deal and something goes wrong, keep at it. Don't take "no" for an answer. Find a way around the problem. Go over it. Go around it. And if none of that works, try barreling right through it.

When hard work brings home a deal and good profit—reward yourself! Have a good meal out or treat yourself to whatever turns you on. By psychologically conditioning yourself with small rewards for jobs well done, you will get as much of a charge out of your accomplishments as from the reward. An actor or performer gets more out of giving a good show and the applause it brings than from his paycheck. So it should be with the Tycoon. Pulling off the good deal is the thrill. Increased wealth is a secondary payoff.

So, go to it. Don't procrastinate. Put the TV in a closet. Cancel your subscription to *Playboy*. Stop all reading that tends to make you think like a consumer instead of a producer. Go to it and start. "Do it now" the voice will tell you. Why wait till mañana?

---

*Play one of my inspirational cassette tapes! See back page for order form. But don't wait till you're feeling down to order.

Now that you have seen some of the barriers people set up to stop themselves from becoming Tycoons, how can you organize yourself for success?

Educate Yourself. Read not only the biographies mentioned earlier, but read all the real estate books you can find. If they give you one good idea, it could be worth thousands. Still, reading is not to replace action. Reading is for sitting on the toilet, getting yourself to sleep, riding on a bus, or while waiting for someone. And there is more to read about than just real estate. Salesmanship, accounting, trade magazines for the apartment house owner, manager, or builder. The public library in a big city will have more specialized magazines than you can dream about. There is a good reading list at the back of this book.

Getting Organized

Having a creative account and a successful business-
oriented lawyer on your team sure doesn't hurt!

Finally, take the most boring course in the world, *Accounting One*. I flunked it, but it was probably the most valuable course I ever took. Sometimes it is given other names, but always take the first basic course. Remember business is in many ways like a game. Accounting is the way you keep score. Without it you just don't know where you are. When you move to bigger deals, a property that looks great and sends goosebumps of ownership pride up your arms would have given you rigor mortis if you could have understood the statements. Community college real estate courses are good too—but not as helpful as a strong basic accounting course.

Learn the Jargon.   Real estate, like every other profession, has its own special vocabulary. Many of the new terms you will come across are explained in this book. Learn them. My *Tycoon Home Study Course* contains a complete glossary of words, expressions, and abbreviations used in the trade.

Stop Consuming.   Ben Franklin, one of the richest self-made men of the colonial era had the right idea. Working in the print shop as a kid, he saw all the other printer's devils take several beer breaks a day. Ben drank water. He ran extra errands for extra pay. Within a few years, Ben had his own print shop. Then he started his own newspaper, while his contemporaries were still taking beer breaks. Ben Franklin was big on saving.

The Five Percent Rule

You can discover a whole new world if you apply the 5% rule. The 5% rule is something to strive for, not to accomplish all at once. When I told a stewardess friend about it, she said I was absolutely crazy and she never wanted to see me again. But I explained to her that it was one of the most important early steps on the trail to Tycoondom. Here it is:

Determine what your gross income is. For example, $1,000 per month.

Take 5%. That would be $50 per month. Plan to spend no more than that on your living expenses and taxes.

That leaves $950 to build your empire. Find a way to channel this entire amount into investments that will double, preferably in a month.

That is the goal. Now there are lots of ways to reach that goal. Let's take Sally, my stewardess friend.

Gross Income	$1,000
Income Taxes	300
Rent	250
Clothes	100
Car Payments	100
Food	100
Entertainment and Travel	200
Medical and Dental	50
Insurance and miscellaneous	100
Total Expenses	$1,200
Net Loss	$ 200

Obviously this girl could never become a Tycoon. Her Christmas bonus was the only way she got out of debt once a year. However, within two years of applying the 5% rule, she owned a thriving basket import business. Sally's tax-free income grew to $70,000 per year. This is how she did it:

If she was going to live on 5% of her gross income, she decided that her gross income was much too small. She began looking for ways to increase that income. At one of her regular stopovers, Manila, there was a native basket weaver who sold rattan fruit baskets for 35¢. Sally brought back a gross, duty-free with her $100 allowance. She had no transportation costs because she was a "stew," and she sold the baskets for $3.50 each. She picked up a few hundred extra every week that way. And that is where most other stews would have stopped.

Then the 5% rule was brought into play. Instead of squandering the extra profit, it was all reinvested in more baskets. To get more capital, she eliminated her rent by (together with her boyfriend) offering to become manager of the apartment building they lived in. Presto, there was another $250 a month to go into the high-profit basket-importing business.

She liked nice clothes and as manager of an apartment building she discovered the cast-off clothing of former tenants—the source I had been using for years. With a new twist, she began trading things that didn't fit her with other stews. Soon she was at the point where she never spent a dime on clothes. A combination of tenants' cast-offs and the trading of garments she couldn't use kept her looking sharp.

Car payments. Sally discovered she could buy a Volkswagen for $3,000, drive it for five years, and sell it for $3,000. Last year she bought a used $10,000 BMW 3.OCS, expecting to do the same in another five years. Though you put up more at first, you can usually break even with a good German car. It has therefore always amazed me that people would buy a brand-new American car and end up with nothing to show for their investment after four or five years. Just a rusted hunk-o-junk. There are several ways to eliminate car expenses. You might sell it and get along without one. Or have a part-time job which gives you a company car. At worst you can shop around for a used car at a good "all cash" price where the car will hold its value if you take care of it.

Food, entertainment, and travel. Sally didn't have to cut down much on these. As the basket business grew, business dinners were turned into deductible business-related expenses which helped reduce her income tax by a third. (Purchasing a small rental property and gaining overflow depreciation deductions got rid of the rest of her tax.)

If she keeps up the good work for a few more years, this stew will be a millionaire—and real estate played only a small part in her story. She owes it all to the 5% rule, which started her thinking of ways to reduce expenses and invest the saved capital in money-making ventures.

How could the 5% rule work for you?

Perhaps you could eliminate much food expense by helping out as a busboy, waiter, or hostess during rush hours. The usual pay is a few dollars plus a free meal. If you can't eliminate an expense, the 5% rule says "find an alternate source of income" that gives you the same effect as if you had saved. In other words, make profitable use of your spare time.

Be creative! Be inventive! There are hundreds of ways to earn extra money if you put your mind to it. Remember: **Find a need and fill it.**

I once came across this money-making scheme, which has to pull a high rank in ingenuity. This card was shoved in my post office mailbox:

DEAR FELLOW BOXHOLDER:

I drag my bones down to the post office each morning to check my box for mail. So while I'm at it, why don't I look through your little window too? If I see that you have some mail, I will call you immediately.

This saves you (literally) dozens and dozens of time-wasting— sometimes fruitless—trips to the post office. So why not join the rest of the folks on my "call sheet" for a couple of weeks to see if you like it? Give me a call at 345–6789.

Yours in rain, sleet, or snow,

Mr. J. FROST   P.O. BOX XYZ   Chicago, IL

Whether Mr. Frost had many takers I don't know. But at least he was trying.

Another way to success is to develop the traits of the successful. Assuming that you haven't quit your job or even made your first real estate offer, start revamping your image or changing it if necessary. Most important, create a reputation for extreme *dependability.* If you have an appointment at noon, don't arrive at two minutes past. Arrive early and stand there looking at your second hand. At precisely noon, ring the bell. If you have promised to return a book or a borrowed dollar on Monday morning, get it there at 9 A.M. Be very punctual. Hold up your end of a bargain or transaction. Don't give excuses to anyone. Do what has to be done. Your reputation for being dependable, prompt, and fanatical at meeting your obligations will be worth more than anything else as you move up in business. It works for the Swiss bankers. It will work for you.

Finally, what is the best, most productive thing you can do to get yourself organized as a real estate Tycoon? *Eat, dream, live* real estate. If you drive past a vacant lot, think of how you might improve and develop it. What would be its best use? When you see a junky or abandoned structure, figure out how you would remodel it and what would bring in the best rents. Stop your car at real estate offices and discuss your ideas with the local realtors. Get to know them all on a first name basis. Let them know that you are in the market for deals.

Let's Get Organized!

The main difference between a Tycoon and the other 99% of the population involves three factors. The first is *ambition*—and I covered ambition, motivation, and persistence in the chapter "Think Like a Tycoon." The second element is *having a workable, realistic plan.* "Realistic" means *not* spinning your wheels on projects that cannot produce a good profit. A nickel and dime business, like a neighborhood gift shop or hot dog stand simply won't make it. You must expend energy only on high-potential projects or education experiences that will give you a very solid return for the hours and money invested. What's a good return? If you can't anticipate a venture making at least $10,000 profit after taxes in a year or less, don't bother. The third factor is *your ability to put this plan into effect.*

Your time and money must be organized in such a way that it is spent only on activities that will produce maximum financial reward. You will notice immediately a great torrent of required paper work. There are lots of records to keep, mainly for the Internal Revenue Service

and other government agencies. If you don't get your paperwork organized *at an early stage* you will find yourself hopelessly buried in
insoluble accounting problems. I know, because it has happened to me.
Again, it will help you to enroll as soon as possible in a course of basic
accounting. Don't take a specialized course like Real Estate Accounting
because it's better to understand the overall basics first.

Remember, business is like any other game. You need a scorecard
to know how your team is doing. The scorecard in business is your
accounting record. Profits or losses are revealed only by good accounts.
Because you may not have taken an accounting course yet, I will give
you enough information here for you to set up a rudimentary accounting
system today. However I still recommend that you take that accounting
course at some future time.

If you hire a certified public accountant to do your tax returns, ask
the same accountant or his staff to help you set up a system of keeping
books and records. Then you can always know where you are and what
the score is. How much do you owe people? When is it due? How much
do your tenants owe you? You should be able to meet all your short-
term financial obligations out of the payments due to you from others. If
you look at the books in the reading list at the back of this book you'll
find that most of the real estate books on that list contain a chapter or
two on accounting. Have a look at them. A particularly good basic book
is *Landlording* by Leigh Robinson, sold in bookstores at about $16.00,
or you can order it by mail from me. (See order form at back of book.)
It has a very good chapter on record keeping plus sample forms you can
use to set up a basic system. When you are ready for some tax-avoidance
tips, order my new book *Win Your Personal Tax Revolt* ($16.00).

A Simple Accounting System

Here is an even more basic record keeping system for those who know
nothing about accounting.

Let's assume you have just closed escrow on your purchase of a
duplex at 1234 Anystreet, Yourtown, North Carolina.

The first thing I like to do is give each of my buildings a name. A
good name can add charm to a property. Personally I like the exotic
touch. But you can name it anything you like. Buy an attractive little
plaque and put it up on the property, for example:

> **Casa Paradiso Apartments**
>
> *For information concerning this property:*
> *Phone 333-3333*

I don't like to use my personal name on a property, or give my home address, because I don't want just anyone dropping in. Yet I want anyone who is interested in buying or renting to have an easy time contacting me. That's why you should have an answering service or phone answering device twenty-four hours a day.

At the start I suggest having a separate bank account for each property. It makes life easier, and at tax time all you have to do is give your accountant the check register and let him figure things out from that. I like to have each account at a different bank too. That keeps things well separated.

At the bank, ask for the checkbook and check register known as "The Executive," and if you have an assistant, spouse, secretary, or other trustworthy person, put them on the signature card for the account in case you are away or out of commission. Have your checks printed:

> **Casa Paradiso Bldg. Account**
> Your Name
> Your Box, Your Town
> Your Phone
> Your Drivers License No.*

This is the way your first few pages of checks and deposits will look:

CHECK NO.	DATE	CHECK ISSUED TO	IN PAYMENT OF	AMOUNT OF CHECK	DATE OF DEPOSIT	AMOUNT OF DEPOSIT	BALANCE
				BALANCE BROUGHT FORWARD			1,476.21
5074	6/23	Sam's Roofing Service	Repair Leaks	375.45			1,100.76
5075	6/26	Virginia Gordon	Cleaning	25.00			1,075.76
5076	6/26	The Banner Daily News	Rental ad	15.—			1,061.01
Deposit	6/29	Security Deposit— Tessie Tenant				600.00	1,661.01
Deposit	7/1	July Rent - Tessie Tenant				400.00	2,061.01
5077	7/5	Howard's Hardware	New locks & keys	52.22			2,113.23
5078	9/7	Sam's Home Improvements	Carport	1,000.—			1,113.23
5079	7/7	Citi-Power + Gas	utilities	15.—			1,098.23
5080	7/7	Allstate	insurance	275.00			823.43
Deposit	7/7	Cash from washing machine				3.75	826.98
5081	8/1	Tax Collector - R.E. Taxes		875.00			
Deposit	8/5	Deposit from Bob Buyer				5,000.00	

*The reason for including your license number is that suppliers always ask you to write it on checks for purchases. This way it is already there.

Naturally you must keep in mind that for income tax purposes, "repairs" in general are immediately tax deductible. They can be used to reduce or offset your taxable income in the year incurred. "Capital improvements" in contrast are not deductible and must be charged off over the remaining life of the building, or the life of the improvement (whichever is shorter). When in doubt, it is always better to have a "repair" than a "capital improvement" because there is more of a tax benefit. Assuming that the check register sample constituted your entire annual income and expense on Casa Paradiso, this is how the summary you would prepare for your accountant should look:

Casa Paradiso—Accounting Summary

Repairs and maintenance

Check # 5074	$ 375.00
5075	25.00
5077	52.00

Advertising

Check # 5076	$ 15.00

Capital improvements
New Carport

Check # 5078	$ 1,000.00

Utilities

Check # 5079	$ 15.00

Insurance

Check # 5080	$ 275.00

Taxes

Check # 5081	$ 875.00

Cash Flow

Rents	$ 400.00
Washing machine	3.75
Security deposits	600.00*
Deposit on sale	5,000.00*

*Not taxable income

I keep all of my fire insurance policies in a safety deposit box (in case of fire). All insurance against fire is in one file titled *Insurance— Fire and Casualty*. Into this I put all fire, earthquake, and other casualty policies. These are filed in alphabetical order by property so that once a month my secretary can review all policies and be sure that they are up-to-date and that the value insured for is the approximate replacement cost of the property. From time to time a mortgage lender will want to physically hold an original insurance policy. He has that right. However, to ensure the accuracy of your filing system, you must request a photocopy for each policy not in your files. Other insurance is broken down into several other categories: *Insurance—Motor Vehicles* (policies and correspondence); *Insurance—Liability* (policies and correspondence).

Billing

As long as you have only one property, keeping expenses and income credited to the proper account is easy. But suppose you have twenty. During a busy day you get a notice that ''your insurance premium on account 2233445566 has not been paid and your policy will lapse in three days.'' Since it would take hours to find out which building the policy refers to, I use this simple trick. The address on each bill should refer to the property by name. In that way the notice on this particular bill would come addressed to:

> Your name
> **Casa Paradiso**
> Your P.O. Box

In my early days, when bills, tax statements, bank statements, etc. came merely addressed to me, I had a devil of a time just allocating them to the proper parcel of real estate.

Filing System

I suggest you purchase two matching standard letter-sized two-drawer files. Not only will they be a convenient and semiportable place for your records, but if you purchase a factory-second flush door as a desktop, you will have acquired an attractive typing table as well. Each property will have about four or five folders, for example:

Casa Paradiso—New Roof. This file might contain your plans, building permits, contractors' bids, a copy of Notice of Non-responsibility for Liens and all else pertaining to this project. When the project is underway, it is kept in an upper drawer. When the new roof is completed and final inspection has been approved and all bills have been paid, it is filed below under ''closed files.''

Casa Paradiso—Tenants. This might contain copies of ads, leases, photocopies of tenants' checks, so that if at any stage they don't pay up you can sue and know in which bank they are likely to have a checking account to have your lawyer attach.

Casa Paradiso—Financing. This would have a copy of the note and trust deeds, showing how much was borrowed, and a payment book or other computer print-out showing how much was paid on principal and how much interest is due each month.

Casa Paradiso—Original Purchase and Depreciation Schedules. This would contain a copy of original escrow statements, any side deals with the owner, and a letter from a real estate broker setting forth his estimate of the percentage of depreciation applicable to land, building, and personal property. It would also contain your bill of sale on the personal property and estimated depreciation schedules for the next five years.

Rents Received. This file would include a list of all properties and a place to enter the rent as it comes in. I set the property address on the left; column two is security deposits; column three is scheduled rents with January, February, March, etc. marked out. Each month I enter the rent received. If there is a special transaction, for example, tenant got $25 off for painting or whatever, a note is made. If a tenant fails to pay—or is late—I mark a yellow circle around his name. If he gets too many circles I might take some action, like having a little talk with the tenant.

More Record Keeping Tips

Your record keeping system should also take into account these tips: Some banks offer *free* checking accounts if you have $100 to $300 minimum in the account. How do you get that first $300? Well, one way is from the security deposit from your tenant. The security deposit from a tenant will usually be a month's rent. (I personally prefer six weeks, but to each his own.) If you put this security deposit in your bank as a minimum deposit, then you should get the free account. If a tenant ever asks you for interest on his deposit, say that *you* don't get interest as the deposit is in a checking account. Therefore he isn't entitled to interest either.

Open a separate account for each property you own. That way every expense and everything relating to a specific property can be assessed easily. If someone else is preparing your account books, this will make it easy for him to figure out what you took in and what was spent on each property.

If you have to pay in cash you can still accomplish the same thing. Keep a record *in the checkbook itself* of *cash paid out.* For example, always note the cash spent, its purpose, and to whom it was paid, just as you would if the transaction had been by check.

When you get a check from a new tenant, have that person make it out to *cash*. That way a tenant cannot stop payment on a check he has already given you. I know you like to trust people, but when you've been around real estate as long as I have, you'll find out a lot of tenants' checks turn out to be "duds." Never keep checks lying around. Cash them immediately. If you are unsure about the signer, take it to the bank it was drawn on and cash it there. That will save a couple of days' waiting. Sometimes checks go bad unintentionally. Tenants overdraw their account—had to buy their mother a present, etc. What should you do? You should re-deposit all bad checks "for collection." That means any bad checks will not be returned to you, but will stay at the debtor's bank for up to ten days or until that person deposits enough to cover it.

I find it a real bother to write out the same checks each month, i.e., the same mortgage payment to the same company month after month. Why not use post-dated checks? If I buy a property and the seller carries the financing, I will write him twelve post-dated checks, each dated January 1, February 1, and so on. Since banks rarely look at dates on checks, I write in bold letters over the top of the check: **Do not cash before . . .** This will cause the banks to notice something special about the check.

Whenever possible I get post-dated checks from my tenants too. That way I don't have to chase them for payment. I have them pinned to the bulletin board and simply pull them off when the payments are due.

Another way to handle things automatically through a checking account is by something called "transmatic." This works when you have an institutional mortgage holder, like if you owe Philadelphia Savings money. Sometimes you forget to write them a check, thereby incurring a substantial late charge. The transmatic plan automatically withdraws a mortgage payment from a checking or savings account. Savings and Loan Associations and most banks will provide this service for you at no extra cost. It saves a lot of time.

If you have a contract of sale and if because the lender can call the loan in the event of a sale you don't want the lender to know that you have acquired property, this must be handled differently. Supposing the lender is Dell Savings and Loan. You go along with Sam Seller and you, Bob Buyer, open up a joint account with Sam. You tell Dell to automatically withdraw all mortgage payments from that savings account. Then, all you, Bob Buyer, have to do is make regular payments into that savings account, which can also be arranged automatically. The loan department will never know it is anyone other than Sam Seller paying the loan.

Next, a very helpful step in any potential Tycoon's career: Join your local association of property owners. In many cities there is a local apartment owners' association. Most counties or towns will have their own associations, such as the Irvine Income Property Owners' Association. If you consult a phone book under "clubs and associations" or ask around, you will find the appropriate group in your area. Join it. These associations probably cost as little as $10 to $20 a year for dues. Besides the obvious advantage of associating with people of similar economic interests, these associations recommend many helpful publications which are cheap or free. They make deals with merchants who will give members big discounts on carpets, drapes, washers and dryers, or whatever you need. These associations also take an interest in laws and regulations that are pending both statewide and local. Their opposition to rent control, for instance, is the only bulwark standing between you as a property owner and the fuzzy-thinking leftists who would like to take all your property away and smother the free enterprise system.

Therefore, one of your first steps in getting organized is to join your local organization like the association of (income) property owners. If your business is single-family homes perhaps you'll also want to join the local association of home owners. This group would have a name like the *Forest Park Improvement Association.* You'll make friends there and if you have problems it is nice to have experienced people to help you out, who are familiar with the local public officials. They'll be your co-members. There is a spirit of camaraderie in these associations and additionally these property owner groups often sponsor low-cost educational forums and seminars. These courses will help you be more effective in buying, selling, managing, and trading up your properties. They also set up tax write-off junkets and conventions in exotic places like Pismo Beach, maybe even Hawaii.

To summarize, borrow all the real estate books from the public library you can find. Acquire paperbacks if you can afford them—they'll be cheap, mostly under $10. All books and lectures should be studied if you feel they will be of value to you. Take an accounting course. Join your local association of property owners. Get on my mailing list for a free newsletter and news of upcoming *Tycoon Classes.*

Here is how to plan your time! First, it's a good idea to list all the things you want to do on a big sheet of paper. Then rearrange the list in order of priority, putting a number 1 next to the things of great importance, and so on down the list. Each specific project on the list should be related to your general plans and goals in life. If your main goal is financial independence, one of your first steps is to get an education, both formal and in the real world, before you jump into a deal.

Get some education in real estate by going to classes or reading books. Most important by far, however, is get out and *look* at the real estate deals available in your community. When you start out, the first thing to do is circle ads with magic markers or clip ads from local newspapers. You organize them, to spend time, perhaps all weekend, looking at properties. Later on priorities may change from looking at new deals to digesting the ones you have. Once you get into owning a few properties, you'll be making needed repairs and improvements or you'll make changes in tenants as appropriate. You should never get up in the morning without going over a plan for what you will accomplish that day and that week. Do not spin your wheels doing things unrelated to your major goals in life. It's so easy to get side-tracked into other diversions. Remember, you have a goal, and that goal is to achieve financial independence in the shortest possible time. Every minute counts and you must do only those things that relate directly to your goal.

That doesn't mean cutting out all pleasure. You must give yourself some treats now and then. But try to arrange going to the Bijou, or whatever else turns you on, as a reward for accomplishing a high priority activity. In other words, if you have ten or fifteen things in the number 1 category to accomplish, do not go to a movie or take time off until you have done those things. Robert Redford can wait. You can't. *Then* treat yourself to a night out. Psychologically it is very helpful to look forward to the reward you promise yourself for closing a deal or doing something important.

I have also found it most essential to get a diary or appointment book with a separate big page for every date. That way I can put down in detail what I want to accomplish that day. At 7 A.M. I have to do one thing, at 7:30 another, and at 8 A.M. still another. Time from now on should be closely scheduled. Your days should be filled up with properties to look at, books to read, people to call, etc. Don't get discouraged if you don't accomplish everything you map out to do on a given day. I always seem to schedule twice as much as I can accomplish and I am usually a little bit behind. I would rather have the feeling that I'm behind than that I have nothing to do.

People sometimes ask me, "Are you really happy?" Frankly, the only unhappy people I have ever met are people who are bored. Often these are rich people with too much leisure time. Just as often, however, they are working people who get home from work and the only thing they can think of doing is to watch television. These days, in our affluent society, even poor folks often have too much leisure time.

Happiness is having a goal and working towards it.

Many people spend money on shrinks instead of doing something productive which would make them happy. The shrink gets happy and rich. But does the patient? Not usually.

In business you may have to devote almost every waking hour to your work if you are going to be extremely successful. You will have to cut out all time-wasters and people who don't have a direct bearing upon your main activity—people who might lead you in wasteful directions. If you are lucky enough to find a boyfriend or girlfriend who shares your interests, they could be a very good influence on you and help you reach your financial objectives. Every race horse has a pace setter. Unfortunately in my life and most of my friends' lives, it is very difficult, if not impossible, to find such a person; someone you like to be with, like to make love with, and also thinks the way you do about acquiring a real estate fortune. If you have such a partner, you are in an ideal situation. Chain that person to your wrist! You might even consider marriage!

Making friends is another aim at real estate courses. Why not place an ad in your local newspaper and find a group of property owners to share experiences and work together on trades. If you are married and have a spouse who is interested in working with you, you might want to join another couple on projects. If your spouse does not share your interest, perhaps you can find another married individual with whom you can work. To keep problems at a minimum, your partner should be of the same sex. On the whole, romance and real estate don't mix. The clinch should be in the deal, not in hanky-panky with your partner. You are out to make money, not whoopee. Real estate deals I have made with compatible partners have been more satisfying and more enjoyable than those I have done alone. It is simply more fun to share your high and low moments with someone else.

So where do you find a compatible partner? Often through ads in the paper. Or you might meet people selling their property or buying yours, at real estate seminars like my *Tycoon Class,* or through groups you join or organize on your own. If you make your desires and interests known, like-minded individuals are guaranteed to come your way.

You can no longer be a consumer. You should never spend your time and money on fashionable clothes. They will have little impact on your business success and will only waste your time and money. There was once a book published called *Dressing for Success.* As if dressing made any difference! A few years ago, a friend and I both used to dress in patchy blue jeans and frayed shirts. We thought about putting out a parody of this book, in which we would be visiting our banker in raggedy jeans. Then, in the same raggedy jeans, we would be looking at property, closing deals, etc. I am convinced that bankers, sellers, and everyone else are more interested in what you have to offer than in the name of your tailor. So don't kill a lot of time worrying about how you look. Just stay neat, clean, and presentable. Again: Put your TV in the closet. They don't call it the "boob-tube" for nothing! If you just *have* to watch the American Bandstand Reunion, then schedule it in. But watch nothing else. TV is a prime time-killer. The same thing is true to a lesser degree of the radio. Instead of listening to music, have a cassette player in your car. Then, when you're driving you can slip a cassette educational course into your player and spend the time learning as well as driving. It just so happens I put out a good set of educational cassettes.

You might also, while you are driving and learning, try flossing your teeth. You can floss with one hand if you use a plastic holder. I give you this helpful hint because most people lose their teeth by the time they are fifty. Not decay—it's the result of gum disease. Nobody wants to buy real estate from a toothless wonder. Flossing with a little plastic holder will keep the gums healthy and your mouth smelling fresher. It will prevent you from wasting time and money on dental work when you could be out looking for property.

I didn't bring up flossing your teeth to be funny. In fact, being healthy is a Tycoon's biggest concern. If you do not work at maintaining a healthy body, all the money in the world can't buy you a new one. Luckily, property ownership means that you can get plenty of exercise by working on your properties. Don't be afraid of strenuous physical activity! Others would have to go to an exercise club or whip themselves into a frenzy playing tennis. But as a property owner you get to do all this healthy work, like shingling, stonework, painting, and landscaping.

Doing it yourself is also probably saving you $50 an hour. Improvements and sweat equal appreciation in the value of your real estate. I much prefer painting a building to playing golf. The paint job may bring me an extra $100 in rents, $10,000 in increased net worth. In the meantime, I am keeping fit.

In the next few years you may want to leave your job. But take that action only after accumulating enough wealth and cash flow to live comfortably. When you leave your job, you will lose your group medical plan. So why not join a group like Kaiser Plan in California? I am sure there is one in your area. With Kaiser you pay a relatively small amount (like $60 a month) for full medical coverage. Unlike medical insurance, where you have to select your own specialist who may turn out to be incompetent, Kaiser will refer you to their own staff specialist. Having paid the basic $60 a month, any extra treatment like x-rays is only $1 or $2. This minimum charge is probably designed to keep the hypochondriacs at bay. Kaiser also has complicated instrument and diagnostic gear that no sole practitioner can afford. Hospitals charge hundreds of dollars for the same tests. Unfortunately, at Kaiser you do have to wait days or weeks for service and the level of service is generally unexceptional. Still, it is cheap and provides a reasonably satisfactory level of service, which I was not able to obtain consistently from private or small groups of practitioners. But you may also be able to *trade* something for medical services. I have found many doctors, particularly younger ones, open to barter. Like getting a break on rent, in exchange for molar work. So always offer a trade, whenever possible. It conserves cash and has obvious tax advantages for all concerned.

One of the most important steps before buying your first property is: Use the *Hundred House Rule.*

Here is what happened to me on *The Bayview:* This was a gorgeous home with a most magnificent view of the San Francisco skyline and all of San Francisco Bay. It was one of the first homes I looked at. Because it was worth about $150,000 at the time, I considered it way out of my league and figured there was no way I could make money on it. It was a very attractive redwood and glass house. Apart from the pink trim, which screamed to me for a coat of Barcelona Brown, there was nothing wrong with the place.

Yet after I had completed my hundred house look, it was still on the market and the price had been reduced to $125,000. I was told it had been vacant for a year or more. I smelled a problem. Inquiring of the neighbors, I learned that a year earlier *two weeks* after she moved in a beautiful young girl had had her throat slashed, reputedly by a mafia don who had caught her in the arms of another man. The man had been strung up in the kitchen in a very unpleasant way. It appeared that the hoodlum had purchased the house for his girlfriend, but after the "incident" had taken off for parts unknown. The heirs of the girl had been notified that they owned the property, but they, wanting nothing to do with the situation, merely told a local lawyer to sell the place for the best possible price and just send them a check. The lawyer had the property appraised ($150,000) and listed it with a broker. From time to time offers were made—mostly by people who were new to the area and who had not heard the murder story. When they heard the grisly tale, they generally backed out of the deal, figuring that the house had bad "kharma." By the time I returned to the house six months later for a closer inspection, the neighbors had even embellished the tale. The girl, it turned out, had been a belly dancer who often did exotic things like stripping to the nude on moonlit nights. According to the neighbors, the ghost of the slain girl was doing her striptease on the front lawn every time there was a full moon. The story was retold and found its way to the papers. Nobody in town would buy the property.

My reaction was a little different than most. I figured if I owned a haunted house with a full moon show of that calibre going on, it would sure beat going to a drive-in. The property had been listed with several brokers and all their listings had now expired. Even the local brokers didn't want to be bothered showing what they regarded as an unsalable property. I asked more questions and ordered a "title report." I learned from the title report that a private loan on the property amounting to $75,000 was in default by several months. It appeared that the people who originally owned the property would get it back in a foreclosure for $75,000, less than half of what it was worth. The owner of the mortgage turned out to be a widow living about two hundred miles south.

I drove down to see her. The information I got might have upset most people, but for me it represented an unusual opportunity. She told me she would under no circumstances take back the property even if she had the legal right. In a foreclosure, if no one bids the amount of the mortgage, the mortgage holder gets the property. If the mortgage holder does not want the property, a person who comes to the sale and bids 3¢ (or anything) gets it. I told her that if she didn't bid for the property it was likely to go for a song, and that I would personally bid $10,000.

I asked her why she didn't just take over the property and rent it out for the $1,000 per month it should rent for. She broke into hysterical tears, but when she had regained a measure of composure told me:

"My husband committed suicide in the bathroom of that house four years ago, just two weeks after we moved in. He shot himself in the mouth with a shotgun. It wasn't pretty. The house was vacant for a long time. Two weeks after Mr. Moravia and his beautiful young wife bought the place from us—well, you know what happened. I don't want to go near the place."

I gulped. But thought to myself, "What the heck . . ." So I offered the lady a deal whereby I would take over the mortgage and tax payments of $600 per month. She agreed that I should bid the full amount of the mortgage at the foreclosure and she would extend the loan for five years. Assuming there were no other bidders at the sale, I would have made my first no-money-down deal.

Feeling I wanted to be sure of my ownership, I placed a long distance call to the heirs of the dead girl. They were resigned to the fact that the house would be taken from them in a foreclosure, and had no interest in doing anything about it. To be sure that there would be no surprises with an outside bidder going against me at the sale, I offered the heirs $300 for a "quit claim" deed. They accepted at once, since that was $300 more than they had expected to get. I became the owner and holder of legal title.

With the permission of the lady who held the loan on the property, I called off the foreclosure sale and moved into the house. I never even thought about the two week curse until fifteen days after I moved in—I got a lot of calls from the mortgage lady and neighbors asking if I was OK. I was, of course, and in the two years I lived in the house I never had an unhappy moment.

The view was great. I watched big ocean liners pass under the Golden Gate Bridge, past Alcatraz and under the Bay Bridge. The house itself was laid out as a duplex and the smaller unit was rented by me to another bachelor who was in the wholesale fine wine business. I got $375 a month, plus $50 in wine for the lower unit. My cash outlay every month for loan and taxes was $600.

$600
375   Rent for lower unit
$225   Net outlay

The place I was occupying had to be worth at least $600 a month rent. It had three bedrooms, two big bathrooms and a super modern kitchen, etc. In fact it was a little too big for me, though with all that wine to drink every month I kept it pretty full with parties three times a week. In due course I painted it, put in some rosewood paneling, expanded the size of the living room, and took in a girl roommate. She paid $275 per month which more than covered utilities and kept snacks in the refrigerator. She was good company too, though to keep the relationship business-like I made another rule which I have always followed: *Never sleep with your tenants.* We were very good friends, and when she was down she could rely on me for a shoulder to cry on. But most of the time our relationship was quite formal and correct. It worked out well, for over a year.

The net result of my first deal, including the roommate's contributions, was that I got a free place to live in, all the good wine that my friends could drink, utilities paid for, free food, usually cooked by my girl roommate, and good company. Not only that, when I went to see my accountant at income tax time, he told me I had a slight tax loss or write-off from the depreciation I was allowed on the property. (See the section on depreciation.)

In two years, the property I bought for $75,000 with nothing down was sold for $275,000. By trading up, a maneuver which is covered later in this book, I got $200,000 cash, tax free. Part of that $200,000 profit was due to the devaluation of the dollar, or inflation. But don't forget, the property was worth $150,000 when I bought it, so as soon as the ink had dried on my purchase contract, I was $75,000 richer. Without any inflation or increase in the general price of property, I would have made $75,000 just as soon as I had changed the image of the house from a deserted, deadly haunted place to a bachelor pad of fun and parties. As it turned out, my first buy had been at the start of the real estate boom in California. But even without a boom this deal would have been a winner.

That's why you must get yourself organized and look at one hundred deals. I'm sure you will find several of your own winners.

The Tycoon's Credo

A Tycoon is:

1. **Organized**
   I will schedule a written program of my activities and objectives and stick to it the entire day.
2. **Dedicated**
   I will do at least one thing I should have done, but have been putting off.
3. **Confident**
   I will feel as good as possible and achieve a sense of well-being by meditating fifteen minutes every day. I will exercise or jog another fifteen minutes.
4. **Appreciative**
   I will tell my family, friends, and business associates "I like you" and *mean* it. I will be generous with praise and compliments.
5. **Optimistic**
   I will not dwell on past failures but will think positively about the present and the future.
6. **Educated**
   I will read something to improve my mind each day, and will keep away from nonproductive and time-consuming people and activities.
7. **Thrifty**
   I will not be a consumer or a taxpayer any more than is absolutely necessary.
8. **Sociable**
   I will be charming and agreeable to everyone and speak badly of no one.
9. **Alert**
   I will be open to new ideas, experiences, and people who might teach me something new, and I will not let myself fall into a rut or routine.
10. **Dependable**
    I will meet all my business, social, and moral obligations punctually, honestly, and honorably.

—Bill "Tycoon" Greene

CHAPTER 10

Finding Super Deals

Did you ever hear of Father Flanagan, the founder of Boys' Town? He is famous for the quote "There's no such thing as a bad boy." Well, here is Bill Greene's variation on the same theme: I say "There's no such thing as a bad real estate deal!" Every deal, every property, is potentially "good" or profitable, but sometimes (read "sometimes" as "usually") the *price* is *too high*. Yet, bought right, and properly leveraged with good loans, *any* property could be an excellent deal. This is why, once you know the market, you should make an offer on virtually every property you look at. Much of this book is concerned with what sort of offers to make. Here we will deal with the process of ferreting out all the deals on the local market. More importantly, you'll learn to flush out deals that are not on the market, but can be yours exclusively.

Making big money in real estate is as easy as falling off a log. But if I told you to fall off a log this minute, you'd have a problem. First you'd have to find a log. Downtown, in some cities, that would be difficult. Then you'd have to find a lake or a stream. The third step, getting the log into the water, would involve a bit of work. Finally, the hardest thing of all, you'd have to stand up on the floating log. After all that, falling off is easy.

Making money in real estate is just as easy as falling off a log. But the problems in getting on are similar. First you must *find* suitable property. It might not be available in your neighborhood, or even in your city. Then you've got to negotiate for it, arrange financing, and close the

Making money is as easy as falling off a log.
Getting *on* the log is the biggest problem.

deal. Finally you must get the property in proper running order. Once all that is done, you'll make nothing but money. Finding the right property, negotiating the deal, and staying on top of it is the hardest part.

Obviously you are nowhere until you find your first property. **If you don't look you'll never find anything!** Let me show you *how* to look for good deals and how to recognize a bargain when you see it.

How can you find or create that elusive first "good deal"? Do you think that if you sit in your living room and watch television, some salesman will come to the door and present you a super deal with a red ribbon on it? And all you'll have to do is write out a check and wait for the profits to roll in? Unfortunately, any deal presented to you by a salesman with a smooth, memorized presentation and four-color brochure isn't worth beans. You'll have to get off your fanny and as a preliminary step you must educate yourself to the point where you can recognize or create a good deal when you see a promising situation. Educating yourself is easy. It costs nothing but a little time and shouldn't take more than four to six weeks. You simply learn and apply the *Hundred House Rule.*

Look at a minimum of one hundred properties for sale. If you are interested in single-family houses, look at one hundred houses. Or you can look at one hundred small apartment houses, one hundred warehouses, or one hundred motels. Look at whatever type of property you would feel comfortable owning and managing. I suggest that you concentrate your attention on run-down or "problem" properties of one to four units for starters. Compare "problem" properties with well-managed, clean income properties that command high rents and top dollar asking prices. Try to figure out the difference between the "good" and "bad" properties. Ask yourself, "How could I improve this particular sick property? How might I cure the problems to make the building worth more rent? What would my changes mean ultimately in terms of market value?"

Remember, until you have actually gone through one hundred properties, both physically and on paper, it's all just six weeks of looking. Mere mental exercise. You do not make any offers. You just ask questions. It's an educational time only. Don't let anyone "sell" you anything. During your hundred house period, explore different neighborhoods. Visit nearby towns and communities. Observe where the growth areas are. By growth I mean new construction and upgrading. Which areas seem to be declining in popularity? Are undesirable elements like bums or porno-massage-pinball parlors moving into nearby shopping areas? Where are the trendy young professionals shopping? How much remodeling is going on? Check out different types of property. Be alert for special situations.

Watch out for special local factors affecting value.

Even though you may be preliminarily interested in buying small apartment units, don't be afraid to look at property containing stores on the lower floors and apartments upstairs. This is called a "mixed use" in real estate. Look at homes, duplexes, apartment buildings, stores, offices, manufacturing buildings, and warehouses. Notice which seem to be the best value for the money. Where do you get the most square footage per dollar? Compare prices for comparable properties in fashionable neighborhoods with prices in up-and-coming areas. Try to notice patterns of change. Consider the possibilities of converting abandoned warehouses into offices or apartments, apartments to offices, or remodeling any type of property for alternate uses. Discuss your ideas with real estate agents, contractors, sellers, and other people already in the business of owning, managing, or remodeling. Look at other developers' successful projects. What makes them work? Look at failed projects, places with a lot of vacancies or into foreclosure. What mistakes can they help you avoid?

To ascertain the prevailing rents in an area, spend time posing as a prospective tenant. Seek to rent various types of property. If landlords are anxious to give concessions like paying your moving expenses and giving three months' free rent, obviously the rental market must be soft. True rents are often not the same as scheduled rents. Scheduled rents are what sellers try to make you believe they can get for their property.

How do you find one hundred properties to look at? The traditional method is simply read ads in the local papers. Probably one-third to one-half of all real estate deals are initiated through newspaper ads. With a magic marker, circle ads for interesting properties. Call. Make appointments with the owners or agent handling the deal. Don't waste time. Arrange your schedule so there is order and flow to your viewing. In other words look at all properties on the north side of town in the morning and on the south side in the afternoon. Stay organized! Don't spend time driving and going back and forth unnecessarily. Use time efficiently. Ask a lot of questions.

What's the local real estate market been like over the past twenty years? Are there more people anxious to sell than there are buyers—or vice versa? How long does it take for fairly priced deals to sell? Where are the schools and churches? Does the town have a master plan? Is there any urban renewal or condemnation activity in store?

Are there special grants-in-aid or subsidized government loans available for owners in the area because it is considered historical or otherwise worth preserving? Is a freeway going through? What new developments are going in? If expensive new apartments are planned for the area, it could be possible that the higher rents scheduled for the new projects will make the older units by comparison more attractive to prospective tenants. A new shopping center or rapid transit stop could make all properties in an area more convenient and therefore more valuable. *Has there been any local agitation for rent control? If so, run in the other direction. Rent controls spell devastation to the area, both physically and economically.*

What improvements made by other real estate operators are most profitable? Perhaps installing a lot of skylights, modern kitchens, and exterior shingles make the difference between a $60,000 and a $100,000 property in some areas. It is up to you to ascertain the costs of value-adding improvements. Call up general contractors. Have them stop over at a property that you are "considering." Let them give you their estimates and suggestions on restoration, remodeling, conversions, or needed repairs. You may see indications that $10,000 in work could give you $30,000 in added value. In many instances merely cleaning up and painting could turn a lemon of a property into a juicy grapefruit. Can you do the work yourself? Being your own contractor, carpenter, and painter can save at least two-thirds on most projects.

The most important thing is that by looking at a hundred or a large number of deals on the market and considering all the possibilities your creative mental juices will start circulating. You will begin to have original ideas on where to buy, how to make profitable improvements and how to best take advantage of the existing situation.

Why did I choose the *Hundred House Rule* instead of the *Fifty House Rule?* Is there any magic in the number *one hundred?* Of course not! If you feel comfortable making your first serious offer after looking at sixty-three properties, do it. If you don't feel you know the market after carefully examining one hundred deals, then look at two hundred. Can you look at too many deals? Yes! As in the search for a spouse, it is impossible to find perfection. The perfect real estate deal doesn't exist either. You can look forever and you'll never find perfection. There's always work to be done, and no guarantees.

Once you are familiar with every property on the local market, you have to take that giant step. *Make an offer on the best deal available.* You must get into the game and do as well as you can. If you wait for perfection in a lover, you'll die a virgin. In real estate there are plenty of virgins who have been "just looking" for forty years.

If everything locally is so high priced that you would rather be unencumbered, it could be a good time to take a trip and see what sort of opportunities exist in Vermont, Hawaii, or wherever attracts you. Before you begin your career as a real estate tycoon, it may well be the opportune moment to move to an area you have always wanted to live in. Real estate investments, at least in the beginning years, will tie you down to a given locality. So you might as well acquire those first properties in a climate you are happy to be in. To make it big in real estate you will probably have to put some roots down in a community for at least a few years.

Earlier, I said that up to 50% of all real estate deals are initiated by ads in the paper. If you are thinking, you might have asked yourself, "Perhaps the other half of deals are initiated in some other, possibly better way?" Right you were! Most of the best deals are never placed on the market or advertised. In my experience, looking at properties with an average real estate agent or responding to ads has been a wonderful way of getting an education; that is, doing the hundred house bit. But once familiar with the market, I quickly discovered better ways of ferreting out super deals.

Get a real estate broker who will do you some good. When you visit real estate offices in response to an ad or just walk in off the street, casually ask whoever you are dealing with "Who is the most successful broker in the office?" The agent on duty or "floor person" will probably point out a busy looking individual on the telephone with three people waiting to see him. Don't call him or waste his time during your hundred house period because he will rapidly size you up as a "looker," not a buyer, and won't have anything to do with you after that. But keep his name and number on a 3 × 5 card for future reference. Once you have clearly in mind the type of property you want, and the prices and terms you are interested in, call this broker. Also call any and every other top-notch broker at every other major firm in your area. Give him your requirements and explain that you are ready, willing, and able to acquire large amounts of property. Any top-notch broker is already very familiar with the Tycoon principles because he and all his heavy-duty clients already use the techniques.

As a top producer, your new agent will have many clients who are interested in trading out of properties as they move up to bigger and better deals. These properties will be available out of trades to buyers who can make quick decisions. Many of these deals will never be listed for public sale because the American tax laws penalize the owners (by making them "dealers") if the property is advertised. Thus they are "available" but not on the public market for sale. You as a buyer will find out about them by attending local trading sessions for professionals in real estate, or getting to know the brokers who specialize in representing the wheeler dealers. These brokers will invariably be the "top producers" in every busy office. They have no time for amateurs, novices, or lookers. They will be among the 5% of brokers who earn 90% of the commissions in an area.

Don't waste their time! Just remember that the best deals are often not advertised, but are called in the trade "pocket listings." Probably because the seller is in the pocket of the broker and the broker keeps the listing in his pocket. He shows it only to his favorite investor clients. The broker does not share the listing (and the potential commission) with the other brokers because he will earn a full (usually 6%) commission on the deal by representing *both* the seller and you as the buyer. If the broker knows exactly what you want, he will call only if a deal pretty close to your requirements materializes. The advantage of dealing with a top producer is that he does not waste your time showing you unsuitable properties.

I have several brokers who only call me once or twice a year. When they do call, I know there will be a deal because they know exactly what I want: Low up front cash requirement, potential for improving the income stream, and pots of money to be made in the ultimate resale or trade up.

The most successful brokers are successful for very good reasons. They know the market and they do not float around wasting their time

Good brokers always have pocket listings!

with sellers who want outrageous prices or who change their minds. They have no use for "buyers" who are only lookers or clients who will try to chisel down or circumvent their commissions. Good brokers will do their best to solve any problems as they come up: they persuade lenders to loan during tight money periods. They convince title companies to waive objections. A successful broker cajoles building departments to approve permits or zoning if these are a contingency. If necessary to close a deal, good brokers are usually flexible about carrying back all or part of their commission in the form of a note. For this they normally ask for and get the buyer's agreement to resell through him.

A good broker is worth his weight in gold. The only problem is that as few as one in fifty of the real estate agents in the business are any good. But the good ones are knowledgeable of the current wrinkles in the tax laws and all current trends in the local market. They probably earn well over $100,000 per year in commissions by handling in excess of two or three million per year in sales. If you are clear about what you want, they will let you know of good deals from time to time. You must be ready to move fast. If they call you at 8 A.M., be ready to meet them at the property at 8:15 and be ready to make an offer by 8:30. The best real estate deals are always snapped up on the day they are offered.

Naturally you are in no position to recognize, much less make such a deal, until you know the market: the best way to know the market quickly is to use the *hundred house rule.* Once you have looked at one hundred properties, make low offers, or no-money-down offers on *every* deal you look at from then on. Remember there is no such thing as a bad real estate deal! At the right price or with good terms, any deal can help make your million.

How about other ways of finding super deals? Going back to the ads, before we pass on to other methods, look particularly for ads that say "for sale by owner." Normally owners have an exaggerated idea of what their property is worth. Often they start out asking well over market prices. But owners will sometimes accept *terms* that brokers would convince them to turn down. Also, many sellers are what I call "non-money motivated." So if you can deal directly with a seller rather than through an agent, you may find that your seller has things other than money in mind when he begins to negotiate with you. A seller represented by a real estate agent generally acts more rationally. In my comments on negotiating, coming right up, I'll give you several hints on dealing directly with sellers. There are definitely different and more creative techniques you can exploit in direct negotiations.

Another type of ad, which I call the *hot tip ad,* is where it says something like "Owner will carry loan." That statement, appearing in many ads, tells you that the seller may be willing to carry *all* the financing on the property. The seller found that if he takes a small cash down payment he will get certain tax benefits. He wants an *installment sale.* The tip off that is important to you is that the seller is mentally prepared to lend you the money to buy his property. He will "carry the paper." To you as a buyer this means that there will be no need for you to qualify for a bank loan. You only have to convince the *seller* that you are reliable, namely that you will make the required monthly payments to him on the mortgage he has carried back.

It may be possible for you to convince a seller advertising "low down" to carry back a 100% loan. For those skeptics who say "it can't be done," I say don't knock it if you have not tried it! Over half of my own deals have been no-money-down deals, with the sellers carrying the entire loan. There may be many good tax reasons why a seller is willing to do this, and I've discussed many of them in the section on no-money-down deals. Here I just stress that where you see a "for sale by owner" ad you can occasionally get property at a super price. More often, you can negotiate creative loans that are very advantageous to you. Where you see "low down" in ads it always means that the seller is willing to carry the financing. If you are just starting out or are overextended, or if for some reason you find it difficult to borrow from financial institutions, "low down" means that you do not have to look too good on paper and you can usually make the deal with a lot less than 10% down. You only have to charm the seller, who seldom requests or requires a financial statement.

Whenever you meet a seller or an agent through a newspaper ad, whether the deal advertised works out for you or not, never fail to ask if they have any other properties that you could look at now or coming up in the near future. Many a property advertised in the paper has been totally unattractive to me. But the owner had another deal around the corner or up his sleeve and I bought the *other* property. Every owner or agent you meet is a contact. And in real estate (as in any other business) it is having contacts who want to deal with you that is important. **A good contact in the business is better than any one deal.**

If someone in business appears to be exceptionally *lucky* time after time, you will find that his or her "luck" is always *other people.* You'll often be presented with a deal or opportunity as a result of knowing someone who knows you are a serious, reliable buyer. Or they simply want to do you a favor. You'll be able to utilize that opportunity or take that deal because you have other contacts to help you do it. In real estate your contacts will range from sellers to handymen and construction people. There will also be potential tenants and financial backers and a whole gamut of acquaintances who can supply the pieces to make a deal work. In your hundred house period you will not only be getting an education, but just as important, you will be cultivating a wide range of potentially useful contacts in the business.

Your preparation or training period should be complete within two months. Thoroughly familiar with the local market, you should at that point be able to do what I call a "second gear appraisal": You hear of a property for sale. You drive by in second gear. If you have done your hundred house homework, you should be able to look at any building from the outside. Within a 5% margin of error, you can estimate the asking price and the price it will actually sell for. Try it a few times. If you are way off, go back to the drawing boards—or rather, the ads—and keep looking and asking questions.

Once you can make "successful second gear appraisals," you have arrived! You are as good as the so called professionals in the area, and you should have full confidence in yourself. If you know the market, you can't make many mistakes.

Now that you are educated and are ready to become a serious shopper and buyer, let's go on to the ways that "insiders." people who really know their way around, get the very best deals.

Multiple Listing Book: "Multiple" is a monthly or weekly picture book put out as a cooperative effort by all the real estate agents in a given community, listing the unsold inventory of properties. Generally the MLB is the last place to look for good deals because after an owner has tried to sell property on his own and it didn't move, he gives it to an agent. The agent shows it to all of his favored investor clients. They don't take the deal because it is overpriced. He advertises, but still no takers. The agent shares it with other agents in his office. None of the other agents want the stinker of a deal, nor do *their* clients. After exposure to several hundred buyers, the broker decides to share his commission; to put it in the Cooperative Multiple Listing Service. That is his last resort. The broker proclaims to the community "I couldn't move this turkey to any of my own clients, so I'll pay half of my 6% commission to any other real estate agent who can find a sucker to take it." Obviously the best deals never get into the Multiple Listing Service. The best deals are the pocket listings or the deals that never get listed at all.

Can you *ever* get a good deal out of Multiple? Of course you can! There are at least two ways I have gotten super deals out of Multiple. The first involves having a real estate agent who is willing to go to the printer or publisher and get the first galleys of the Multiple Listing Book just as they come off the press.

Here's how an occasional winner gets on Multiple. Picture this: Little, old, incompetent broker doesn't know the market, has no clients, is in real estate only to have a one man office to get away from the wife and play cards with his cronies. This bloke hits it lucky and a listing comes into his office at a price well below market value. Not recognizing the good deal for what it is, nor having any clients to show it to, he puts it into Multiple. When it is published, the broker is immediately deluged with dozens of full price offers. Legally the seller is obligated to sell at the first full price offer by virtue of the contract with the Multiple Listing Service. He thinks the broker did a swell job by bringing in so many offers. The seller doesn't realize that his agent made a terrible blunder by listing too low. But the point is, you have to be the first offer. In a decent sized community, there may be one or two sleepers a week coming out in Multiple. To take advantage of them you have to get the sheets early!

Getting to those rare underpriced offerings before the crowd is one way to get good deals out of Multiple. Being first is the best way. However, being last is another way: Every listing in Multiple carries an expiration date printed right above the photograph of the listed house. If you

Getting multiple listings before the ink is dry

call the listed owner a few days before the expiration date and ascertain that the property is not sold, you can deduce several useful bits of information. These can be used to discuss and later draw up an offer to be presented one day after the expiration date. If the asking price was $50,000 you know the seller was willing to pay out $3,000 for the standard 6% commission. He doesn't have to pay the broker commission after the listing expires. There was probably a factor in the asking price for negotiation: at least 10%. So an offer of $40,000 to $43,000 net would likely be accepted. But since the property didn't sell in three to six months, the owner may be more than a little discouraged. He may be desperate to unload. That could mean he's willing to carry secondary financing or to lower the price drastically.

Therefore, to get a good deal out of Multiple, often all you do is call the owner of an expiring listing a few days before it expires and feel him out. If the owner intends to relist the property (as most do) ask him to specifically exclude any deal with you from any new listing agreement he signs. That way there will be no commission payable on a sale eventually concluded with you, even if the property is listed with another agent. Once the earlier listing expires you have a clear shot at the seller, can sit down with him and present an offer for say $30,000. You may be able to walk away from the closing with cash in hand. Who knows what sort of a deal you can make? It is all in the negotiating. And in real estate negotiating you can offer anything. A dejected seller may accept whatever you offer.

I once bought a property this way. The asking price was $50,000. I offered $18,000 cash. To my surprise, this offer was immediately accepted. I bought with an unsecured bank loan. In a few months I repaid the unsecured loan because I had obtained a $25,000 long term bank loan. Within three years I sold the property for $88,000. Why did I get the property so cheap? There was a divorce going on. The wife wanted to keep the house as long as possible, so she refused to sign a listing unless it was over priced at $50,000. She figured that pricing it out of the market would enable her to live in it longer. The property was actually worth closer to $30,000. Six months passed. The husband moved out and didn't make payments. The wife later moved out and the mortgage people had about $16,000 past due.

The place was a "yuck house." It was dirty, the yard was full of weeds, and it smelled of cat pee. The lenders from Upright Savings and Loan told the wife she'd better take the first offer that came along over $16,000 or they'd take over the property and she'd get nothing. Mr. and

Mrs. Yuck could have sold at $30,000 and split an equity of $14,000. But the wife in this case was happy to have screwed her husband out of his half of a $14,000 equity. He was equally pleased that she didn't get any money in the divorce. There were no assets besides the house. It was your typical American divorce—both sides were vindictive and angry. They let their assets go to hell and to their lawyers. But there's always a budding Tycoon around to pick up the broken pieces: In the right place at the right time, with the right offer. There are dozens of deals like this being made every day. For you to get your share, you just have to be there, looking and making offers.

If you drive through almost any neighborhood you'll see "for sale," "for rent," or "open house" signs on property. For me it's as regular a habit as breathing to come to a screeching halt, knock on the door, and talk to the owner or the agent handling the deal. Every inquiry gives you more information on market prices, rents asked, etc. Just as important, it will create an ever widening circle of contacts. Never fail to ask the magic question "What *else* do you have for sale or rent?" It

The "Yuck" House

will lead to other deals, further information and more contacts. Never stop asking questions! If it's a rental sign, ask the owner "Did you ever consider selling this place so you wouldn't have to go through the bother of renting it?" If it's a "for sale" sign and the deal is obviously not for you, ask "What are the comparable properties currently on the market? Are any of your neighbors thinking of selling or moving?"

One of my best deals resulted from going up to a door to read a tiny calling card with the cryptic message "For information on this place, call—phone number." Hardly the way to get maximum exposure for the seller, but it permitted me to negotiate an excellent deal with a seller who didn't want to be bothered with hordes of lookers. He figured that anyone who took the time to climb twenty stairs to read his little card would have to be a serious buyer.

Real estate is traded in what the economists call a very imperfect market. Every property is unique and every buyer and seller has peculiarities or motivations. *You* can regularly buy properties at well below their market value if: 1. You know the market. 2. You can learn of special situations through your network of contacts.

Auctions—Probates—Conservatorships
Partition suits—Foreclosures—Tax Sales

All of the above come under my general heading of distress sales.* If you are looking for bargain basement prices, distress sales is where you'll find them. You learn about these situations in several ways. In most communities, banks, savings and loan associations, trust companies, the public administrator, auction houses and even the IRS will put you on their free mailing list. Most county courthouses have bulletin boards where all probate estates, trustees' sales (foreclosures) must, by law, be posted. They must also be advertised in a newspaper of "general circulation." In every community there is an obscure legal paper that almost nobody reads. It will have a name like the *Law Bulletin* or *Legal Advertiser.* It's the favored place for publishing notices of these sales. Also you could simply go to the local courthouse regularly to check their bulletin boards where the same notices are posted. Check the postings and read the newspapers containing legal notices for those pertaining to real estate. If you call the law firm mentioned in an ad or posted notice you will get the details of appraised value, location, and problems and decide whether you want to bid on the deal. Obviously you must always go to inspect the property physically.

*I have written an extensive technical manual about acquiring distress property in California. See back page to order.

There are technical rules for each type of sale and before bidding you must ascertain whether you must have "all cash" with you at the auction in the form of a cashier's check, or just a deposit. Sometimes a cash deposit (such as 10% in probates) will do. When only a deposit is needed, the closing can generally be scheduled for thirty to sixty days after the successful bid is accepted and confirmed. At that point you need to pay out the rest of the price in cash. Each state has slight variations.

The main problem with distress or estate property is that it is generally impossible to get a seller to help with the financing by carrying back a loan for part of the purchase price. The nature of distress or probate property is that the seller needs all cash in order to pay his own debts or make distribution to the heirs. Thus until you have a line of unsecured credit, it is necessary to bid real money to take advantage of the generally lower than market prices for distress property.

Usually there is no room for creative negotiations with trustees or estate administrators who merely put property up for the best all-cash bid in a public auction type sale. Yet you should be on the lookout for special situations. From time to time the property is such a dog that no bidders materialize at the sale. Or, the best bid for a substantial property is so low, it is unacceptable. In those cases, (often occurring in a half-finished construction project or vandalized building) it may be possible to get a very cheap price—an option or at least a large mortgage from the estate. You can then control the property without significant investment.

When you get property cheap, it is very cheap! At a delinquent property tax auction, I once bought a half acre in San Anselmo, California, for $10. At the time similar-sized lots were selling for $30,000! Why was this one so cheap? For starters it was landlocked—that is, there was no access to it from any road. No road could be built because most of the surrounding properties had homes on them and all the adjacent owners refused to give an easement to pass over their land. Equally significant, at least half of my lot was under a creek in a community that did not permit construction on underwater lots. Other people at the auction thought it was worthless, so I bid the minimum. For $10, I figured, how wrong could I go?

I didn't go too far wrong, because two years later I sold that lot for $10,000. I did it by picking up an adjacent parcel at a fair price. Combining two sub-standard parcels, I created one excellent creek-side apartment building site. The two sites together had proper square footage and enough above-water land to get a building permit. Moral to this story: If you watch all the published and posted legal notices and check them out carefully, all sorts of opportunities will come your way.

The annual delinquent real estate tax sales and public land disposi-
tions produce all sorts of weird slivers and parcels that nobody seems to
be interested in. They can be picked up for peanuts. I generally bid the
minimum on all of them, figuring that if worse comes to worse, I can
grow a weed garden or use them in a trade (see *No-Money-Down-
Deals*). What usually happens is that the owner of an adjoining property
will pay me at least one hundred times my ten-buck investment. In the
story I just told you I made a return of one thousand times my investment. In the real estate business that sort of thing happens every day.
Just keep your eyes and ears open, read the notices, attend and bid at
the sales, and then think creatively about what you can do with the
property. It's as easy as falling off a log.

H.U.D. Auctions, F.H.A., Foreclosures, Government Deals

Another category of auctions will not be posted in the county courthouse. But you can get on the federal government's mailing list or find
out what sort of deals they have by keeping in touch with the local office
of the federal government's department of Housing and Urban Development, the Federal Housing Administration, and your local housing
authority. There are myriads of federal loan programs, subsidies, gimmicks, and give-aways, the bill for which is all subsidized by the taxpayer. To catch the gravy train and get your share, just call up the local
numbers listed in the phone book. It would take another book of several
volumes to go through all the government real estate programs. For our
purposes, I just want to make you aware that if you are "low income,"
have a handicapped child or elderly person to support, or are blind,
deprived, or disadvantaged in any way, the government probably has a
special give-away program just for you. For ordinary, unhandicapped
folks, there are plenty of opportunities too.

For instance, when a government loan is foreclosed, the home or
apartment building in question is often refurbished at government expense to high FHA standards, before it is put up for resale. The deal to
the buyer often involves little or no money down with goodies like forty-
year, 3% loans. The government always pays a commission to the broker
who represents you, even if it's a no-money-down deal. If the broker is
your wife or business partner, you can see that the family could close a
deal and be net cash ahead sometimes.

On some deals, like low-rent housing and historic area preservation,
super fast depreciation (five years) and investment tax credits are allowed
as additional tax incentives. On others, the financing can be at almost

unbelievable terms. If these government-subsidized deals are so good, why aren't more people into them? A lot of people are into them. Even me. But I don't like them. For one thing, the laws and complex regulations under which you must operate (as with all government programs) are almost incomprehensible. Profits are often limited by law to a lot less than you could make in the private sector. Rents may be controlled at arbitrarily low levels. The resale of property may be limited or restricted. And if you wittingly or unwittingly violate the law, the Feds play very rough and might give you a two-year paid vacation in a federal prison. As always, the main problem in dealing with the government is that the paper work, red tape, regulations, and time consumed in dealing with bureaucrats usually just aren't worth the prize. But many people do it and do just fine.

The Dirty Window Gambit

Would you believe that looking for dirty windows could make you a fortune in real estate? It has certainly helped me. I don't mean your ordinary garden variety of dirty windows—I mean really filthy, cracked, or broken windows. They are usually found on a house or property that has a front yard full of weeds, peeling paint, signs of vandalism, graffiti, or an abandoned looking car in the drive—in short, abandoned or *neglected* property.

The owner of neglected property may be in a nursing home, the French Foreign Legion, or dead. He may have heirs thousands of miles away who'd love to get any offer to purchase a property they might not even know they own. In one case, I discovered that the owners of a derelict property were scattered heirs, all of whom, when contacted, wanted to sell. But one heir in Poland, Vladimir Dzerwinkovitch, didn't answer my letters, telegrams, or phone calls. I figured if I could buy deeds for three-quarters of the property and take possession, there would have to be a way to get the other one-quarter, whether the Polish heir wanted to sell or not. So I paid rather nominal sums, about $500 per deed, to three out of the four heirs. I recorded the deeds and went to the lawbooks. There were several ways to proceed. I had the choice of ignoring the interest of Vladimir for seven years after which, if I rented out the property and paid my real estate taxes, the property would be entirely mine by virtue of the laws of adverse possession. But that seemed risky. The missing heir might turn up in the sixth year. Also I'd be tied up for seven years. Another possibility was an immediate legal action against the Pole called a "quiet title" or "partition suit."

So I filed suit. This involved publishing a notice in the *Law Bulletin* that Vladimir's interest would be sold on a certain day at the request of myself as a tenant in common. The law has always given a remedy to partners who don't get along. In due course the property went up for public sale at my request. In this case, controlling three-quarters at the sale, I only had to put up cash representing one-quarter of my bid. Fortunately I was the only bidder at $10. The Polish heir, good old Vladimir, was credited with a deposit of $2.50, which I assume the county treasurer is still holding for him.

If you had come to that auction, you might have bid me up to the $20,000 I was prepared to offer for the property. $20,000 wouldn't have been a bad price either, because three years later it was on the market at $115,000. My cost: $1,500 to the heirs, $2.50 to the recalcitrant heir, $375 in legal fees, and a lot of research, phone calls, and running around.

An uncared for property is often an unwanted property. Someone else's discards can make you a fortune. If a property isn't cared for physically it probably isn't being cared for financially either. I have a way of finding those financially abandoned and unloved properties that is even more efficient than cruising the streets looking for dirty windows. As mentioned earlier, you should always watch the courthouse bulletin

Think creatively!

boards for notices of foreclosure and the "notice of default" that is posted when a property owner doesn't meet his obligations under a trust deed or mortgage. Someone who can't pay his mortgage is a good prospect for a buy-out. But suppose the property is free and clear. There is no mortgage to default on. How can you discover financially distressed owners of free and clear property? Simple. You go to the records of the County Tax Collector and compile a list of properties where the taxes have been delinquent for a year or more. You send the owners (their addresses can be found on the public records) a friendly letter noting that their tax is delinquent and suggesting that you would consider making them an attractive offer for their property. I have found that a mass mailing to this particular list of property owners brings almost a 25% positive response, and when things are slow it's one of my old faithful methods of stirring up a few good deals. If you go beyond a mere mailing and trace owners whose mail is returned as undeliverable, and telephone the rest, you'd get even more prospective deals.

While you are tediously going through the public records for owners of tax delinquent properties, I suggest that you also prepare a list of out-of-state owners. They, as a group, are often eager to sell and reinvest proceeds in their own area. In a letter explain to them the possibility of their being able to trade their property, tax free (see chapter on "1031 Exchanges"), for equivalent property in their own area selected by themselves. You will find that 4% to 6% will have a high degree of interest in working out a deal with you.

Personal Contacts

Last and most important are personal contacts! My local Fuller Brush salesman makes about $10,000 a year selling hairbrushes and brooms door-to-door. He makes another half-million a year trading real estate. He knows all the older people who plan on moving to Sunshine Retirement City. He's on a first name basis with all the pregnant women who will soon be pressuring their husbands to get them a bigger house. He is on top of job transfers, births, marriages, deaths, divorces, and all the factors that cause people to make a change in their living or investment situations. His door-to-door selling job is literally worth half a million a year to him because it puts him in touch with everybody in the community.

You may not want to sell brushes, Shaklee vitamins, or Avon cosmetics door-to-door—but you should consider it. You must make and keep up your contacts some way. Other alternatives: Become a real estate agent and constantly solicit listings; political door-to-door canvassing is good. You could be on a payroll doing appraisals for local lenders.

At the very least, you should join the local National Guard, Masons, Knights of Columbus, Rotarians, or Jaycees so that you will know lots of people. And lots of people must be made aware that you are interested in any real estate an owner wishes to sell before it is listed or advertised. Make a standing offer of a bottle of champagne for any such tip. Your friend gets at least a hundred dollars for any tip that results in a deal.

Put a Smile on Their Face

Many times, real estate agents, in the course of soliciting possible sellers for listings, find that a seller is willing to sell but does not want to sign a listing contract. The property owner tells the broker, "Bring me an offer of X dollars and I'll sell." The broker is then in a bind. If he alerts a client to the deal without a listing, it may be difficult for him to collect his commission from the seller (who traditionally pays 6% of the sales price).

Brokers have been burned so often by this type of seller that they will usually not take any action to inform anyone of the deal without a written listing guaranteeing their commission. For every written listing, brokers may know of ten or fifteen possibilities of the type just mentioned. How do you take advantage of the situation and gain knowledge of them? Simple! Every broker you become friendly with should get the following offer from you: "Charlie, if you tip me off to a good deal, whether you have a listing or not, there's $300 cash in it for you if I buy the property. And when I go to sell or trade, I'll put another smile on your face with another little bonus or a listing on the way out."

If you get a reputation for never trying to perform a commission-dectomy on brokers (that's where you cut out the broker's commission on deals that you close) but instead are known for always leaving these ladies and gentlemen with a smile on their faces, you phone will ring constantly as your bird-dogs bring you more good deals that you can handle.

If you become a trustworthy wheeler-dealer, what happened to me last year will happen to you. Amos, a broker, woke me up at 6 A.M. with a phone call. In conspiratorial tones he said, "Greene, I've got a hot one for you."

"What is it?" I mumbled, half asleep.

"I want $4,000—if you buy it."

"The deal was $300. I offered you a flat $300 for hot tips."

"But this is a *real* hot one. Take it or leave it!"

"O.K." I said. "I'll take it: 1) if I don't already know about it, and 2) if you'll agree that I pay $4,000 only if I buy the house."

I figured there was no harm in looking at the deal. Whatever price was set, I'd just mentally add $4,000 to the cost. If it was worth it, I'd take it.

"Done," said Amos. "I'll pick you up in half an hour."

Amos took me to a mansion I knew about. It had been on the market for years at $120,000. Very overpriced.

"What's the story?" I said.

"The mortgage has been foreclosed and you can buy it at 10 A.M. for $30,000 from the Bank of America. I want $4,000 cash at the closing. There's a public sale scheduled, but the time and place was given wrong in the papers. Only I know that the sale is on for this morning. You'll be the only bidder."

I almost didn't believe him, but as he had been a reliable source in the past, I toddled along with Amos to the Bank of America, picking up two cashier's checks as unsecured loans on the lower floor of the bank. One check was for $30,000 and one for $4,000. Amos introduced me to the trust officer handling the deal, I made the only bid and handed $30,000 to the trust officer. At 10:02 I was given a trustee's deed to certify that I owned the property. It was easily worth $90,000. I slipped Amos his $4,000 on the way out.

The same day, I called a few of my own real estate investor friends and offered it to them at $64,000 "as is," all cash, quick close. A week later I sold the property at a $30,000 profit. I gave Amos another hundred dollar bill.

Amos had a smile on his face.

I had a smile on my face.

I made $30,000 in a week and I owed it all to knowing the market, having good contacts, and having a reputation for spreading smiles and sunshine wherever I go. **Now You Do It!**

CHAPTER 11

Negotiating Tips and Ploys

You have heard people say, "Never take *no* for an answer." Sometimes you can get the answer you want, that is the *yes* answer, by merely asking the question right. When you are looking for property and you spot an owner working on his property, you *could* say to him in a negative way, "You probably *don't* want to sell your property right now, do you?" You've already given in your question a suggestion of the answer. The logical answer is, "Yes, that's right. I don't want to sell my property." Why not think like a Tycoon and ask the question in a positive way?

You could do it much more effectively this way: "If I can show you how to trade up for a much better property tax free without taking a dime out of your pocket or paying a broker's commission, would you be interested?" Of course, in the case of most sellers, their ears would perk up, and they would be eager to know what you had in mind. And if you could show that fellow how to trade up, using section 1031 of the Internal Revenue Code as explained in this book, he'd probably be willing to sell and move himself up to a bigger and better property.

Another way of posing a proposition positively is, for example, approaching a potential seller and saying to him, "If I can show you how to get much more rent money and more depreciation than you are getting now, would you be interested in listening to me?" Now, how many potential sellers would refuse to listen to your proposition? Even if they were not considering the sale of their property, you now have the opportunity to talk to them about installment sales; or you could con-

132

vince them that by selling their property to you and by acquiring a different, larger property in a tax-free trade, it would bring them in more rents and enhance their own financial position. It should be obvious that if an owner asks you to outline a plan for doing better, and you help him do this, he will feel psychologically committed to deal with you when he implements the plan. But if you got a *no* answer in the first place and tried to carry on a further conversation by explaining your plans, you might meet a wall of resistance.

When you are trying to get someone to interact with you, to work effectively with you, or to make a deal with you, remember: *People are not generally interested in your needs.* It's up to you to show them what you can do for *them,* where you can do it, when you can do it, and how you can do it. How can *they* profit by dealing with you? What are the benefits to *them?* What are the risks they may want to avoid? How can they protect themselves against loss? The Tycoon anticipates needs, fears, and all questions before negotiating.

It is true that you should seldom take "no" for an answer in a business relationship. But to get a "yes" you must structure your proposition so that the person you are dealing with has no choice but, in *his best interest,* to accept your offer. In other words, like the Godfather said, "Make 'em an offer they can't refuse."

The same approach can be used outside of real estate. Suppose you're looking for a job and the employer says "I don't need you. My overhead is already too high. I can't afford another employee." Your answer will be, "That's true—I agree with you, I see your point, *but* I will work for you for *free* for two weeks. If in two weeks I haven't made you far more than the salary I'll need, then you don't have to use me. Now, how can you refuse an offer like that? I'll work for you and make you profits of more than $1,000 a week and you don't have to pay me anything. And if I do work out for you, all I ask is that you pay me a part of what I make you." When you make your offers to people in such a way that it is difficult for them to refuse to deal with you, you'll find that if you perform you will always have success.

If the person from whom you want to buy a property has some objections to selling to you, treat those objections with respect. Never argue. Always *agree* with what they have to say then add, *but . . .* and take it from there. For instance, if a person does not want to sell their property to you because the place they would buy with the proceeds would cost them more in taxes, you can say: "The taxes on the next place will indeed be high, but you can get enough extra income from the new higher rents you will be collecting to more than cover those taxes."

Another pointer is, after you have an agreement that gives you what you want, don't talk beyond the sale. Sometimes, once the person on the other side has done what you wanted, if you keep talking, he may have a change of heart. All you should do in a real estate deal once the person has agreed to sell is to both sign an informal written contract. It can be innocuously titled "memorandum." Remember that in real estate all contracts are meaningless unless they are in writing. After signing the "memorandum," and again after every closing, you should say something to encourage the seller that he did the right thing. One of my favorite remarks is, "Boy, Mr. Seller, I certainly didn't intend to come up to your price of $100,000. I didn't think I'd have to go over $85,000. You did very well with me on this particular deal." In that way the seller's opinion that he got the best of you is confirmed. Give him that satisfaction!

Obviously if you had said at the closing, "I was prepared to go to $110,000 on your deal. I'm sure glad you sold to me for $100,000," you would, by your uncalled for remark, cause him to renege or speak ill of you for decades.

Regardless of the contract you may have with someone, remember a contract is only as good as the people who make it. If either side to the contract wants to get out of it, they can always do so. Once they do, all you have left is a law suit. In the process of negotiating, never lose your cool or give up, no matter how great an idiot you are dealing with.

Sometimes it is wise to use testimonials as to your good character and reliability. Rather than giving a reference to be used later, I found it very effective in negotiations to say to the person opposite me, "Look, Mr. Jones at the First National Bank has dealt with me successfully many times. I'm sure he will give me a good reference. I'd be happy to step out of the room while you call Mr. Jones for a reference on me."

That way, if you can supply the name of a person who is respected in the community, you may be able to close a deal that otherwise would have been impossible because the seller in question thought you were some sort of a flake. Developing good references and using the name of someone well respected in the community, like the local banker, is particularly useful to younger Tycoons, who at the age of twenty to twenty-six perhaps might not be taken seriously by older sellers of substantial property. Don't appear too wealthy, bright, slick, or money hungry. Being sincere, understanding, helpful, and interested in the *other* person's problems is your best negotiating stance.

CHAPTER 12
The Magic Question

O nce you have made a bit of money, in spite of valiant attempts to keep a low profile, word of your prosperity will leak out. Then investors, promoters, and con-men of all shapes, colors, and sizes will convincingly offer to triple your money. The deals touted will be wonderfully entertaining. But don't part with a dime unless you want to lose it! Listen to their stories. Let them wine and dine you. But remember, there are more than the two choices most people make when approached by a pie-in-the-sky salesman. Obviously you could say a firm "No thank you and goodbye." Or, you might be a fool, take the deal offered and lose your shirt. Here's a third alternative that has made me a little richer, several times. Not to mention psychological rewards! There is nothing quite as satisfying as out-conning a confidence man. When a hot-shot salesperson departs from my home leaving *his* money behind, a warm glow radiates from me for days! Here's how you can take the money of fast talking salespeople.

Ask the *Magic Question:* "If this deal is so good, why don't you keep it all for yourself?"

The answer will always be: "I would if I could, but I just don't have the money."

Here is where you turn the tables. You say: "Instead of investing in your deal, Mr. Conniver, I'll *lend* you the money in return for half of the profits you just promised me. That way you, Mr. Conniver, can multiply my borrowed money and keep half of the gains for yourself without putting up a cent. You will take the risk of course, but as you've told me . . . *It's a sure thing.* All I want is some security pledged plus your personal note and a postdated check due six months from now." You should casually throw out some bait with the comment, "If and when this deal works out, I will probably invest lots more money on similar deals."

Why should you offer to make a loan to every promoter and why must you always ask for security?

Most promoters, inventors, and syndicate fund raisers will be personally broke and totally worthless to you. They will (if you let them) take your hard earned cash. Usually you will never see any of it again. Sometimes the *Magic Question* will give you the opportunity to create a profit for yourself. If the conniver in our example has any assets at all, and if he really believes in his scheme, then one time out of a hundred you *both* will make a profit. But whatever happens, even if his deal goes sour, *you'll* come out smiling.

First: Find out what assets the con-artist has control of. Car? House? Listed stocks? Perhaps his wife has a diamond engagement ring. Maybe he has a fine oriental carpet or a Picasso. Anything of value will serve your purposes. My favorite security is a deed or trust deed on real estate. A home is good if conniver's "equity" over his mortgage or the net value involved is at least triple the amount of money he wants from you.

Second: After establishing that old super-salesman has an object worth $15,000, you can offer to lend, or rather "invest" one-third of that value—say $5,000.

Third: The sample contract on page 138 is one that you might use to close a deal.

You might properly comment that these contracts were the strangest loan package you ever saw. It looked more like you bought a car at a bargain price, and got a 50% interest in a risky venture thrown in as a gift. Actually, you *did* buy a car, diamond, house, or whatever at a bargain price. Conniver will probably lose it to you as well as losing *his* shirt on the deal he was trying to sell you. He will not be able to raise the cash to exercise his option in 95% of all cases, and you will end up with his property at a bargain price. In my experience, as a result of this type of deal, I have ended up with many goodies.

Once I got a nice sports car at a bargain price from an operator who was going to triple "our" money in three months. His scheme was to open a chain of massage parlors in Alaska to service the boys working on the Alaska Pipe Line. For one reason or another, as I predicted, it didn't work out. In a different deal I got a $50,000 house for $33,000 cash when I bought it from a self-proclaimed wheeler dealer for $3,000 over his mortgage of $30,000.

In the first case, I was told that Alaska had the best cops money could buy, but they didn't stay bought and unexpectedly shut down the rub-down emporiums. In the second situation, the big profit was supposed to be made by buying silver coins at near their face value from a "secret source" and reselling immediately at their "collector value" of triple the cost. But instead of buying silver coins, the wheeler dealer (without informing me of his alternate plan) bought a plane load of Colombian marijuana and other similar items. The dope was hijacked in Mexico (of course!). In this case, however, the dealer "saved" enough cocaine to offer me two pounds in lieu of $3,000 needed to repurchase the house. Terrific! I politely refused his offer (as I suggest you do in any deal involving illegal substances). Not that I have any great moral feelings against cocaine. I personally believe it should be legal to drink Draino or do anything else your heart desires. But life is just too short for me to traffic in anything illegal unless survival depended on it.

To sum up this *Magic Question* bit: If and when some person comes to you with a *Red Ribbon Deal* where all you do is hand over your money to get a fabulous, absolutely safe, super-return in a short time, remember: ninety-nine times out of a hundred, you will lose every penny that you put up. The loss can result from incompetence, dishonesty, and most often an ill-advised, illegal venture. The person trying to sell you a deal often does not own the proverbial pot to pee in, but sometimes he does have assets. In those cases there is often an opportunity for *you* to make a risk-free profit. It will work out well for you in those comparatively few instances where:

1. The promoter believes in the project.

2. He or she has assets.

3. Where a con-man with assets wants to get you involved and is willing to give you a handsome phoney profit on your first venture hoping to sucker you in more heavily without security on the next deal.

Don't be a sucker. The sting (loss) will come at a time when you are holding no security. Grab the first profit and run!

To repeat, even if you make out like a bandit on your first deal—**do not assume that you can have a repeat performance** without the same security agreement.

Can you trust anyone?

I used to say you can't trust anyone except a major Swiss banker. Then in 1977 a Swiss banker, manager of Swiss Bank Corporation's Chiasso (Switzerland) branch was found to have diverted almost one billion dollars into personal and disastrous speculations.* He went to the pokey. Today I have *no exceptions.* Don't trust anyone!

Agreement

1. For the sum of $5,000 Mr. U *(that's you)* has purchased from Mr. Conniver one 300 SL Mercedes Benz Gull Wing Serial No. 12345, 1959 Model.

(Note: You should comply with all local sales formalities. You take physical possession of the car and the title documents. Let Conniver pay the sales tax.)

2. It is further agreed that if, for any reason, Mr. Conniver wishes to repurchase said vehicle within six months he may do so, at a price of $7,000.

(Note: The value of the property is $15,000, triple what you are paying. Thus the buyback price should always be about 50% of market value.)

Dated: _____   Signed: _____

_____

Subscribed and sworn to
before me:

Nancy Notary _____

Notary Public in and for the
State of California.
My commission expires 1982.

At the signing, as part of the deal Conniver must give you a check for $7,000 dated six months ahead. You also execute this "side deal."

Agreement

For a valuable consideration, plus time and effort invested by John U in connection with *(describe venture in detail)*, Sam Conniver of 123 Ace Lane, Yourtown, does hereby agree to give John U a 50% interest in the gross profits and sales price of said *(invention, restaurant, massage parlor, etc.)* with profits or losses to be distributed and fully accounted for monthly. Conniver is to be the general partner or active participant in this venture, and John U is to be a silent investor without personal liability. John U is to have access to the books and records of the business at all times.

Dated: _____   Signed: _____

_____

Subscribed and sworn to
before me:

Nancy Notary _____

Notary Public in and for the
State of California.
My commission expires 1982.

* The bank however covered all losses to their clients. You *can* trust a big Swiss bank.

How to Avoid Lending Money

If someone approaches you with a request to borrow money, always assume that one or more of the following will happen:

A. The person pushing the deal is involved in something illegal and soon will be in jail.

B. Within ten minutes of getting your money, your new partner or debtor will:

a. Be abandoned by a lover. He'll decide life isn't worth living and will split the scene (with your cash) for Brazil. Or perhaps he'll go to an even more celestial region by jumping from the top of a skyscraper.

b. His mother, father, sister, brother, spouse, and children will simultaneously be afflicted with terminal leukemia or other fatal disease. Meeting their medical bills will become far more important than returning your money.

c. He will turn into a certified lunatic or have an accident that will make him an incoherent vegetable.

d. He will be murdered or fatally injured.

e. A person that *he* trusted with the investment will be a thief, disappearing not only with your money, but with your partner's or debtor's alleged life savings, those of his widowed mother, and so on.

f. The business deal that was so highly touted in the initial meeting just ". . . didn't work out."

After hearing those stories in at least fifty deals, I vowed never again to invest in a Red Ribbon Deal or lend out money.

A basic rule to remember in dealing with other people is: **If anything can possibly go wrong, it will!** Assume that all of the above (and more) will really happen in every deal, loan, or investment. Protect yourself in advance. With a little bit of luck, you'll do a lot better than I did, particularly if you meet an inventor.

The most dangerous person you'll ever meet in your business career is not a robber, murderer, or even a representative of the IRS. The most dangerous person you'll have the misfortune to encounter will be an *inventor*. Once an inventor has you believing in his new product or process, your entire fortune and all your prospects will go down the tubes. The time demanded of you to promote the invention and attract other investors will become an endless treadmill; your money will go into a bottomless pit!

I want to repress all memories of the time I became involved with the inventor of a solar panel. The small scale prototype was convincing: It produced usable heat/energy in arctic climates with only a few hours of sunlight per week. Once installed, fuel and operating costs were almost nil. Because of federal income tax credits and a financing package available to the buyer, any user of these panels would actually *make money* from day one. Nothing could possibly go wrong. Wealthy Arabs had already been after the patents for $3 million, but the inventor didn't want them shelving his project in order to sell the world more of their oil. That was *his* story anyway. . . .

It seemed like the opportunity of a lifetime. The inventor's projections showed that my $10,000 investment would return a million a year. Of course once production began, there were a few "minor bugs" to be worked out. Three more $10,000 contributions were required—each one to "turn the corner." To my sorrow, the corner never was turned—and probably never would be turned. I kissed my $40,000 goodbye.

What went wrong? In my case, the invention in large size just never worked nearly as well as the doll-house-sized prototype. But with your inventor friend, it might be anything. See "How to Avoid Lending Money" a few pages back. Those are a few of the things that can go wrong.

Dealing with a product that works is tough enough, but backing an unproven item—a new invention—will give you what I got from my solar panel: a lot of useless hot air.

DuPont or IBM can afford research and development. They can afford a dead loss on ninety-nine out of a hundred ideas because of the one product that makes it big. You are not in that league. Don't be a pioneer!

A sound rule to follow: **If someone wants your money (inventor or otherwise), ask the "magic question." If you can't be placed in a 100% secured position, run like hell in the opposite direction!**

The sad truth is that most inventions, like most movies, most oil wells, most real estate syndicates, most new products, and most commodity options never make the novice investor a dime.

The only "sure thing" in an investment is probably in your back yard. Let's move from the exotic to the mundane. I'll show you how to buy the house next door without investing or risking anything of significance.

CHAPTER 13

Buying Property without Money

In a no-money-down deal you acquire property without putting up any of your own money. The first type of no-money-down deal is an option. People don't tend to think of options as a way of getting property for no money down, but it certainly is a way of doing just that. Using options to get control of real estate is one of the least risky and most profitable ways to deal in real estate.

An option is the right to buy a given piece of property for a set period of time—say six months or five years—at a fixed price. Any item, whether it's real estate or personal property or stock, could be the subject of an option. Every option has a definite time period. It gives you the right to buy a specific property in the future for a certain time period, for a certain price, both clearly stated in the contract.

You could, for instance, get control of a $100,000 property for $100 (or even $1!) and tie it up for a year. During that year, if you are able to sell the parcel to a third party for $150,000, you could make $50,000 on your investment. Results will often be that spectacular! So, options are a method of 100% financing you should be familiar with.

Let me give you another example of how to use an option to make big money: Suppose that you are about to become a tenant in a three-flat apartment building in Oakland. At the time that you move in, the property is worth about $70,000. In the process of negotiating with the landlord for a two-year lease, you say to the landlord, "I would like the right to buy this property during the term of my lease for the price of

$70,000." The landlord may be willing to give you that right, or he may say, "No, I'd sell only for $80,000." He may charge you $1 for the option, $100, or $1,000. Often the price of the option will be deductible from the price of the property. However, it won't be unless you provide in the contract that the amount paid for the option is to be applied against the purchase price.

In a more typical landlord/tenant option, you the tenant might lease a single-family home for a period of two years at $400 a month rent. During these two years the landlord might agree by writing on the lease that you have the right to buy that home for $40,000. The consideration (there always has to be a consideration for any contract) is the fact that you are leasing it and paying rent. You don't really need to pay an extra $1 to the landlord to have the right to buy the property in that two-year period. But I always pay at least $1 for an option. That way, if you default on the lease by missing a rent payment or moving early the option is still good.

How do you get a lease option? You simply ask for one. Tell the landlord you would like to buy his property. Ask, "What would you sell it for?" Merely by asking any potential seller for an option, you may get one. Perhaps the seller is willing to sell to you for $40,000, but at the moment you are not able to qualify for a loan or you don't have quite enough money for the down payment. Then you ask your seller if he will give you a few months to raise the down payment or arrange for the mortgage. Very often the owner of a property will be willing to give someone a six-month option in this type of situation. That gives you time to get your deal together and the details of the option are limited only by your (and the landlord's) imagination.

In many cases where an option is negotiated, the rent charged is the fair rent, and the entire fair rent is deductible from a reasonable option price if it is exercised during the first year. That sort of option is a very good deal for the tenant. The landlord may want to raise your rent as consideration for the option. But he may also give you credit for the extra rent off the option price. You could counter by asking for a cumulative monthly credit. There's no limit to the ways of working out an option contract.

When you get an option contract from a landlord it is very important that you have it notarized and recorded with the county recorder of deeds. Why? Because recording protects you against the seller's change of heart.

Let's say you have an option to buy a property for $40,000 and during the course of the next year the landlord simply forgot about it. It slipped his mind; perhaps because he got a better offer from an outsider of maybe $50,000, totally forgetting about your option to buy the property for $40,000. If you didn't have your option contract notarized and recorded, the new buyer would own the property free and clear. You might have a claim against the landlord and you would certainly have a good lawsuit. But you want to avoid lawsuits, and if you've had that option contract recorded, a new buyer would only be able to get control of the property by buying you out.

Now, suppose you have an option on a property at $40,000. You've been lucky. It's gone up in value to $100,000. That sort of thing isn't as unusual as you may think. Especially if it was a commercial property and you also had the lease. You may have had a long-term lease, perhaps for five years. During a three- to five-year period a price rise from $40,000 to $100,000 isn't unusual at all. Still, you may exercise this wonderful option to buy a $100,000 property for $40,000 even if you do not have $40,000. At this point you have several choices. You could let the option expire. That would not do you any good. You would not own the property and the landlord would regain full rights. (An option *must* be exercised before it expires!) In this case you would have lost $60,000. That is your potential profit: $60,000. Therefore I don't recommend this choice.

Or, you could go to the seller and say, "Mr. Seller, let's take out a loan to refinance your property. Now that it's worth $100,000 you won't have any problem getting a loan for $50,000 on it. Then I will take over the property and assume your new loan."

The seller would say, "Why should I do that? What's in it for me? You have the right to buy my property at $40,000. If you want it you can have it. But why should I borrow for you and sign a note for $50,000?"

You will have to make it worth the seller's while. You may want to offer him $5,000 extra for his property. And if your seller got a $50,000 loan under these circumstances, it would be in your favor too. You could walk away with an extra $5,000 cash at the close. All you do is assume the seller's new loan of $50,000 and make all payments on it thereafter. Result? You bought property with $45,000 that the seller borrowed. To get your seller to cooperate with you, you will of course have to convince him that you are a reliable person and won't default on the loan.

If you have an option and the property has gone up in value above your option price, the more common thing to do is to put up a "for sale" sign and sell it to a third party. Perhaps you are lucky enough to find a buyer at $100,000. Then $40,000 goes to the landlord and you make $60,000 on the deal. All that profit is your return on the price of the option.

You may ask, "Is it legal? It seems too good to be true." The answer is yes, because that's what an option is all about! You do not have to own the property to sell it if you have an option. An option is transferable during the entire time-period of the option. So you could sell the property to someone else, or you could just sell the option.

An option contract is very simple. Here's how to prepare one: Take a blank sheet of paper and title it *Option Contract.*

Option Contract

I, Larry Landlord, for the sum of $1 *(or other agreed sum)* hereby sell to Tom Tenant an option to purchase my four-plex at 44 Montgomery Street, San Francisco, California, for a full price of $40,000 from this date until January 1st, 1985.

Terms: All cash to seller.

_____   _____
Larry Landlord   Date

_____   _____
Accepted, *Tom Tenant*   Date

(It is very important that the option contract be dated and acknowledged before a notary public or a witness on the same date. After acknowledgment take the option to the county recorder and record it. It will cost you $3 and will be the best $3 you ever spent.)

Some people will tell you that, as the buyer, you don't have to sign the option contract. This is true. However, I recommend that you always *do* sign it. This indicates that you and the landlord (option seller) had a "meeting of the minds" so to speak and that you both knew exactly what you were doing. Larry Landlord, your seller on the other hand, *must* sign it. If he or she is married, the spouse must also sign it. The option contract might be enforceable without a spouse's signature, but it could get you into court. The most important thing about court is to avoid it at all costs. Once the contract is recorded with the county no one else can buy the property without being on notice of your interest in it.

One of the first deals in my career involved the use of a kind of option. One of the hundred houses I had looked at during my self-education period was a little summer hiker's cabin in the woods. To some, it was a "yuck" house because the floors tilted at a 10° angle, the heavy redwood plank walls were of single thickness with cracks and knot-holes to let in plenty of wind and rain. The fixtures and fittings were "early

American pioneer" and had been put in about 1895. But the cottage had charm. The lot was an acre on a sunny hillside in an area which had become the setting for many a wealthy San Francisco family's mountain hideaway. The average price for an old summer home was $75,000.

Here was a charming little unlivable cabin for sale at an asking price of $25,000. It was livable perhaps if your name was Thoreau, but I imagined that it would be pretty difficult to rent. I made inquiries about the property with neighbors and real estate agents. It seemed there had been a few offers near to the asking price, but all were dependent upon 80% financing. Unfortunately no bank or savings and loan would lend anything unless the buyer came up with architect's plans to put in a new foundation, expand the house from one tiny bedroom to a more conventional three bedrooms, put in a garage, and spent about $50,000. Since a ready-built home in the area could be had for $75,000, I was told that no one wanted to tackle a major construction project and what might be worse—all the paperwork of getting building permits, environmental impact reports, and other red tape. So the house sat vacant.

As you should know by now, when a property has been on the market for a long period of time, the owner is usually amenable to "unusual" offers that would initially have been rejected. My first step was to talk to a local lender.

"Would you lend me anything on the place if I put in a foundation, straightened up the floors, made the place barely livable, and was able to sell it for $34,000?" The banker said, "Because of its unusually good location we'd go to 50%." That was the banker-talk meaning a loan of $17,000 could be obtained.

I knew I could put the place into shape for $3,000 with my lightning technique in a weekend. I didn't expect the building inspector would catch me. No permits to be applied for. My next step was to contact the owner. My offer, shown at the top of the next page, had a personal check for $300 attached.

My offer was much lower than the asking price. But it was a direct principal to principal offer. Without the usual 6% commission, it was equivalent of $1,000 more than an offer through a real estate broker. I stressed this point to him. Furthermore, I explained to him what he already knew. The property had been on the market for six months and people poor enough to want to live in, and fix up a house of its nature, didn't have $16,000 cash. They couldn't qualify for a loan, and even if someone qualified for a loan, banks wouldn't lend on that particular property without a fortune being spent on a foundation and improvements.

146

Offer to Purchase Real Estate

The undersigned, William Greene, hereby offers to purchase the house at 10 Redwood Lane, Mill Valley, further identified as Assessor's Parcel No. 4545 for a full price of $16,000, all cash to seller.

The sum of $300 is attached herewith and may be cashed by seller upon acceptance of this offer. Upon acceptance, possession of the property shall go to buyer in order that buyer may put in a foundation and otherwise improve said property in order to qualify for a bank loan which will enable him to complete the purchase within six months.

In the event that the balance is not fully paid to the seller for any reason within six months, the seller shall have the right to repossess the property, retain any improvements made by the buyer, and keep the buyer's $300 deposit.

(signed) _____

William Greene

Accepted

_____

Sam Seller

(Note: A standard notary public acknowledgment should be obtained in all contracts regarding the sale of real property. Then the contract should be recorded.)

My plan was to buy for $16,000—with only $300 down. I would improve the property by working on it myself and spending about $3,000. I was going to get those costs and more by taking out an $8,000 home improvement loan on the place where I lived. After I completed the improvements, my plan was to get my promised loan of $17,000, rent the place out for $275 per month, and have enough rent coming in to pay off both the $17,000 first loan on the property and the $8,000 home improvement loan on my own place. Here is how the cash flow would have worked:

Cash Outflow		Cash Inflow	
$ 300	For down payment	$ 8,000	Home improvement
3,000	For improvements		loan
16,000	Price of house	17,000	First loan
1,000	Closing costs, reserve		
$20,300	**Total**	**$25,000**	**Total**

Yes, within six months I would end up with almost $5,000 in my pocket; the loans would all be paid back by the tenant; I would own the property, be cash ahead, and get tax benefits that would shelter other income.

That was the plan, but something even better was to happen as a fluke: I put up a little card inside a front window so that it could be seen from the outside. (If you post notices outside, someone is sure to pull them off.) The card said:

> **For information regarding**
> **the sale or rental of this property**
> **contact: W. Greene, owner.**
> **Phone 777-7777**

(Why make it hard for people who might want to make you an offer you can't refuse?)

Here is what happened: The old owner signed my contract on a Thursday morning. I posted the sign at about noon. At 3 o'clock I got a call from Helen, a real estate lady I had dated occasionally and knew pretty well.

"I heard you've got an option on Redwood Lane for $16,000." She made me a firm offer. "I'll take it over from you for a thousand profit. I'll give you $1,300 today for your option."

I explained to my friend Helen that I would like to deal with her, but that I had a plan for fixing up the property and hoped to sell it for around $34,000. I hoped to make a profit of more like $15,000.

She told me that I was crazy, that it wasn't worth it. Helen then got abusive. She said, "I've had my eye on the property for over six months and now you've stolen it from me." She said she was getting all set to offer $17,500 all cash to the seller, and I would be the meanest, cruelest man alive if I didn't sell to her. She threatened never to speak to me again if I didn't sell to her at once. Now Real-Estate Helen was no dummy. She was into house speculation two years before I was, and I felt if she was willing to offer $17,500 real money in cash, I must have pulled off a coup by getting it for $16,000 on an almost no-money-down deal.

I told Helen to cut the hysterics, that I hadn't even known she was interested, consequently I didn't steal her property, and that if she was getting all set to make an offer, she should have made the offer instead of keeping it a secret. Helen slammed the phone down and has been bad mouthing me in real estate circles ever since.

In any event, as soon as Helen hung up on me, someone else called. He had seen my card on the property and he also had been planning to make an offer when the owner was more desperate. He too was planning to offer $17,500. I told him that I had a firm contract to buy the place at $16,000, had received an offer of $17,300 a few minutes earlier and had turned it down without hesitation because I hoped to sell the property for $34,000 as soon as I had fixed it up. This chap then said he'd offer $18,500, all cash. I said, "I will consider it and call you back."

An hour later, another, even higher, offer came in. I wondered why all these offers had been hiding in the woodwork, and when I later asked, the answer was that people were timid about "insulting the seller" by offering so much below the asking price of $25,000. But once they heard that I tied the property up for $16,000, they felt very good about offering me a quick profit. Thus my advice to budding Tycoons is: **Never be afraid to make a low offer. Forget your psychological problems, just make the offer. The seller may be delighted that someone wants his property. If he refuses, what did you lose?**

Getting back to our tale, the property I had bought at $16,000 was absolutely the lowest-priced home in town. The house next in line, offered on the multiple listing service, was $35,000. Thus, every buyer searching for a cheap house had seen Redwood Lane, but everybody waited till my deal went through and *then* got interested.

I had the hottest property in town. In the next three days I got a dozen more calls and eventually sold my contract for a $5,000 profit. The lady who bought it from me (at an effective price to her of $21,000 cash) didn't do a thing to the property, rented it for $200 a month, and three years later sold it for $34,000.

As for me—I had invested $300 and gotten back $5,300 in a few days. I had never made that much return in such a short space of time in stocks, commissions, or anything. At that point I was hooked on real estate.

Another method of getting property for no money down is with 100% loans. A few years ago I came across some charming old cabins in the country. They were very rustic, surrounded by redwood trees near a stream, but very run down. I had heard that the owner, a retired gentleman of about seventy, had told neighbors, "I'm really tired of fixing up that place and running after the tenants for rent. There's always something wrong. I'm working all my days repairing things and I would sure like to sell." I knew that on this particular property, lenders would not give a conventional loan because they were run-down sixty-year-old cabins. Lenders and bankers generally don't like charm. Only tenants do.

So I went to the seller. We talked and I did the most important thing you as a buyer should always do. *I quickly found out what the seller wanted.* I simply asked, "What are your plans if you sell this place? What do you want to do?" Basically he wanted to move to a retirement community up north and have a comfortable extra income in addition to his pension. That was his real need. By telling him about my career and engaging in friendly conversations during the course of a number of visits, I won his confidence. I let him know I wasn't a flake, that I had some other property and was regular in my mortgage payments. He soon realized that I was a dependable person. He felt that if we did negotiate a deal and he gave me a mortgage, he could rest secure that in his golden years, he could depend on a check coming in from me every month.

At first he hemmed and hawed about chasing me for late payments. I countered with: "Look, I'm prepared to give you post-dated checks for two years on these mortgage payments. As you know, it's a criminal offense to pass a bum check, so I will give you whatever mortgage we agree upon in the form of post-dated checks. You will have a big stack of them and be very secure that they will be paid on time. When you get half way through your stack of checks, I'll give you another stack of checks. That way you'll always be at least a year ahead." That offer seemed to turn him on.

Then we had to negotiate price. We had established that the present rents from the property were about $750 a month. (For the sake of this example, let's assume that this was *net,* after expenses.) So I said to him, "Look, would you like to get exactly what you're making now in the form of loan payments? *I'll* give you that $750 a month without you having to do any repairs—no work, no vacancy problems, no chasing tenants for rent. In other words, you'll be getting exactly what you're getting now, without any work for the rest of your life. That's my offer."

"Great," he said, "but for how long do I get that $750 a month?"

I said, "Look, you're seventy years old now—how does ten years sound?"

The owner said, "I might be around in ten years, in fact, I hope to be around in thirty." In the end we compromised at twenty years.

Then we went to the *Blue Book,** checked the amortization tables, and looked for the figures *$750* and *twenty years.* That came out to a 7½% loan on $93,000, fully amortized or paid off over twenty years. Basically that's how we set the price—with the help of the *Blue Book.* We agreed on a dollar amount—$93,000—and twenty years. My seller got exactly what he wanted—$750 trouble-free net cash every month. I became the proud owner of the Dipsea Cabins.

Why was I willing to give him exactly what he was getting in rent with the buildings in such rough shape? Because I knew that if I improved

* See the reading list at the end of this book.

the cabins just a little I could raise those rents up from $750 a month and almost from the very beginning have a little profit each month for myself.

Three years later, I still own the Dipsea Cabins. The monthly net is now $2,750. I am making a $2,000 a month net cash flow out of the building I bought for no money down, and at the same time I'm paying off the loan. In seventeen years more I'll own the property free and clear—and think what the rents will be then!

The seller is well pleased. He's up in his Sonoma County retirement home getting $750 a month. He feels secure with my post-dated checks. He *is* secure. He sold to me for no money down—gave me a 100% loan—yet he couldn't be any happier. We're good friends. I talk to him on the phone about every six months.

As mentioned, I bought the Dipsea Cabins in rough shape. During the last few years I built up what I call sweat equity. In other words I went out there personally on weekends. I took out rotten boards, I put in some sun decks, I added ivy, I took good care of the place; did all needed repairs and painting. The place is in much better shape now.

Three months ago I put it on the market for $450,000. The loan was $93,000. I put no money down, I've been taking $2,000 a month out for almost a year and have been getting a nice tax loss because of the depreciation the IRS gives me. When I walk away from that deal for $450,000 I'll have over $350,000 as my profit. Where else can you make over $100,000 a year without any investment? Only in real estate! Of course I will never sell it. I would always *trade* up to a bigger and better deal using my $350,000 equity as a down payment on a $1 or $2 million property.

Now, going back to those original purchase negotiations, supposing the same seller liked everything I proposed but said, "Bill, I just have to get some cash out of the closing. Can't you come up with some cash? I would like to get at least $40,000 up front to buy my new retirement home free and clear." If I had a fairly good credit standing I could have gone to the bank with the seller and probably have borrowed $40,000 on a first loan. Then I'd have made arrangements with the seller to give me a $60,000 second loan. So I would get the net effect of a no-money-down deal, except that I would owe one loan payment each month to a savings and loan and one loan payment to the seller. That's how to deal with the situation when the seller wants money up front.

Here is another variation. Let's assume your credit is bad. Until now you have been a slow payer or a nonpayer. You don't have a good reputation and lenders would consider you a bad risk. (Incidentally, *change your ways:* if you want to make it in real estate you must develop a good reputation for meeting your obligations.) Here's a little gimmick you can use to get the seller the cash he wants. I could have said, "Before we make the deal, Mr. Seller, you get the property refinanced." In other words, get the seller to go to a banker, preferably one he has a relationship with and get whatever loan they will give. Here, we're talking about a $93,000 property. Even when money is tight and things aren't so good, you can always get a 20% loan or a 30 or 40% loan. It's the 80 or 90% loan that you don't get when money is tight or the property is run down.

So the seller could have gone to his friendly savings and loan to say he wanted some cash just before he sold to you. He could then have refinanced the property using his credit and not yours. In that case you might want to be a cosigner. But if your credit was really bad you wouldn't want the bank to know your name. You could then take over the property from the seller on a *Contract of Sale.* With a contract of sale, which I will talk more about later, the seller retains legal title. In every other way it is a sale. You collect rents; you take all the deductions.

The secret of 100% financing or 120% financing is finding someone who will carry the loan. Most often it will be the seller who carries the entire loan, but sometimes a bank or savings and loan will make a first loan, and the seller will carry the second. Sometimes outside lenders will be brought in. But the key to making a no-money-down deal is a 100% loan.

Suppose you found an owner who has a building for which he wants $100,000. You are going to get an $80,000 loan from a lender, but you don't have $20,000 for the down payment. You give the owner a $20,000 second loan on properties you already own. Obviously this suggestion can apply only to people who already own property. In other words you could create a lien on your own home or other property you already own shortly before the closing. The seller would give you his check for $20,000. You give him an IOU or note for $20,000 secured by property you already own. Then you use his check as the down payment on the new place.

Everything in this world is negotiable. The seller might say something like, "I don't really want to take a second mortgage on your home as a down payment. I want $10,000 cash. I don't care how you do it." A lot of sellers just don't want to do fancy deals. You can show him that at the closing he would be getting $80,000 cash from the bank. But the seller still may not want to lend you the $20,000 for the down payment.

Here's one way to get him "all cash." You will need the seller's cooperation. You give the seller the second on your property, as in the last example. Only this time you raise it to $25,000. You tell him the truth

—there is a big market out there for second mortgages. People are trading second mortgages at a discount all the time. All you have to do is look in the Sunday newspaper or the phone book to get a long list of people who are actively in the second mortgage business. I would say without any doubt that you could always sell a relatively short-term $25,000 note for at least $20,000. Generally a 10 or 20% discount is what you'll run into in discounting second mortgage paper. So you tell your seller he'll get his $80,000 from the savings and loan and he'll get his $20,000 out of that second mortgage. I always personally guarantee that my $25,000 second mortgage can be sold at a discount to a third person.

Many small loan or finance companies will issue a written commitment to purchase the second loan in our example for $20,000 cash. So there should be no reason why you shouldn't be able to raise that $20,000 by creating a new $25,000 second mortgage on property you already own before the deal closes. As mentioned there are plenty of people out there dealing in second mortgages, and like real estate, it is a very big field in itself. There are a surprising number of older people who don't want to deal with rental property, but who love wheeling and dealing in second mortgages at discounts. An ad in the paper might bring them in. Once you get involved in the market, you'll get familiar with it. So, if you put an ad in your local paper saying "second mortgage, $25,000, 20% interest, two years, well-secured. Will sell for $20,000," you'll get lots and lots of calls if the return is attractive.

Of course it would be much more convenient and cheaper for you if your seller takes the $20,000 note at face value as the down payment. But if he doesn't, you can always raise the value and discount it to a third party to come up with the $20,000 that you need.

There is another problem that can arise. The seller may say to you, "Look, I know and love the property I'm selling to you. I'm prepared to take a second loan on *that* property, but I don't want a second on your own home or any other property of yours that I don't know anything about." You would go along with that. There is no problem for you, and this offer gives you a no-money-down deal. But the problem is the *lender*. Often the bank or savings and loan who's making an 80% first loan will not finance a no-money-down deal if they know about it. They seem to feel that people who don't have anything invested will walk away from deals to leave the bank holding an empty bag.

I think the lenders are dead wrong in this attitude. If I were a banker I would rather hold a first loan in a situation where there is a second loan held by a wealthy seller. Why? Because the holder of a big second will pick up the property and make the payments on the first loan if the owner goes under and the first goes into default. If the seller doesn't keep up payments he loses the money that is due him on the second mortgage.

In the case of the seller who wants a second on the property he is selling you, here is how to handle the deal. You issue him the note and trust deed as in our previous example. The security is property you already own. You write on it: "This trust deed is transferrable at seller's option to the property on Oak Lane at any time after thirty days."

So we solved the problem of getting the $20,000 cash down payment you needed to buy the $100,000 property—you got that $20,000 by creating a note and trust deed on property you already own. As before you have to own property already in order to make this deal. Now the seller has never seen your home, but he does know and love his own place. He's willing to take a second loan on that, but you can't give him a second loan simultaneously because the bank that's making the first loan won't let the deal go through if you do it that way. They just don't want to make loans on no-money-down deals—at least in California. They might do it in Las Vegas or Reno where I hear the bankers are real swingers. But in California they won't. You start out by creating a note or trust deed on your own property or home. That's legal. The bank won't object to that.

You make this deal with the seller: A month after closing he is to transfer security for the note from your home to his. That means he releases your home, and has the same note secured by a trust deed on the place he's selling you. If you do that maneuver anytime after the closing of the new property, it will work out. You get the lien released from your old property and it is placed against the new property you have just bought.

A title company will show you exactly how to handle the technicalities of releasing one property and putting a loan against the other property. A good title company will always help a customer on any paperwork problems without charge.

The most usual and traditional way of getting a no-money-down deal happens to be illegal. It is fraud and I am not suggesting that you use that method. Why? Because there are always legal ways of doing almost anything you want to do. The fraud that goes on between a lot of professional real estate owners and bankers is that a buyer and seller meet and agree that the price for a certain property is $80,000. The buyer will pay $80,000 to the seller and the seller will sell for $80,000, but they make a side agreement to tell the bank that the price is

$100,000. So on paper they draw up a phoney deal showing the price as $100,000 subject to getting an 80% first loan. The closing comes along. A nonexistent $20,000 changes hands, the bank lends $80,000, and, as you can see, the bank has financed the deal 100%.

Things like this are done every day, but I *stress* that you shouldn't do it that way. It is very simple, but it is also fraudulent. Though you probably wouldn't get caught on such a deal—it's called "pumping" or inflating the price—you could get into big trouble if there was financial difficulty and you couldn't pay off the loan. In most Western states there is no liability on purchase loans on property. That is, in a legitimate deal where you borrow money to buy property, if things go sour, you can walk away from that deal with *no personal liability*. The lender cannot come after your other personal assets to satisfy that debt. They can only take over the property given as security. But when there has been fraud, they can proceed against you personally. Thus if a lender discovers that you made a fraudulent deal and got 100% financing by giving him a false statement, he might grab your other assets and try to send you to jail. I don't think the risks are worth doing a fraudulent deal. Particularly since you don't have to take any risk. There is a way of doing exactly the same thing, legally.

Suppose you are negotiating for a property. The seller is asking for $100,000. You have a feeling he'll take $80,000. So you say to the seller, "Look, I'll take your property for $100,000," and his eyes will widen because he was expecting you to offer a lot less than that. "Yes, I'm going to give you $80,000 cash but part of the deal is that I want you to buy from me my antique Wedgewood coffee set for $20,000." He says, "What are you talking about? I don't want a coffee set." Then you tell him, "I have these antique cups, an empty lot, or paintings, or an oriental rug" (something that should be of value to somebody but that isn't necessarily of value to you). You tell the seller that it's part of the deal, that you are going to use your antique cup as a down payment and that we will establish the price of the cup at $20,000. "You want me to buy your turkey of a building for $100,000, so you've got to buy my turkey of a coffee cup set for $20,000."

The seller will think about it, and perhaps realize that you are offering him the $80,000 he really wants for his property. This is what lawyers call an "arm's-length deal." If he takes it he will give you a check or receipt for your coffee cup set for $20,000. Or he may give you a receipt saying he has received $20,000 outside of escrow as down payment on his property at Oak Lane. Now you go to the bank and show them the price of $100,000 and ask for an $80,000 loan. That will be legal because the price really *is* $100,000, and it was negotiated at arm's length.

It just so happened that you used personal property in trade as all or part of the down payment. Your lawyer might raise an eyebrow at this, but I know that old hands in the real estate game do it all the time. Their favorite trading vehicle is an empty lot, or some odd-shaped parcel of land they picked up for a song at a tax sale. Like an art work, these parcels are difficult if not impossible to value. On your first trade deal of this type you should confer with an experienced real estate lawyer or agent and get an outside opinion on how to handle the paperwork. Escrow officers who have been around for a few years are always very helpful, and they don't charge a fee for advice if you get title insurance through their office.

There is another variation on the no-money-down theme that I picked up on by accident. A few years back I bought a place with the standard 20% cash down, financed with an 80% institutional first loan. Naturally the $20,000 had been borrowed unsecured, but that's another story. In this deal, when the seller moved out his possessions and I took over, I was shocked to discover that the floors looked like Lake Michigan on a windy day. That is to say they were seriously warped. The waves in the floors had been caused by annual floods. But the strategic placement of oriental rugs and furnishings had totally concealed this condition during my inspection of the place.

I wrote the seller immediately upon discovering the damage: "Dear Mr. Seller, I am giving you a choice of taking back your building, El Warpo, or sending me $25,000 immediately as an allowance for repairs. I have just found out that you intentionally concealed material faults in the property including severely warped floors and a faulty drainage system which promises to flood the place each spring. If I do not hear from you in twenty-four hours, I will retain counsel and bring an action against you for rescission of contract."

In real life you never settle anything with one letter, but to make a long story short, eventually I got $22,500 out of the gyp-artist seller. Later I did part of the repairs myself. I never spent anywhere near the $22,500 I received. After building a $1,000 concrete spillway to prevent future flooding, I was happy to keep the wavy floors, cover them with thick-pad carpeting, and kid around with future tenants that they had been put in at great cost by Mr. Wavy Gravy, a rock star. But the net result of the deal was that I picked up over $21,000 tax free on the deal. Why was it tax free? Because recoveries of damage claims in lawsuits are tax free, by definition.* Now doesn't that give you a lot of ideas?

---

*Technically speaking, this payment resulted in a "reduction of basis" by $22,500.

You might have a similar situation sort of prearranged, like this: A sale is agreed upon at $100,000 but you make up a long list of expensive repairs that the seller is to take care of before the closing. You both value this work at $20,000. At the closing of the deal guess what? The seller has not gotten around to doing the repairs he agreed to do. I can't see any legal reason that without telling the institutional lender a thing he simply rebates $20,000 to you. I have been to many a real closing—even one where the bank knew of the rebate—and they let the deal go through, assuming that the buyer would use the money to make the repairs. A more sophisticated bank would have held back $20,000 of the loan pending completion of the repairs.

If you made a deal with a seller that he was going to give you a rebate for repairs—and it was informally understood that the reason for this was just to get the lender to come up with more money—and if the rebate arrangement is not disclosed—then you are beginning to get into the gray area. But this situation is not the blatant fraud of establishing fictional contracts and a phoney sales price for the bank, and keeping the real deal in a separate secret contract. Just as in tax matters, the substance of a deal can be one thing—but the form in which it is done, the "appearances," can make one transaction legal, while a slight variation is fraud.

It is best, in my opinion, never to wave red flags in front of lenders. They like simple, easy-to-understand contracts and never want to wade through a lot of side deals. You should therefore consider making disclosure so that the lender can't later claim he wasn't put on notice that some repairs were to be done. I would suggest something innocuous like a clause in the deposit receipt: "Seller agrees to put the property into first-class shape before delivery to buyer." The private rebate agreement (the clarification of this clause) then spells out what first-class shape means, exactly what repairs are contemplated, and provides that the seller is going to pay the buyer $20,000 if he fails to deliver the property in first-class shape.

The way you can handle a no-money-down deal is limited only by your imagination. There are millions of ways of doing it since every real estate deal is different. Getting money back at a closing—that is actually getting cash out of a deal at the start—is accomplished by more aggressive use of exactly the same methods. The most important thing for you to realize is that it can be done, it is being done every day, and that you can do it. Get your mind working in the right direction! Soon you will control a highly leveraged real estate empire having acquired it in exactly the same manner as countless other successful Tycoons.

Getting off your fanny and overcoming inertia is all you have to do. You now have the knowledge!

To summarize: A no-money-down deal is any acquisition of property where you don't put up significant sums of your own money. I would put in this category a deal where you buy property for all cash with an unsecured loan, and shortly after the close arrange for a combination of first, second, and possibly third loans to arrive at the point where you have none of your own money in the deal. Many deals require several steps until you get your money out by refinancing; others require little or no cash to begin with. Let's look at them in the order I regard as most preferable to the buyer:

A. Seller gives buyer option to purchase at a reasonable price for a lengthy period of time. The contract provides that buyer gets possession at a low rent during the option period.
B. Outright sale with seller carrying back a loan for the entire purchase price. Often sellers will insist that this be done with a contract of sale by which the seller retains title as security for buyer's meeting his obligations.
C. Sale with seller taking as down payment the buyer's personal or secured note—or a legitimate investment property in trade. The balance of financing (usually 70 to 95%) comes from a lending institution.
D. Down payment borrowed from an outside lender by seller who refinances property. Buyer assumes loan and seller carries balance.
E. Down payment borrowed from outside lender either as an unsecured note or secured by the property buyer already owns.
F. Property is 100% (or more) financed by an institutional lender. The most common ways of obtaining such a loan are:
   1. Outright fraud in manufacturing phoney documents establishing a higher-than-actual sale price. *This emphatically not recommended* though it goes on in perhaps 20% of all commercial deals.
   2. Over-valuation of property or odd-ball assets used to put together a trade.
   3. Rebate for repairs from the seller or other imaginative schemes to transfer part of purchase price back to buyer at or shortly after closing.
   4. Drastically increasing value of property by some action taken by buyer between time of contract and closing, for example, favor-

able rezoning, lot split, or issuance of building permits; evicting undesirable tenants or establishing new and favorable leases; subdividing; establishing higher and better use for property. Item 4 is preferred by me.

G. Property bought with substantial down payment (or all cash) and this cash is recouped shortly after purchase by refinancing.

H. You use investor-partners for cash. They get half of the deal.

Why should you try to make no-money-down deals? The answer is that it is possible to acquire a large number of properties having a high dollar value in a relatively short time. In the West, the laws of many states make purchase-money loans "nonrecourse." That means if the deal goes sour you can walk away from it. There is no downside risk. No one can claim your other assets. In Eastern states, the same risk-free status can be obtained using land trusts, straw men, corporations, and other legal entities to insulate the buyer from personal liability. If inflation continues, as it probably will, you can become a millionaire in one year or less. All you have to do is buy a lot of property and sit back and wait. Your debts will become insignificant, rents will go up, and your equity will soon be a million or more.

Nice Guys Finish Last!

Let's take this scenario: Assume a temporary dip in real estate prices. Mr. Nice Guy believed his friendly banker's advice that it is more conservative to buy one four-plex with a large down payment than to "speculate" in several four-plexes with the same amount of money.

So Mr. Nice Guy buys a $100,000 four-plex with a $30,000 down payment, taking out a $70,000 loan with the Friendly Bank. He didn't even consider the possibility of a no-money-down deal. As it happens, Mr. Nice Guy bought at the top of a period of escalating prices, just before a local rent-control law, economic adversity, or other problems forced him to roll back his rents slightly. To make matters worse, Mr. Nice Guy lost his job. The combination of circumstances causes him to be unable to meet his mortgage payments of $700 per month. Mr. Nice Guy can barely squeeze together $400 per month, leaving him $300 short each month.

At the same time, Miss Tycoon, who also had $30,000 cash to start with, decided to buy six four-plexes. She told a little white lie to the Friendly Bank and five other banks, and (see chapter 13 on no-money-down deals) was able to acquire six small apartment buildings, each for $100,000 and each with a $95,000 loan. Miss Tycoon was hit with exactly the same temporary crisis, viz., rent controls and the loss of her job, and like Mr. Nice Guy is barely able (under the new rent-control laws) to come up with $400 per month on each loan, even though in her case, $950 per month is due on each loan.

Real estate price levels have dropped drastically, and the buildings can be liquidated quickly in a slumping market for about $70,000 to "all cash" buyers.

This is what would happen in the real world: The friendly banker would assess the situation. Money is tight. The bank, like everyone else needs money to keep afloat. "Where to get it?" asks the friendly banker.

He sees on Miss Tycoon's deal that if the bank foreclosed it would get a $70,000 four-plex and be able to realize $70,000 cash, but that would mean writing off a $95,000 loan and taking a $25,000 loss on the books. Under these circumstances, a banker would be very friendly to Miss Tycoon and offer to take lower payments of interest only until the local economy recovered. That way the bank wouldn't take a loss. Nobody likes to take losses, especially bankers who might lose their jobs if the stockholders objected to their having made too high a loan relative to the security involved.

But Mr. Nice Guy has a different situation: The bank can foreclose, sell the property, and get $70,000 cash. They take no loss whatsoever. Thus there is no reason at all to be friendly to Mr. Nice Guy. This is what happens in the real world. The bank "works with" the Tycoons and forecloses on the "nice guy."

A year or two later, when the market recovers and four-plexes can be sold for $120,000 each, here is what happens: Mr. Nice Guy was wiped out. He started with $30,000 but is now out of the game. He has lost his $30,000, and his credit is lousy because he must now admit on new loan applications that he went through a foreclosure. Miss Tycoon sells or trades up her six buildings for a handsome profit of $120,000 (6 × $20,000). The bankers love her because she had "staying power" and helped them ride through a difficult period by sticking with her properties. She did not cause them any litigation or losses. On her $30,000 investment she made a 400% profit. Everybody loves a winner!

CHAPTER 14

How to Use a Contract of Sale

Until recently a *contract of sale,* sometimes called a land contract, was not popular in the Western states. It was and still can be dangerous for both buyer and seller. But it became very popular in California after the 1974 case of *Tucker v Lassen Savings and Loan Association* knocked out the "due on sale" clause. This decision by the California Supreme Court made virtually every loan in the state assumable—*if* the deal was drawn up as a contract of sale. The position of almost all banks and savings and loan institutions in California today is that they will not "call" a loan if the seller who was the *original borrower* transfers the property by contract of sale, *retaining title* to the property as security for the payment of the debts secured by the property.

Let's look at an example that will make it clear when a contract of sale can be used to your advantage: In 1978 Sam decided to buy Blackacre, a home, apartment building, or whatever. The price was $100,000 and Upright Savings and Loan lent Sam $80,000 of his purchase money for thirty years at 10% interest. Upright insisted on a clause in the loan agreement that said if Sam should sell Blackacre, the balance due on the $80,000 note will come due then and there.

This is the "due on sale" clause that gives property owners trouble. Lenders may want a due on sale clause* because it forces a new buyer to apply for a new loan. That, in turn, means that the lender, Upright, can get another set of appraisal fees, points, prepayment penalties, and a higher interest rate, if rates have gone up.

In 1982, Sam wants to sell. Sam and Bob Buyer make a deal where

---

* With the newer "Variable Interest Rate Loans" most lenders don't care about due on sale clauses.

Bob offers to pay Sam $125,000 for his property, contingent upon a new 80% loan at Upright. Upright turns down Bob's application for a new loan, but agrees to let Bob assume the old loan of $80,000 if the interest rate is raised to 15% and if Bob pays a loan assumption fee and costs amounting to $4,000. Bob figures the extra 5% in the interest amounts to about $400 per month and the extra $20,000 cash required (because Upright would lend only $80,000, not the $100,000 requested) makes the deal very unattractive to Bob. Bob goes back to Sam and says, "Tear up my offer. The deal is off."

However, Sam has another idea. He will make Bob an offer he cannot refuse. He says, "Bob Buyer, you were willing to pay me $25,000 cash down. You were going to pay at least $3,000 in closing costs, and were probably willing to pay 15% interest on the $100,000 debt. I, Sam Seller, will make it all possible with a contract of sale on even better terms."

Sam explains that under the rule of *Tucker v Lassen,* "ownership" of the property can be transferred by a piece of paper known as a *contract of sale,* but title on the public records stays in the name of Sam Seller until the fulfillment of certain conditions. Those conditions are usually payment in full of any debt to Sam Seller, and the payment of the debt to Upright Savings and Loan.

The main purpose of a contract of sale is to allow a buyer of real estate to assume existing financing on property without the payment of fees or higher interest rates which may be prevailing in the marketplace. The contract of sale also sets forth the obligations of the buyer to the seller.

The danger of a contract of sale to the **seller** is that if the buyer does not perform, the seller's only remedy to enforce the contract may be in a court of law. It could take years and cost a bundle. In contrast, the procedure for foreclosing on a standard deed of trust is speedy (about 120 days), familiar, and does not involve the law courts.*

The danger of a contract of sale to the **buyer** is that if the seller dies, gets a judgment against him, or goes bankrupt, the buyer may have extreme difficulty in getting clear title to the property. The seller will be incapable of delivering a valid deed once he is dead.

Bearing all these risks in mind, the buyer and seller may still want to enter into a contract of sale. From the seller's point of view the risk of

*In some states foreclosing on a contract of sale may be easier than on a standard loan. Check with a local lawyer.

getting into a lawsuit is not great if he is dealing with a buyer of good reputation for meeting financial obligations. Additionally, the seller in our example is going to get all his original $20,000 investment money plus $5,000 cash profit out of the deal. It is a lot easier psychologically for a seller to take the risk that he may have to wait or sue for the balance of his *profits,* than for "real money."

Also, certain safeguards can be incorporated into the contract. From the buyer's point of view, if the seller is a responsible business man, it's unlikely he will go bankrupt. And if the seller is not too old, it is not likely he will die before the property is resold or refinanced. In the event of death or bankruptcy, while it may take time to get a deed out of a trustee in bankruptcy or an administrator of an estate, the main risk is one of delay and some legal costs. However, the contract buyer would normally not be in much danger of losing the property. In fact, death or bankruptcy of the original contract seller could offer a time of opportunity to settle the debt for something less than the value of the contract.

A serious problem I once had with a contract of sale wouldn't happen to you because it's been solved with a provision I suggest you use in every contract of sale that you're involved with.

I was Bob Buyer. I bought a little office building for $125,000 under a contract of sale. For two years I made my payments to the lender, Upright Savings and Sam Seller, the gent who had sold to me on a no-money-down deal. Then I negotiated a resale with Tim Thirdparty. The price to Tim was $145,000. Tim got a $115,000 loan commitment from the Third National Bank and was to put up the rest in cash. All I needed to close the deal was Sam's deed transferring title to Tim Thirdparty. I called up Sam Seller to give him the good news that he was going to be paid in full, and to arrange to pick up Sam's deed. Phone disconnected! It turns out Sam had moved to Mexico. His last known address was in a little town where he had no phone.

Mail service in Mexico (to put it mildly) is undependable. Several telegrams brought no response. So I bought a $500 round-trip ticket for our girl at the title company. I told her to go down to Mexico and get Sam's deed. Two weeks later she comes back with a nice tan but no deed. Sam, she tells me, was out with his camper and would not be back for several months. This she had learned from neighbors. Tim Thirdparty's loan commitment ran out and the resale died. Months later when I was finally able to locate Sam and get his deed, I was obliged to sell to someone else at a lower price.

The problem of the "unavailable seller" has now been solved by a clause in my contracts of sale providing that a *fully executed deed from the seller be deposited with a local title company.* The seller leaves instructions that if payment in full for him is deposited with the title company, they must release the deed to the buyer. Also I have the seller give a power of attorney to a dependable local lawyer "just in case."

When I made my first contract of sale deals, I looked and looked for a "standard form" but soon learned that there was no such thing. Each deal seemed to require a form that was tailor-made. And when I went to lawyers to prepare such a document the results were uniformly unsatisfactory. So for your benefit, here is a sample form I whipped together. It's a composite of the forms I used on my own deals. It should be tailored by you, your company, your lawyer, and, of course, the other party to the transaction to fit your needs.

Contract of Sale for Land

(This sample agreement is provided as an example only and should not be used unless fully understood.)

1. The parties to this agreement, made in duplicate on January 3rd, 1981, are Sam Seller, a single man, 1234 Spring Street, Springfield, California 99922 (Phone 413/334-4324), hereafter known as "Seller," and Bob Buyer and Mary Buyer, his wife, of 555 Ligonberry Lane, Grapefruit Grove, California 99922 (Phone 415/331-9753) hereafter known as "Buyer." Buyers have agreed to hold the property and later to take title as joint tenants with full rights of survivorship and not as tenants in common.

2. Seller has agreed to sell, and Buyer has agreed to buy, in its present condition, without warranties, the following described property, commonly known as 1, 3, and 5 Blackacre Court, Springfield, California, said property being Assessor's Parcel Numbers 2248 and 2249, and further legally described as:

> Lots 429 and 430 of Higgins Manor, according to the official plan thereof filed in the office of the Recorder of Glenn County, California, on November 10, 1967, in Book 5 of Maps as Map Number 328.

3. Buyer has this date paid seller cash in the amount of $25,000, receipt of which is acknowledged, and has further agreed to pay Seller $200 or more per month at the above address of seller on the first day of every month starting February 3rd, 1981, and continuing for a period of ten years until February 3rd, 1991, on which date the balance due on the principal amount as set forth below shall be fully due and payable. Said sums were paid or agreed to be paid on a full purchase price of:

$125,000 (One Hundred and Twenty-five Thousand Dollars)

Subject to:

$80,000.00 Note of seller to Upright Savings and Loan payable at $600 per month, 8% interest, thirty-year amortization, starting February 3rd, 1981, which is assumed by Buyer.

$20,000.00 Obligation of Buyer to Seller, payable $200 or more per month at 9% interest, balance all due ten years from date.

$25,000.00 Cash Paid.

4. Seller agrees that when the $20,000 debt herein plus accrued interest has been paid, he will deliver a properly executed grant deed to the buyer. Simultaneously with the execution of this contract, Seller deposits with the Transatlantic Title Company (hereafter TTC) the promised deed, together with a copy of this contract, and instructions to TTC to deliver this deed on Seller's behalf to Buyer upon showing (by cancelled checks, receipts, and/or cash deposits with TTC) that Buyer has made or is making the required payment of the balance due to TTC. TTC is authorized to accept the balance due on my behalf, to release said deed, and is held harmless by me for any errors in handling said transaction. Upon payment or proof of payment having been made, TTC is irrevocably instructed to deliver said deed to Bob Buyer or Mary Buyer, or their successors or assignees. Said deed is not to be delivered back to Seller except in the event of default by Buyer under paragraph 5.

5. Buyer agrees that as security for his performance herein, he has delivered to TTC as escrow agent his quit claim deed to the property. TTC is irrevocably instructed to deliver said deed to Seller, his successors or assignees in the event of default by Buyer. Default shall consist of not making a current payment as required herein on either the obligation to Seller or the underlying loan to Upright Savings and Loan, or being behind in payments totaling over $2400.

6. Possession of the premises shall be transferred to Buyer and proration of rents and expenses shall be as of January 3rd, 1981. Said prorations shall be prepared by TTC. All charges by TTC shall be paid by Seller.

7. Buyer agrees that in the event any installment of money due to Seller is paid more than ten days after the date due, he will pay Seller a 5% late charge. Seller will also pay any late charges imposed by Upright Savings and Loan together with extended coverage for fire and liability insurance premiums (fire coverage no less than $125,000). Seller will pay when due all real estate taxes, special assessments, and all other of his obligations which are or might become a lein upon said property.

8. It is agreed that if Seller accepts payment from Buyer of less than the amounts due hereunder, said partial payment will in no way affect the rights of Seller under paragraph 5 herein or any other remedies available to Seller for default. It is expressly understood that in the event Buyer is more than $2,400 behind in any required payments herein, Seller shall have the right to receive Buyer's deed from TTC and to record said deed, and by doing so, to declare a forfeiture of this contract and of any rights Buyer might have in the premises. Buyer and Seller further agree that in the event of litigation over this contract, or default hereunder, the prevailing party shall recover, in addition to damages, all reasonable attorneys' fees expended. Provided however that in the event of a default in a required payment being the cause of litigation, Buyer shall have no right to recover his attorneys' fees as the party who by his default caused the litigation to begin.

9. Buyer expressly agrees before the signing hereof to set up a savings account at Upright Savings and Loan as a joint account with Seller, and to deposit in said account the sum of $2,400, being three months of Buyer's debt obligations. Seller will keep passbook to said account, and Buyer agrees that he will at all times maintain a balance of at least $2,400 in this account. Upright Savings and Loan will be instructed to withdraw automatically when due the $600 monthly payment due Upright on its secured loan on Blackacre. Seller will withdraw his $200 monthly payment from the same account on the third day of each month. Any interest earned by said account shall accrue to the benefit of Buyer. This agreement will be in default if the balance in said account falls below $1600 at any time.

10. Buyer may repay loan to Seller in full or in part at any time without penalty.

11. This agreement may be assigned one time by Buyer, but in the event of assignment, Buyer shall remain personally liable for all obligations of this contract.

12. Buyer agrees to make requests of institutional lenders for financing of said property upon written demand of seller and if a loan in excess of $99,000 is available at an interest rate of 11% or less, Buyer agrees to accept said loan and to use the proceeds received in excess of the Upright loan to retire the loan balance due Seller. As an inducement to Buyer to refinance as soon as possible, Seller agrees to pay all points, closing costs, or other charges in connection with such loan up to $4,000.00 during 1981, $3,000.00 in 1982, and $2,000.00 thereafter.

13. Buyer agrees to keep said property in a good state of repair, and to not make any structural changes without the written permission of Seller.

14. Seller shall, at his sole option, have the right to make necessary repairs, to pay taxes or insurance premiums, or to take other such action as in his sole judgment may be required to protect his interest in said property, and to demand reimbursement therefore from Buyer, together with interest at 10% per annum.

15. In addition to Seller's other remedies herein, in the event of default by Buyer, Seller shall have the right, upon failure of Buyer to remedy the default himself within five days after written notice, to thereafter be released from all obligations to Buyer. At Seller's sole option after default and five days notice, Seller may reenter the premises, take legal possession of the premises without legal process, Buyer becoming at once a tenant at will of Seller, with Buyer thereupon forfeiting as liquidated damages for the nonperformance of this contract, any and all payments previously made by Buyer. Or, Seller, at his sole option, upon default of Buyer and upon five days written notice to Buyer, may declare the entire balance due hereunder at once all due and payable, and may elect to treat this contract as if it were a note and mortgage or trust deed, and pass title to Buyer, and proceed to foreclose immediately in accordance with the laws of California, and have said property sold, with the proceeds applied to the payment of balances owing, including costs and attorneys' fees; and Seller shall have judgment for any deficiency. In the event of foreclosure, Buyer agrees that, upon filing, all rents are assigned to Seller, that he will immediately vacate the premises, and that Seller shall be entitled to appointment of a receiver or to take possession of the property during any redemption period provided for by law.

16. It is agreed that time is the essence of this agreement.

17. In the event there are liens or encumbrances on the property at the present date, which have not been disclosed to Buyer, or if other liens or encumbrances shall become a lien due to acts or neglect of Seller, Buyer at his sole option may pay off said liens or encumbrances and suspend payments to Seller until such suspended payments shall equal any sums advanced as aforesaid. Said action by Buyer will not be considered a "default" by Buyer under this agreement.

18. Irrespective of arrangements made with TTC, Seller agrees to deliver upon demand to Buyer or his assigns any deed or other documents which may be required for the successful operation of the property or to pass title once all sums due Seller have been paid. Seller agrees to keep Seller's own lawyer, Jonathan P. Moneygrabber, 13 Lawyer's Tower, Sacramento, California, informed at all times of Seller's whereabouts and by this document, Seller instructs J.P.M. to inform Buyer of Seller's whereabouts at any time upon

request. Seller also has deposited with J.P.M. a full power-of-attorney and has instructed J.P.M. to cooperate fully with Buyer in the signing of any deeds or other documents which might require the signature of the titleholder during this contract of sale, in the event that Seller is indisposed or temporarily unavailable. J.P.M. is instructed to cooperate with Buyer in all matters requiring Seller's signature that do not prejudice Seller's interest in the property.

19. Buyer agrees to hold Seller harmless against all claims of the Upright Savings and Loan or any other claimant against Seller as title holder of the property, whether through negligence or otherwise. To this end Buyer agrees to obtain and pay for liability insurance with a face amount of $1,000,000 or more in coverage from the XYZ Company, naming Bob Buyer and Sam Seller as the insured parties. Buyer will also keep said property insured against fire, flood, earthquake, and vandalism to the extend of $130,000, and will provide seller with a copy of said policy.

20. This agreement constitutes the entire agreement of the parties and all prior negotiations, insofar as they are applicable, have been incorporated herein.

All parties to this agreement have signed hereunder:

Robert Buyer	Date	Sam Seller,	Date
		A single man.	

Mary Buyer	Date

State of California
County of Glenn

On this 3rd day of January, 1981, before me, the undersigned, a Notary Public in and for said county and state, personally appeared Robert Buyer, Mary Buyer, and Sam Seller, known to me to be the persons whose names are subscribed to the document and they acknowledged to me that they executed same.

Lilly White	Date

Notary Public

Jonathan P. Moneygrabber acknowledges receipt of copy of this agreement, and a power of attorney from Sam Seller.

Johathan P. Moneygrabber	Date

Attorney at Law

Transatlantic Title Company acknowledges receipt of a copy of this agreement, deeds from Buyer and Seller, and instructions covering delivery of said deeds in the event of satisfaction of the debt herein in which case Seller's deed goes to Buyer, or default hereunder, in which case Buyer's deed goes to Seller. TTC acknowledges receipt of $122.50 from Seller as full payment for escrow fees in this matter, and $340 from Buyer for a title insurance binder on this property, and $300 from Buyer for recording the attached "Memorandum of Installment Contract for Purchase of Real Property."

Eleanor Escrow	Date

Officer for: TTC

Note: It is unnecessary and generally inadvisable to record the actual in-stallment contract. For maximum privacy and low profile, it is best to re-cord a "Memorandum" which puts the world on notice of your interest in the property without actually spelling out the nature of your interest.

Memorandum of Contract for the Purchase of Real Property

This memorandum is a notice of the following: By contract dates January 1, 1981, Sam Seller (Seller) has agreed to sell to Robert and Mary Buyer (Buyer) who have agreed to buy the real property located in Glenn County, California, more fully described as:

(Insert legal description)

All terms and conditions of said contract of sale for land are incorporated herein by reference.

Dated January 3, 1981

_____
Sam Seller

Notary's Acknowledgment

_____
Bob Buyer

(To be recorded with the
Recorder of Deeds)

_____
Mary Buyer

Special Note The California Supreme Court, in a September, 1978, case affecting California only (*Wellenkamp v Bank of America*) has decided, in effect, that most "Due on Sale" clauses in California are void. This means that most institutional loans on real estate are assumable by subsequent purchasers, so long as the security of the lender is not impaired.

The effect of *Wellenkamp* and similar cases in about 50% of the other states is great for us as real estate buyers. It makes it possible to do no-money-down deals in a new way. Example: The seller wants $100,000 and is willing to carry back $20,000. Buyer does not qualify for an $80,000 loan. New technique after *Wellenkamp:* Seller refi-nances, gets $80,000—tax free refinancing proceeds—then sells to buy-er and trades up. Buyer can take title and doesn't have to go through the complex *contract of sale* procedure anymore. He can take title to the property, pay the old lender directly, and doesn't have to pretend to the lender that he is "not really" the owner to avoid the "due on sale" clause. No points or assumption fees to pay.

The *Wellenkamp* case eliminates the main reason for using a contract of sale in California—but remember, this case applies *only* to California-chartered savings and loans or banks—not to private lenders, federal or out-of-state savings and loans. The contract of sale will still be useful to avoid "due on sale" where those lenders are involved. Also, the contract of sale is still useful to sellers who receive little or no down payment, and for that reason are reluctant to give up title. In California, Transamerica Title and Steward Title Company are now willing to insure the nontitle or contract interest of contract purchasers. They are also willing to handle foreclosures for a contract seller as if they were "trustee's sales" if the escrow and contract of sale was done with them.

The contract of sale is also going to remain useful in deferred exchanges under Section 1031 of the Internal Revenue Code.

CHAPTER 15

Installment Sales

The installment sale is a *tax concept* and should not be confused with the contract of sale. A contract of sale is a method of selling real estate where the seller retains title to the property sold. An installment sale is a method of selling property that gets favorable tax treatment. An installment sale can be by contract of sale, but doesn't have to be.

To get preferential tax treatment as an *installment sale,* the seller of real estate or personal property must be paid in either "trade-in real estate" or notes providing for installment payments. Any portion of the sales price not paid in cash is not subject to tax until the cash is actually received. The preferential treatment is that in an installment sale, the gain on sale is not taxed until it is actually received. Only a portion of each dollar received is treated as taxable gain; the remainder is treated as nontaxable return of basis.

I rarely advise my Tycoons to sell their properties on installment sales. Reason? Being a creditor where we have 20% p/a inflation doesn't make sense. Inflation and taxes allow you to just break even with a 40% yield on your mortgage paper. But the new installment sales rule, adopted October 1980, may make installment sales useful in some situations.

The new rule says, in effect, that you can defer taxes on any gain when you sell property, on any portion of the purchase price that isn't received in cash. The old "29% Down" restrictions are out the window, and are now nothing but ancient history. You can now take lower value property as a down payment in putting together your installment sale.

169

Let's suppose that in your holdings you have a problem property that isn't going up in value because the neighborhood is declining. Tenants, building inspectors and so on are giving you ulcers. It was a nearly "no money down deal" for you three years ago and you bought your problems for $450,000 with $450,000 in loans. You've already written off $150,000 in depreciation, so your basis is $300,000. Problem is, if you sold for no money down at your cost, you'd get stuck with a tax on $150,000 in "loan relief" or "recapture of depreciation," if the new buyer assumed your loan.

There are several ways to get out of this problem. But let's look at the new opportunities presented by the revised installment sales rules of 1980.

Suggestion: Find a buyer with equity of say $50,000 in his property. The trade-in property can be either free and clear, or have a mortgage on it. Your object is to dump your problem property for a problem-free income property in a "trade-down." The deal is drawn up as a regular 1031 Exchange from the point of view of the buyer (who thus has no tax to pay on the profit on the disposition of his house). The price of your problem property is set at $500,000. The buyer deeds you his $50,000 equity and takes *subject to* your $450,000 in loans. Since you got "like kind property" and no cash, under the new rules you've got an installment sale on which no tax would be due until you sold your new little house. You probably don't have to "recapture" the $150,000 depreciation you took earlier. Naturally, you could always trade up later, avoiding the tax forever. Run this idea by your accountant if you feel that "trading down" is something that would benefit you. I'd like your feedback on this concept or variations made possible by "loopholes" in the new installment sales rules.

CHAPTER 16

Managing Property and Problem Tenants

O nce you become a landlord, your major challenge will be getting and keeping good tenants. You'll note I said "challenge" and not "problem," because, as in every aspect of your career, mental attitude is extremely significant. If you can meet the challenge of picking good tenants, you will preside over a smooth-running operation. Rents will be mailed in on time. There will be a cordial tenant relationship, low turnover, and a minimal vacancy factor.

When you buy your first rental property, existing tenants normally come with the building as part of the package. As soon as you take over management, adjust rents to market levels and evict undesirables immediately. Tenants expect it when ownership changes. If you procrastinate before introducing your new policies tenants will be more apt to argue or feel resentment.

What is an undesirable tenant? If you are already a landlord, I don't have to tell you. If you are a novice, you'll discover that problem tenants come in two major categories:

A. Irresponsible deadbeats

B. Inconsiderate slobs

Often these qualities will be found combined in one tenant. When you inspect each apartment in a building you are about to purchase, the slobs will be easy to recognize. A slight mess doesn't worry me, but if I

The kind of tenant you don't want

were to describe the sort of visual and nasal experience you can expect now and then—sometimes even in middle-class buildings—I might scare you out of being a landlord at all. But suffice it to say that you'll definitely recognize a slob's style of living when you see it. You want them out at once, if not sooner.

The second category is the deadbeat—someone who won't pay their rent when due. They can't be detected by sight or smell, but during negotiations most sellers will be glad to give you a thumbnail sketch of their tenants. Some will be prompt payers, others late payers. But no-payers are the ones to get rid of. If your seller doesn't tell the truth, you'll know the deadbeats on the next rent-due date. You want to re-form the slow-pays with a rent discount arrangement like the one in my sample rental agreement.

Generally, tenants you want to get rid of will leave without court proceedings if you give them proper notice. Notices of various types are at the end of this chapter, with a suggested rental agreement. Buyers of this book may copy and use my forms.

Once your bad tenants are gone, you will begin to show the unit to new prospects. Don't ever show an apartment inhabited by a problem tenant until he is out and the place is cleaned, fumigated, and re-painted. If you show a pig-sty to a prospect, everyone except other slobs will be turned off. However, you may be able to develop rapport with another tenant in an identical apartment, and show that one. Obviously, a day of vacancy represents an irretrievable loss. Still, it's better to have a vacancy than to rent to a loser. A bad tenant could be so annoying to his neighbors that you could lose all your good tenants. And if you get a deadbeat/slob/fuzzy-thinking leftist as your tenant, it will give you gray hair. Not only will he let the property run down and refuse to pay rent, but he will have legal-aid lawyers wear you out with frivolous legal proceedings that take up inordinate amounts of time, money, and energy. You could even lose the building if Mr. Deadbeat's rent was your only source of meeting the mortgage liabilities.

All of these problems can be avoided by careful tenant selection. Follow these suggestions, and you will seldom, if ever, have tenant problems or problem tenants.

Advertise appropriately in places likely to reach the market you seek. If you want gay tenants (who are usually pretty good) there are newspapers and publications read solely by that market. Local neighborhood papers are much cheaper and often more effective than the large metropolitan dailies. Your ad should be attractive and designed to weed out undesirables before they apply. Here's one of mine:

> **—Romantic Cabin in the Woods—**
> $400/mo. Fireplace, Deck, 2 Bdrms, 2 Baths. Adults. No dogs. Tenants must be employed w/good references. Call 332-2345 from 6 P.M. to 10 P.M.

When the prospect calls, you should interview further to ascertain his desirability. If you detect a hostile attitude towards landlords or a tendency towards litigation, it's best to suggest that he seek other accommodations. It is hard to reject a potentially bad tenant. But you must weed out problem tenants in order to have a successful real estate management program. Set up two specific times per week for all prospects to come at once to look at the property. There are several reasons for having all your prospects come at once. They first is that at least half of your phone prospects will not show up for their appointment. Thus, rather than wasting time going to and from the rental unit, if you set up a generally convenient time such as noon on Sunday for everyone, even if five out of ten are "no-shows," you will not have made five useless trips.

Psychologically, if there are several prospects at the same place, you create an atmosphere of competition for the rental. Hopefully at least one desirable prospect will feel it necessary to make a speedy decision rather than say, "I will think about it and call you back." If any prospect is interested in the property, have them fill out a rental application form. Reading over their application carefully will help you weed out undesirables. Check the references! Call not only the present landlord of the prospect, but also the predecessor landlord. The reason is that the present landlord may be so anxious to get rid of a loser that he will give him a wonderful send-off, even though he is the worst deadbeat or slob imaginable. The prior landlord, on the other hand, has nothing to lose by telling the truth about your applicant. Always call the named employer and the bank of the prospect to ascertain his general level of responsibility and to verify the fact that he is employed and does have a bank account.

If you, as landlord, pay a surprise visit to the tenant at his own home, you can quickly determine whether his style of living is acceptable. You also discover, rather quickly, if the tenant has a large collection of dogs or disreputable friends camping in the living room. When a tenant who looks good has completed a rental application, I always ask if it's OK for me to accompany him back to his home. After a quick look you can determine whether he is suitable or not. That takes care of selecting qualified tenants. Next we'll cover money.

Don't make the mistake of accepting sex or dope in lieu of rent.
Never get sexually or illegally involved with your tenants.

Never agree to hold a rental unit for a prospect without a substantial deposit, up-front. A substantial deposit to me is at least one month's rent, but preferably six weeks' rent, my standard security deposit. Normally this sum will be paid in the form of a check. Until that check has cleared, the prospect should not get keys to the unit. The law is such that once you give a tenant possession of property, even if he gives you a bum check, you will have the problem of evicting him. That could take up to two months.

When you have obtained the proper deposit and have checked out your tenant thoroughly, there is still one step more: Go through the apartment with the prospect. Fill out an inventory and condition check list. I have found that most arguments with tenants occur in connection with the refund of their security deposit. The tenant leaves unclean areas, broken windows, or other damage. The invariable argument: "It was that way when I moved in." With a condition and inventory check list, signed by the tenant, you can refer to that document and quickly ascertain if the tenant is correct. You have a description of the property at move in time in black and white. Reference to this document makes it possible to deduct the cost of any damage or clean-up from the security deposit without further discussion.

Now, for those who have a problem tenant in spite of all precautions: Money is the problem 95% of the time. But, sometimes you get a tenant who is breaking his rental agreement by doing something undesirable, like dealing heroin, or keeping twelve puppies that are poopooing on your new wall-to-wall carpeting. You want to get rid of a bad tenant, and you want him out as quickly as possible. First you consider "self-help." Did you know that it's financially very risky to forcibly throw a tenant out without a court order? Nor can you go to the apartment, unscrew the doors, and remove the windows. You can't shut off utilities. You can't harrass the tenant. You can't pop in at any time you feel like it and you can't bother him unreasonably for the rent. You can't do any of that without risking being sued yourself for very substantial damages. So, stay away from that sort of self-help. But there is something you can do before going to court. You can visit your tenant—and you'd be surprised how often this works—appeal to his sense of fair play. Tell him that things aren't working out and you would like him to move out. Ask him how much time he needs. In many cases, a very reasonable approach works. The tenant agrees to move in a few days. You'd be surprised what you get by just asking politely.

Sometimes the tenant will tell you he doesn't have the money to move. If he's already behind in rent, maybe you'd be able to make a

WRONG!   RIGHT!

Be reasonable! Be rational!

deal something like this. You say to him, "Look, I will pay for your moving. You just be out of here by ten o'clock tomorrow morning and this $100 bill is yours. The place is to be left clean. You get moving money after I put a new lock on the door." That $100 bribe may be your best bet, rather than waiting the four to eight weeks it could take you to get a tenant evicted legally. During that time you'd lose more than $100 in rent, not to mention time and aggravation. So, the first thing to do when you have a problem tenant is to talk to him—be reasonable, be rational. Appeal to whatever it is that you can appeal to in that tenant and try to talk him out. Also, keep your cool. It's only money. Don't get all emotional. Leave if an argument develops. Sometimes you can find a new place for your tenant by making a few phone calls yourself.

Now, let's assume that Plan 1—talking—doesn't work. When you go to talk you should have with you the basic form that starts eviction proceedings. This is the "Three-day notice to pay rent or quit the premises" found at the end of this chapter. You need to serve that on a tenant before you can file a lawsuit.

Now, let's assume just for the moment that your tenant isn't behind in rent but is breaking his rental agreement in some other way. Change the title of that form. Instead of three-day notice to pay rent or quit the premises, you'd give a three-day notice to quit the premises or "perform covenant." Then you write in the body of the notice what the tenant is doing that bothers you, like having a dog in violation of the lease.

There are certain things that you cannot object to. Every community has its own rules. In San Francisco, for example, you cannot kick out tenants because they have a child. If a childless couple moved into an all adult complex in San Francisco and then had a child in the natural course of things, you could not tell them to get rid of the kid or move. In other cities you can. You can't kick anyone out, anywhere in the USA, because of race, creed, religious preference, or national origin. Nor can you discriminate against potential tenants for those reasons.

You can't do something that is called a "retaliatory eviction." For instance, a tenant has complained to the building department that you don't supply enough heat or that there are rats. You cannot get a tenant out through court proceedings just because he has made an official complaint against you. He has a legal right to complain to the building or the health departments. You cannot evict him for this reason.

But, suppose that you want to get rid of a trouble maker—a bad egg—who is organizing a rent strike, calling you up with unjustified complaints every day, and so on. Simply give him thirty days notice to move. Assume this tenant has made a complaint to the building department but you really want him out on general principles. For your day in court you'd better keep in mind only the *other* reasons you want him out (like he has a dog, or he's too noisy, or there have been tenant complaints about him). In a thirty-day notice you are *not* obliged to tell a tenant what it is that bothers you. In court or in your conversations don't even mention that he made a building department complaint or else the judge may accept his retaliation eviction defense. You don't need a reason to ask a tenant to move *if he doesn't have a lease.* But if the court finds you have an improper reason for asking a tenant to move, that tenant can stay.

178

Rental Agreement

THIS RENTAL AGREEMENT IS BETWEEN _Mary Tenant_ HEREAFTER TENANT (T) AND THE OWNERS OF _2 Hometown Dr., S.F., CA._ (Address of rental property) HEREAFTER LANDLORD (L), as represented by the agent whose signature appears below:

Received of T the sum of $ _600_ as a security deposit, and $ _300_ as rent from _8/1_ to _8/31/81_. Balance due $ _-0-_ on or before _____ .

This agreement establishes a month-to-month tenancy, however tenant may stay on premises without any increase in rent for 12 months from the date hereof, at which time rent shall automatically be increased by 6%, unless notice of other arrangements are given to tenant. _Rent shall be $ 335_ per month, payable in advance, but T may take advantage of a discount and pay only $ _300_ if the following conditions are met: A) Rent is actually received prior to the first day of the month at W. G. Properties, P.O. Box 408, Mill Valley, CA 94941, and B) All conditions of this agreement are met by T.

T agrees to pay the full rent on the first of the month, and a late charge of $5 per day for each day after the 3rd of the month, and $5 for each dishonored check. If more than one prospective tenant has signed this rental agreement, all shall be responsible individually for the total rent payments and all other provisions of this lease. T shall be responsible for the payment of ALL utilities including water, PG&E, Cable, garbage and sewer charges if any. There shall be _no pets_ on the property except with the express written permission of L and if any pets are brought upon the property without permission, _T agrees to pay $300 per month for the Pet even if the Pet is on the premises only one day or one part of the day._ New locks or security devices may be installed only if L is supplied with keys. L to have access at all times for inspection, maintenance of the property, and showing to prospective purchasers and tenants during daylight hours. The Security Deposit is not to be used for last month's rent under any circumstances, and if it is, T agrees to pay a double last month's rent. Security deposit will be refunded in full 14 days after move-out only if premises are left in pristine condition with windows washed, walls and ceilings repainted if marred, carpets shampooed, all appliances and fixtures sparkling clean, all utility bills paid in full, floors cleaned and waxed, all damage repaired, all weeds in garden pulled, and if T moves before the end of one year, it shall be T's responsibility to either give 60 days notice of departure or provide L with an acceptable replacement tenant at a 10% increase in rent. T agrees that (s)he will be the only person(s) living on the premises, and agree to pay $10 per day for any other persons staying overnight on the property without written permission. T agrees that if he is given 3-day notice for nonpayment of rent, he will vacate the premises within 3 days, and if he does not, will thereafter be liable for, and will pay rent for the premises on a daily basis of $30 per day; T also agrees that in the event it is necessary to go to court to evict him, he will pay L the sum of $250 for attorney's fees or for L's time and trouble if L acts as his own attorney. L agrees to pay T, and T agrees to accept as maximum damages and attorney's fees, the sum of $250 in the event T should prevail or L be guilty of wrongful eviction. _If T is absent from the premises for more than 3 consecutive days while rent is in default, T hereby instructs L to consider the premises abandoned, and to dispose of any property left on the premises as L sees fit, without liability to T._ L shall not be liable to T for any damages or injury

Rental Agreement, *continued*

to T or his guests on this property. T is deemed to have exclusive control of the premises and therefor T agrees to hold L harmless from any claim for damages no matter how or to whom caused during the duration of this rental agreement or possession by T. L may retain security deposit as liquidated damages if T fails to pay rent on time, or to keep the premises in good condition. L's acceptance of any payment for less than the amounts due hereunder shall not be a waiver of L's right to the full amount, or L's right to declare a default for failure to pay or perform. Notice may be served on L at the above address, and upon T at the rented property by certified mail, the registration slip, and not the return receipt shall be conclusive evidence of the proper service of such notice. *T shall be responsible for keeping appliances in working order, repairing stopped-up drains, garbage disposal units, broken windows, damaged counter tops, fixtures, walls or ceilings or floors.* Working light bulbs will be provided by L at move-in, and must be supplied or paid for by T at move-out. T agrees to furnish property attractively. Waterbeds are OK only if T agrees to take full responsibility for any damage or leakage and to use only underwriter approved waterbeds with innerliners. L is responsible for roof leaks and exterior painting only. *T can terminate this agreement upon 60 days' notice, or 30 days if he gets a replacement tenant. L can terminate this agreement upon 60 days' notice, for any reason, or no reason at all at his sole option.* Interest on the security deposit at 6% per year will be paid to T only if T has promptly paid the full (undiscounted) rent for the duration of the tenancy. T agrees not to remove or damage the following items on the property, and if he does, to pay the amounts set forth next to the item named: $500 for any tree cut down or killed, $50 for any shrub or plant or the actual replacement cost, if lower, of any fixture. Control of insects or animals on property shall be T's sole responsibility, except for termites, which shall be L's responsibility to eradicate. Procedure on repairs: T should get bids from 2-3 repairmen of his choice. L will pay for any repairs that are his responsibility *after* work has been completed to satisfaction of T and L. It is expected that T will handle all his own minor repairs (under $30) and will treat the property as his own. A higher level of tenant responsibility is expected in the rental of this home than in an apartment building where a resident manager is on the premises. T understands that property is owned by an absentee landlord and no ready staff is available for repairs. If the tenant is not ready to accept a very low level of service, he should not sign this rental agreement. T agrees to keep roof and drains clear and if he does not, L may have the work done once a year at T's expense ($9 per hour estimated). L will generally pay for materials if T wishes to paint (white) or make permanent improvements to the property. All such work or any changes on the property must be approved in writing before any work is started. This sheet constitutes the entire agreement between the parties except for additional provisions written here: _____

_____

_____

Sally Secretary _____ 7/25/80 *Mary Tenant* _____
Phone: 383-3229
AGENT FOR LANDLORD

180

Application to Rent

Return to: William Greene, P.O. Box 810, Mill Valley, CA 94942/Phone: 383-8264

TENANT ONE (NAME)   **TENANT TWO (NAME)**

Anticipated length of stay _____

Full Name and Date of Birth _____

Present Address _____

How Long There _____

Office Address_____

Office Phone _____

Present Home Phone _____

Name of Immediate Superior_____

Company Name and Division _____

Job Description _____

Approximate Salary _____

Marital Status _____

Proposed Occupants of Unit
   (give names and ages) _____

Pets? Give Name and Description _____

It is clearly understood that $300 per month per dog on premises for any part of a month, or other pet, will be due, unless otherwise agreed on this sheet, right here: NO PETS ALLOWED!

Drivers License
   (give state and number) _____

Social Security Number _____

Car License Plates
   (give state and number) _____

Make/Model Car, Year, and Color _____

Nearest Relative in Area
   (name, address, phone) _____

Closest Personal Friend in Area
   (name, address, phone) _____

Business or Credit Reference
   (name, address, phone) _____

Name, Address,and Phone of Last
   Two Landlords, and Dates
   You Were There_____

Bank and Branch (Checking) _____

Approximate Balance _____

Bank or S&L (Savings Account) _____

Approximate Balance _____

Parents' Name, Address, and Phone
   (or guardian or older relative
   you want notified in case of
   accident or death) _____

Were you ever evicted from any tenancy? _____

Were you ever bankrupt? _____

Have you ever not paid rent when due?_____

Application to Rent, *continued*

I declare the above application information to be true under penalty of perjury and agree that my landlord may immediately terminate any tenancy entered into in reliance upon misinformation given on this application.

I agree to lease the unit on the terms on the reverse of this sheet, and agree that in the event I have been accepted by the landlord's signature on the reverse, and *I change my mind* and do not move into the premises or stop payment on my initial deposit check, the sum of one month's rent will be due as liquidated damages since other prospective tenants will have been turned away, and it will be necessary for L to readvertise the property, and reevaluate other tenants.

Sign here on this side for application to rent. Other side is lease to be signed also.

Dated:_____   Dated:_____

_____   _____
Applicant   Applicant

Three-Day Notice to Pay Rent or Quit the Premises
and
Notice Terminating Tenancy

To: _____*(name of tenant[s])*_____ and all others in possession of the premises
at: ____*(Street Address, Apartment Number, City or Town, County)*____ , California

Take notice that rent for the above described premises amounting to $_____
is now past due for the month(s) of_____, _____   Year_____

The period for which rent is now past due is _____ to _____. You are notified that if the amount of $_____ is not paid within three days after the service of this notice upon you, and/or you do not deliver vacant possession to the owner within three days, an action in unlawful detainer will be filed against you together with an action for damages as provided by law. California laws provide for the recovery of treble damages in the event that rent is willfully and wrongfully withheld.

In addition to the foregoing notice, and without prejudice thereto, you are also notified that in any event, your tenancy of the above premises is terminated thirty days after the service of this notice, and you are required to vacate at the expiration of said period of time.

Dated:_____   _____

Served on: _____   Signed by Owner

By: _____

Date and time: _____   Copies: 1. Tenant(s)
                                                                     2. Court File
Place: _____   3. Owner's File

I declare under penalty of perjury that I served the above notice as indicated above, and that I am over 18 years of age.

_____
Signed by Server of Process

CHAPTER 17

Pay No Taxes
Ever Again—Legally!

If someone told you that Bill Greene could wave a magic wand to help you manage your financial affairs so that you would never need to pay income taxes again, you'd say they were crazy. But I'm going to show you how to do just that: Pay no taxes, ever again, for the rest of your life —legally!

For ten years, in spite of intensive scrutiny by the Internal Revenue Service, I've paid virtually no taxes, while accumulating several million dollars in assets. The methods I am about to outline will show you how do to it too, in simple nontechnical terms. With minimal effort on your part, you can not only eliminate all future income tax liabilities, but also get a refund of taxes you have paid during the past three years.

More than one United States president has said that the income tax laws of America are a disgrace to the human race. For example, Jimmy Carter, during his first campaign, frequently maintained that our income tax laws were unfair and unduly complicated. He promised vast reforms that were necessary. Yet, after his election, the 1976 reforms introduced by him—the so-called Tax Simplification Act—only made things more complicated. Accountants and lawyers lovingly call it their Full Employment Act!

In many ways the 1976 reforms made taxes even more burdensome to the ordinary middle-class wage-slave. More than ever, productive people are getting taxed to death by a system nobody likes. The IRS, in

My accountant and lawyer celebrating the 1981
Economic Recovery Tax Act. "Reforms" like this
just make our tax code longer and more complicated.
That's good for lawyers, accountants, and bureaucrats.

its collection and enforcement proceedings, often operates like the Gestapo or Secret Police, incorporating in its methods midnight raids, rewards to informers, burglars, and female secret agents who use sex to pry out information from suspected tax evaders.

These days the IRS is even trying to pass regulations taxing people for such things as the "value" of the parking space they get when they park! Our Constitution and Bill of Rights have been so eroded by IRS practices that our founding fathers must be turning over in their graves.

We might as well be living in a totalitarian dictatorship, for all the voice we have in our tax system. Certain politicians express wonderment that overtaxed, basically honest citizens are turning to any device in their fight for survival. Even the lunatic fringe tax rebels who refuse to pay any taxes and file "Fifth Amendment" returns have several million supporters these days. The growing subterranean economy of nontaxpayers who earn money but don't file any returns or even officially exist "on paper" is estimated to produce one-tenth of our gross national product. It's all cash, no questions asked. No W-2 forms, no checks, please.

Of course, the members of the subterranean economy are *tax evaders*. There's a risk of actually going to jail if they are informed on and caught. But legal tax avoidance—what we talk about here— for many people is a game with no risk. The rules guarantee you will win. You simply learn the rules. Find a good coach and manager, your lawyer and your accountant, and get on with the game. Look for openings. Never give up. Hang tough. Play to win. Beat your opponent. You can't lose. You don't have to pay any taxes again, ever! You never go to jail in this game unless there is an *intent to defraud*. Everything I'm going to tell you about and everything I do in my personal life involves *no intent to defraud* the IRS—I am merely using the present laws as they stand. These same unfair laws allow big corporations like Syntex, the oil companies, and rich guys like me, to earn millions and pay no taxes whatsoever.

The IRS doesn't like the Bill Greenes of the world telling Mr. Average Taxpayer these secrets. They've tried to shut *me* down instead of the loopholes. But I contend the loopholes I talk about will stay. Why? Because most Senators and Congressmen use them. They pay no taxes. If

you play by their rules, you won't pay taxes either. When Ronald Reagan was governor of California there was a flap because he paid no federal or state income taxes. Nixon managed to keep his taxes at zero by falsifying deductions (clearly tax evasion) for which he quietly received a full presidential pardon.

You might remember from the papers that during his first year in office Jimmy Carter made a small cash gift of $6,000 to the U.S. government because he was so "embarrassed" at having no taxes due. As if he hadn't planned it that way! I submit that a large proportion of our senators and congressmen enjoy allowances and incomes of $500,000 a year from the public, and most of them pay little or no taxes. After reading this, if you ever pay any income taxes you deserve a dunce cap. America today is like France before the French Revolution: A few aristocrats and politicians control 95% of the wealth and they pay no taxes. The workers and small businessmen pay all the taxes. But you can get smart and join the tax-free class now!

I'm going to show you how to get on the bandwagon. In just one chapter, I can't cover every detail. But by making you aware of the opportunities, the different tax shelters, the books and literature available, I *can* enable you to get out in the world to ask the right questions. Then you will be able to make these tax-avoidance principles apply to yourself. Remember, you can become a millionaire quickly only if you don't pay any taxes.

Let's run through a basic outline of one way to eliminate, or at least save substantially, on your taxes. It will also make you considerably richer because the main focus of the plan saves taxes but represents a very good investment. Let's take an example. We will assume that it is the first of the year. You're a working person, or couple, and you make around $25,000 a year. You don't own any small businesses or investment property. You are that unenviable person—the wage-slave, the consumer, the taxpayer. You are a person who goes to a regular job at 9 A.M. and gets out at 5 P.M. You get a paycheck and find that about one-third of it is deducted for federal tax, maybe 10% for state tax, another 10% for Social Security and other deductions. Little or no chance to finagle. What do you take home? Less than half your earnings. A large part of that goes for sales taxes, gasoline taxes, property taxes on your home, and so on. Worse than that, even if you get a salary raise of 10% or more every year, the extra wage throws you in a higher tax bracket resulting in more taxes than ever.

Combine the evergrowing tax burden with the fact that inflation continuously reduces the purchasing power of every dollar you receive.

The net effect of all this is that your standard of living declines every year even with cost-of-living raises from the boss. What can you do about it? There's a heck of a lot you can do about it!

Following the procedures developed in my *Tycoon Class* and explained in this book or on my cassette tapes, you can negotiate your way into the purchase of real property. You'll end up reducing the tax on your $25,000 regular-income job to zero. For example, take a $100,000 four-plex located in Anytown, USA. This four-plex you select is old, grungy, and in need of lots of cosmetic work, like painting, repairs, and maintenance. It also has worn carpets and drapes, and if you're lucky, perhaps some scruffy furniture. These physical defects are the ideal ones you are seeking. Financially, the closer you can get to a no-money-down deal on the four-plex, the better your tax benefits will be.

In connection with our $100,000 four-plex example, let's assume you bought it with no money down because you assumed a $80,000 first mortgage from a savings and loan association. You got a $24,000 second loan from the seller of that property. The extra $4,000 over cost was to provide enough to cover the closing costs. So, on January 1, 1982, you take title to this income property without taking a dime out of your pocket. We'll assume that rents covered expenses during 1982, your first year of ownership. Now let's skip to April 15 of the following year, 1983, and look at your tax return. Remember, that tax return is a summary of your income and expenses for the year ending December 31, 1982. Let's see what the effect of buying this one property has had on your income tax.

First of all, you must be aware that the IRS has a concept known as depreciation. Even though the value of your building may be going up by 20% per year in the real world, the IRS, for tax purposes, will let you write off, as a tax-deductible expense, a portion of its value per year, as if it were losing cash money. The fact that you did not spend a dime of your own money, but used only borrowed money to buy this property, is totally irrelevant to the depreciation you're allowed to take. The 1981 Tax Act lets you depreciate real estate over 15 years regardless of "useful life." At your option you can take accelerated depreciation of up to 1.75 times straight line.

Let me show you how this first property (and others like it that you might buy this year) will be a magic wand to eliminate your taxes. Because of depreciation allowances, and a few other goodies you can legally claim, you won't have to pay *any* taxes this year or ever again. In fact, if you do two or three real estate deals this year you'll get a refund of all the taxes you have paid for the past three years as well. I'll run through it now to show you exactly how the system works.

The first thing you do after you have closed your deal is set up depreciation schedules. The IRS will not try to change your figures if you use a 15 year "useful life" times 1.75 and stay away from component depreciation. Of course, if you're not audited within three years, your figures stand and can't be challenged. This is due to the three year statute of limitations.

The purchase price of the example property was $100,000. You must break it down into various components to get the most deductions. First of all, estimate what represents the value of the land. You want it to be a low percentage, say 10% of the total. The IRS would like it to be high, because you can't depreciate land. In our example, let's give the land a value of $10,000, the structure $70,000, and the furnishings (drapes, carpets, stoves, and refrigerators) another $20,000. The important thing to remember is that you want to choose a value for the structure that is relatively high as compared with the land value. Obviously you couldn't get a 10% land/90% building ratio if you were dealing with a little old farm house on a fifty-acre farm. The value of the land would probably exceed the value of the building by far.

What do you look for to get the best depreciation? Small lots with tall buildings, not too much land, plenty of bricks and wood. With urban property where you have a structure that occupies most of the lot you will find that the IRS will go along with your setting a land value of around 20% of the price you paid with 80% allocated to the building and furnishings. Who sets up this allocation? **You do.** This allocation will be challenged by the IRS only if you are audited, only if they look at it, and only if it is unreasonable. Once you come up with any evidence showing that your estimate was based upon a reasonable set of assumptions, the burden is on the IRS to show that your estimated useful life and allocation of land value to building value is unreasonable. If you want to be totally on the safe side and allocate in a way that will never be challenged, your county property tax bill generally values the structure and the land separately. The IRS will seldom question the ratio set by these independent "experts."

However, with many properties I feel the ratio arbitrarily selected by the county assessor is wrong, often in our favor, with a low land value, sometimes in favor of the IRS. You are free to develop a ratio which is more favorable to you. What's all this for? Once you've estimated the land value and deducted it from the cost of the property, the remainder is the value of the structure and contents. Valuing the structure itself at, say, $70,000, and using the new Accelerated Cost Recovery System which provides for deductions of 1/15 times 1.75, you will come up with [$70,000 ÷ 15 × 1.75] an $8,167 per year deduction. Then, using the straight-line depreciation method, you have a $7,000 per year depreciation loss which you can use to offset other income on your tax return. Even though that building may be going up in value by $10,000 or $20,000 a year in the real world, you're allowed to *depreciate* the building—that is, take a loss on your tax return. The effect of this for tax purposes is just as if your salary had been reduced by $7,000. Depreciation gives you a loss that isn't really a loss. It is a loss for accounting purposes only.

Let's assume that with the deal you got drapes, carpets, furniture, and removable fixtures (such as refrigerators) that you and the prior property owner by contract agreed were worth another $20,000. Getting a high value on any personal property is best for you. You can also depreciate these fixtures and furnishings. The 3 year life of personal property is much shorter than the 15 year allowed life of a structure. So, let's say you bought this four-plex and allocated $70,000 to the value of the structure and $20,000 to the value of the personal property inside the building.

You will notice that this leaves $10,000 for the value of the land. Land according to IRS rules does not depreciate at all. Therefore, one thing I like to look for is real estate on leased land. Actually, if that lease at a reasonable "ground rent" runs for a very long time (like ninety-nine years), you then have the use of that property for as long as you live, but you get maximum depreciation. Why? Because the entire cost of the deal was for depreciable assets.

Let's get back to the depreciation on personal property. The IRS under the 1981 reforms lets you get away with a three year depreciation schedule. The cost or basis of the personal property is $20,000. On any personal property the IRS will let you take a 6% tax credit the first year. Why? I guess the IRS wants to encourage the purchase of used junk. That's the rule. That 6% of $20,000 obviously gives you an extra $1200 in first-year tax credits on the personal property. That will be deductible from your regular income tax. Then you get 20,000 ÷ 3 or $6,660 in depreciation. So you see how a $13,660 depreciation "loss" was created: $7,000 on the structure, $6,660 regular depreciation on the contents.

If after all this depreciation and the tax credits, you still need more losses, the next thing to do towards the year-end is to arrange for an improvement loan. You borrow $10,000 for repairs and painting on your four-plex.

Borrowed Money Is Never Taxable

You can do what you want with it, but by definition, borrowed money is not income and therefore not taxable. So here we are on December 30.

You borrow $10,000 and on the same day you write out a check to the Victorian House Painting Co. for a $10,000 interior and exterior paint job. Guess what that accomplishes? You've got a $10,000 deduction for the money you've borrowed to repair, cosmetically improve, or paint the property. Out of pocket, you've spent nothing. But now, in addition to the $11,000 depreciation deductions, you've got another $10,000 deduction.

That's only the beginning. Perhaps you bought a new car or pickup truck in 1981. Before you got into the real estate business a car used for pleasure or driving to and from work wouldn't have resulted in any deductions at all. But now that you're in a business where that car is used, you will not only be able to deduct most or all of your car expenses, you'll be able to get an investment tax credit! What is an investment tax credit? Very simply (and brushing aside a lot of the bull) an investment tax credit gives you a bottom line deduction from your taxes of approximately 6% of the cost of that car. Your accountant will do the paperwork. So, assuming you bought a relatively cheap car, a nice economical Honda for $5,000 to use in connection with looking around for properties and managing the properties purchased in 1982, you get $300 off your tax bill *plus* all actual costs of operation. Best of all you can write off (up to $5,000) the *entire* cost of any personal property you use in business.

So here it is, December 30, and you have generated these deductions: $10,000 repairs, $11,000 depreciation, $5,000 car expense, $500 tax credit, and you have reduced the tax on your $25,000 regular job income to zero. Your excess depreciation can be carried back three years to get you tax refunds, or carried forward up to 15 years to eliminate future taxes.

As you see, the acquisition of one small piece of real estate generated enough deductions to eliminate your taxes entirely and possibly get refunds for taxes paid in prior years.

What was the secret? What was the formula? Acquire run-down buildings, not vacant land, but income property, with as little as possible of your own money in the deal. You'll get the same deductions even if you put your own money in the deal, but from an investment point of view, aside from tax considerations, the less money you have into a project the less you can lose and the less risk you have. For that reason I emphasize making no-money-down deals. These deals can usually be structured so you have no personal liability. As a result, if the project doesn't work out you can always walk away from the property and you have lost nothing except your credit rating.

Once you own property you will collect rental income. You will use rents to pay your loans and expenses and in a year or two all sorts of magical things will happen in terms of making tax-free money. First, when a tenant moves out and you get another one, you're going to get from the new tenant a very big security deposit. The old landlord probably made the mistake of getting a deposit for what he called "first and last month's" rent. Thus, for example, he got $300 for the first and $300 for the last month's rent, and that counted as taxable income to him. But, you put in your rental agreement that you'll give the tenant the first month free. Then you take an amount equal to the first and last months' rent plus $150 as a security deposit (in this case $750). Guess what? Any "security deposit" you take in is tax-free money. Why? Because it's not income you are collecting. At least as far as the IRS is concerned, you're going to have to return it some day!

In the real world, will you ever have to return it? No! "Some day" will never come! When that first tenant moves out and a new tenant moves in, the new tenant's security deposit will replace the deposit you have to return. In other words, when "Tenant 2" moves in many years from now, he'll be obliged to give you an even larger security deposit and you'll use that new deposit to pay off the $750 that's due to "Tenant 1." Result? All security deposits collected by you will, in effect, be tax-free money.

One IRS agent, auditing a friend, took the very unreasonable position that for security deposits to be tax-free money, the landlord had to keep them in a separate segregated trust account. Such Bull! But, if you want to be super conservative and meet the IRS's latest brainstorm, setting up a trust account really doesn't cramp your style much. All you have to do is put that money in a savings and loan association. Keep it nicely segregated from your operating funds and play money. As a matter of course, the savings and loan will allow you to borrow against that money immediately. Many savings institutions will give you the money right back at one point higher than they pay you. So, if you deposit it in a typical savings and loan at 6%, they'll lend you that money back indefinitely at essentially 1% a year. In the case of our $750 security-deposit example, the net loan cost of $7.50 a year will be fully deductible, of course, so you get the use of $750 indefinitely as your play money. The interest income isn't taxable because it is held "in trust" for tenant claims while you borrow and use it. The tax benefits of a property owner are just beginning for you now.

Let's go back to auto expenses. When you were a wage-slave you drove your car to and from work; you got no benefits and no deductions whatsoever. But now that you are in the business of owning and operating property, a certain large percentage of the use of your auto will be applicable to your business. The IRS makes it easy for you. It says take 25¢ per mile as a deduction. Once again, this is an arbitrary figure set by the IRS, just like the depreciation figure. It rises every year with inflation, so be sure to use the current figure.

Let's say that in the course of a year's time, you drive 10,000 miles in your car. A certain amount of that will be personal use. You have a social life and you drive over and pick up Suzy to go dancing. That is not business mileage. However, if it is reasonable to assume that you use your car 50% for business (which you should document in some way, either by keeping records in a diary or however you want to do it) then you take 25¢ a mile or $2,500 as a deduction allowed off your other income. Now we assumed that you bought a Honda. Remember? That particular car at forty-five miles per gallon is cheap to run and doesn't need any repairs. The cost of the gas and oil and very minor repairs will average 10¢ a mile. In our inflation-ridden world Hondas don't go down in value when you sell—their value may go up 20% per year. The real cost to you in running that car for a business is at most 10¢ X 10,000 miles or $1,000. The real cost doesn't make any difference to the IRS. The government says you can take $2,500, and of course you should take it. The rule as I understand it (and I always stand ready to be corrected) is that you get a deduction of 25¢ a mile on the first 15,000 miles regardless of the fact that your actual costs may have been far less and your car appreciated in value during the year. When you were a working stiff there was no way that you could deduct car expenses as a business expense. Now you can legally deduct more than you actually spent. Of course, if you own an expensive car, taking investment tax credits, depreciation and actual expenses will be more tax advantageous than using the mileage allowance.

Another good deduction is your telephone bill. Most of us get phone bills of $40 or $50 a month. Once into real estate or any small business you can deduct a reasonable percentage (shall we say half?) of your phone bill. Why? Because you've been calling people who might want to sell or trade their building. You've been calling tenants. You've been calling plumbers, suppliers, and workmen all in connection with your business. Those are all deductible business calls. As a result, a reasonable portion of your phone bill is now also deductible for income tax purposes.

There are lots of other deductions, such as depreciation and investment tax credits on that portion of your home furnishings set aside exclusively for your property management office. These deductions are limited only by your imagination and resourcefulness. As long as they come within the IRS definition of having been ordinary and necessary to the sort of business you are in, they are legal and you should take them. When you were a working stiff you had a shop in your basement. Suppose you wanted to buy a lathe or expensive wood-working equipment to make yourself a desk or piece of furniture. You spent $5,000 on the wood-working equipment—hammers, nails, drills, and that sort of thing, none of which was deductible because it was a hobby. Now it is, because you use it to fix up your investment property. The cost of small tools is immediately deductible. If you were to buy a $5,000 Shopsmith, drill press, lathe, and band saw, you could possibly borrow the entire purchase price and have the loan payable over a long period of time. You'd get an immediate investment tax credit and a deduction for tax purposes that would save you several thousands in taxes.

Once you own real estate you can deduct
many expenses to reduce your income tax, and
the IRS Vampires can't do a thing about it.

You can even deduct the cost of some clothes. The IRS can get a little picky on this. You can't deduct the cost of a suit, tie, vest, and white shirt. The rules say you can't deduct the cost of clothes you can wear outside the particular requirements of your profession or trade. Thus you still can't deduct the cost of a new suit you could wear to church on Sunday. However, if you bought a pair of studded bib overalls—which are very fashionable with the disco set—for the specific purpose of working on your building, this clothing expense is (in my opinion and according to cases I've studied) another deductible expense. Then, of course, there's the typewriter, furniture, and all the supplies you would need in the course of running your real estate business.

Can you deduct groceries? Lunches? Certainly you can deduct cleaning supplies, soap, and what you feed prospective tenants and business contacts. I'll tell you how. At Christmastime, if it is your custom to give your tenants a bottle of wine, there is no reason why you can't deduct the cost of a case of wine as a business expense. If it is your custom to invite prospective tenants to your home for lunch to gain their goodwill before renting an apartment, there is no reason that drinks or food you serve at home (or pay for in a restaurant) can't be deductible. Certainly if you invite your handyman out to lunch or entertain a potential secretary or a person who might be interested in renting your property, these outlays are all deductible business expenses.

How about a trip to Mexico? Unfortunately, if you fly to Puerto Vallarta with the idea of looking at property that you *might* buy, the IRS won't let you deduct the cost as a business expense. However, you do get the deduction if you go to a meeting of the California Apartment Owners Association, or a Bill Greene *Tycoon Class* that happens to be held in sunny Puerto Vallarta.* Many organizations hold conventions or educational seminars in resorty locales. With certain minor limitations, these travel expenses for "education" are deductible.

Now let's assume you purchased another four-plex or even two four-plexes in the course of the following year. That shouldn't be too hard. You can acquire three properties in a year with ease. During my very active period I did as many as three deals a *week*. Most of them required little or no money. Sometimes I was able to walk away from a closing with the proceeds of overfinancing. It was as easy as falling off a log. Every deal generated more and more tax losses till I had far more than I needed.

You'll note that even if you buy property on the very last day of the

---

*Be sure to get on our mailing list for tax deductible junkets.

year, you still get a large first-year depreciation allowance on personal property using the "six month convention" which allows you to take six months' depreciation no matter when you purchased the property. The $10,000 loss you generated by borrowing money for repairs or painting could have been done on the last day of the year. Also there is the investment tax credit on basement power tools or the car used in your business. All these tax benefits can be obtained by purchasing "capital assets" up to the last day of the year. Straight-line depreciation on the *structure itself* has to be allocated equally throughout the useful life of the property, so you get the *most* depreciation if the property is purchased on January first, and only one-twelfth as much if you bought on December first. How to account for all this is explained in the chapter titled "Get Yourself Organized" and the book *101 Loopholes,* which may be ordered by mail from us.

In my hypothetical example I presumed that your job-related income was $25,000 per year. You saw how easy it was to shelter that entire income from tax by merely acquiring one property. If you bought three more properties, assuming the same facts, you'd generate tax losses in excess of $74,000. Why bother? What can you do with excess of "overflow depreciation" that more than shelters all your current income? Simple! You can use the excess depreciation generated by real estate acquisitions to get a refund of all taxes you've paid in the past three years. Here's how: Let's suppose that in your first year you bought several small buildings to generate accounting "losses" of $75,000 more, for a total of $100,000.

If you earned $25,000 a year during the past three years, guess what? That $100,000 of losses can not only shelter your current year's income of $25,000 but can also be *carried back* three years. You don't pay any tax this year, and you also get back every cent you paid in income taxes for the past three years. Not only that, you get *interest* from the federal government along with your tax refund. The interest varies with the market rate.

So let's review the assumptions:

1. You earned about $25,000 this year and in each of the past three years.
2. On the average you paid a $10,000 federal and state income tax in each of the past three years.
3. This year you acquired (with little or no investment) one or more older income properties that break even financially, but generate a

total of $100,000 in overflow depreciation or "tax shelter."

4. You file your current year's tax return showing the $100,000 "loss."

5. On your tax return your $100,000 "loss" gets you a refund of all taxes paid during the *past* three years.

Result?

1. No tax due for the current year. The $10,000 that was withheld or prepaid is returned to you in full.

2. The $10,000 that was paid in income taxes last year comes back to you in the form of a U.S. Treasury check for $10,000 plus about $900 in interest.

3. The $10,000 you paid in taxes two years ago is also mailed to you in the form of another U.S. Treasury check for $10,000 plus $1,800 (two years') interest.

4. The $10,000 you paid in taxes three years ago is refunded with about $2,700 in interest.

What you want is to plan and structure losses so they always just balance your income. In the beginning you'll need to take maximum allowable depreciation and create deductions that can carry back for three years. After a while, though, what you want is just enough losses to cancel out your income. That way, total earnings from your outside job and rents would just equal losses and you wouldn't waste depreciation you might need in the future. In other words, why take more than you need?

In my own case, because of the large number of properties I owned, I could (by taking shorter lives or accelerated depreciation) generate two or three times as much depreciation as I needed to shelter all my income. By taking less depreciation than what was legally allowed, I saved it up to shelter future profits. Accounting is not a science, it is an art. At first you'll need the help of a Certified Public Accountant. Later you'll develop all the required talents yourself. The art of filing a proper tax return lies in constructing reasonable depreciation schedules that will be honored by the IRS which, at the same time, will put you in a position of not having to pay income taxes.

Everything I have been talking about so far is *strictly legal* tax avoidance. Some people would call it tax deferral. It's very different from tax evasion, which is *illegal.* You can go to jail for evasion if the blue meanies catch you. Let me give you an example of tax evasion: Assume that you collect $25,000 in fees, and you *intentionally* do not report it. If you really owe a tax on that money (because you don't have any tax shelters), and your lover or spouse gets very mad at you, that person could report you for the standard IRS 10% Blood Money Reward. For this money, the ex-lover might testify in court that you *intentionally* did not report $25,000 in income. With an informant's fee at stake, he/she may even amplify or lie for the IRS. That's the sort of thing you could go to jail for. That's tax evasion.

Avoidance is legal! Taking a ten-year life on a property that the IRS feels you should have taken a fifteen-year life on is not tax evasion, it's just a matter of differing opinion. You're not anywhere near the gray area of criminal prosecution. If you are audited the IRS likes to argue almost every aspect of your return. Once you become a large-scale property owner, expect to be audited almost every year. IRS agents will probably fiddle around with your depreciation schedules and suggest all kinds of inane and typically bureaucratic changes they want to make on your return. However, the rules of the game are on your side. You can now take straight-line depreciation of fifteen years without running any risk of audit.

If the IRS does get tough about any aspect of your tax return, as a property owner, you can always increase deductions dramatically by taking accelerated depreciation. You merely take 175% of straight-line, and that is also allowable. The only disadvantage is that when you sell the property, you must "recover" accelerated depreciation as ordinary income, not capital gain. As I mentioned, in your first year of operations, high deductions might be more significant because you want to generate enough depreciation losses to carry back three years in order to get that big refund. But, once you've got a substantial number of properties you will find that your overflow depreciation will be so much that you can become very conservative and still have all the depreciation you need. Strangely enough, the IRS never fights when you use conservative figures. If the rules say the life of the building is 15 years and you take a thirty-five-year life, they don't argue. But if they say it's fifteen and you take ten, they may give you some static. When push comes to shove, if you really need that high depreciation and they do knock out the figures you chose, then threaten to use accelerated depreciation to come out with a better result than you had before.

In the example I just gave you'll have many other deductions, too:

1. interest paid on money borrowed
2. real estate taxes
3. maintenance expenses.

The taxpayer in the real estate business is in a game rigged in his favor, if he knows the rules. In the course of being in this business a lot of other tax opportunities will come your way if you keep up with the latest gimmicks by reading books like this one, taking courses like mine, and keeping up with all the current literature in the field. For instance, the *Wall Street Journal* has a "Tax Tips" column appearing on its front page once a week. Read it! Apply it!

I'm assuming that in all the buildings you buy, rents and expenses are just about even. Thus for tax purposes it's the depreciation figures that loom important. This depreciation never catches up with you. Conventional wisdom goes something like this: You can shelter your outside (non-real estate) income with the real estate overflow depreciation. Your ordinary income from your job or outside earnings would have been taxed at ordinary income rates, but you sheltered all the income. Later on when you sell the property you must recapture the tax savings, but you do so at the (lower) capital gains rates. For instance, if after ten years you sell the property for what it cost ($100,000) and you had depreciated it to zero, you would have to pay a tax on the whole $100,000 received as capital gains. However, as I say, this is *conventional wisdom*. The $100,000 profit theoretically would be taxed at capital gains rates, which are less than your ordinary income tax rate. The IRS rules say that each year you take $10,000 in depreciation your "basis" goes down by $10,000. So if you sell it in year 1 for $100,000 after taking $10,000 depreciation, you would have a $90,000 basis and a taxable capital gain of $10,000. If you sell it in year 2 after taking $20,000 in depreciation, you'd have a capital gain (profit) of $20,000. This is, of course, if you sell at the price you bought it at.

Most accountants will say that the net effect of investing in real estate is that "today's income escapes current taxation to be taxed later at capital gains rates." But I say you'll never have to pay any taxes during all your life because, like Vincent Astor, you should never sell your properties! Ever! You can pull money out by tax-free refinancing. The IRS will allow you to go through a maneuver called "trading up." This is covered quite clearly by (for a refreshing change) Internal Revenue Code section 1031. For all practical purposes, this law tells you to find a new property and arrange for the sale of old property to close the same day. If you do the paperwork right, there is no tax consequence whatsoever. I cover this in great detail in the chapter on 1031 exchanges. But for now let me show you how it works: Let's assume that a few years ago you bought a four-plex for $100,000. You depreciated it to zero but it's still really worth $100,000. You now find a building that is worth $1,000,000 that requires a $100,000 down payment. You arrange for the sale of your $100,000 building to be simultaneous with your purchase of the million dollar building. The $100,000 cash you get for your old building goes to the seller of the $1,000,000 building as his down payment. If you do it just that way, there is no tax consequence to you.

Instead of starting depreciation at one million on the new building, you start at $900,000 because you carry over the used-up ($100,000) depreciation or basis from the old property into the new. In real life the figures would never be simple, but I'm giving you this only as an example.

Let's recap. The original property bought for $100,000 you depreciated to zero. $100,000 in depreciation was used up. When you buy that new $1,000,000 building the depreciation that you took on the original property is taken off the price you pay for the new building. This is called a $100,000 reduction in basis. Your "basis" for depreciation starts at $900,000.

When you trade up you should try to trade up in value as dramatically as in this example. Let's look at what happens if you go from a $100,000 building to a $1,000,000 building. From the $100,000 building you took $10,000 a year depreciation each year for ten years. At the end of the ten years, if you buy a $1,000,000 building (without a dime out of your pocket) you begin to generate $90,000 a year depreciation, assuming a ten-year life on the trade-up property. Can you see how trading up gives you new depreciation every time you do it? The depreciation in the new deal can be many times more than what you had before. That's why any real estate investor who has been at the game for a while keeps trading up regularly.

Actually, the rules of the tax game as they now stand *force* you to trade up. If you don't trade up and your depreciation runs out, all those rents coming in become taxable income. A Tycoon wants to shelter *all* his income *all* the time. Real estate is tax shelter that you can create for yourself.

Now that I have given you the basics, let's get a little more sophisticated and go into the subject of generating maximum deductions in real estate.

Suppose that one of your tenants puts an unsightly chip in the bathtub. You have to spend $60 to replace that broken bathtub with a new one. Because it's a relatively small expense, I'm quite sure that the IRS, even if fully informed, would not make you capitalize the bathtub and depreciate it over six years at $10 per year. As picky and unreasonable as they are, they'd probably allow you to write off the entire $60 in the year the broken bathtub was replaced. Likewise if in a later year the same thing happened to a commode or a toilet fixture, you could probably replace it and write it off immediately.

Bear in mind that if you were to do a major remodeling job all at once—take out the fixtures, retile, put in new fixtures, and basically build a brand new $5,000 bathroom—the IRS would say that's a capital improvement. Remodeling must be depreciated over the life of the new bathroom, which might be twenty years. Therefore, remember: To get maximum deductions you want to expense the costs of improvements, that is, write it off immediately as a repair. However, once you have all the losses you need you may want to drag out those deductions by capitalizing them. The IRS will never argue if you capitalize a repair, but they may fight you if you are trying to expense something they think is a capital improvement.

The IRS does issue guidelines and there are books to help you decide what's a capital improvement and what's a repair. In those years you need deductions be sure to classify expenses as repairs, not capital improvements. Is there a choice? Let me give you one example: If you have a house with a four-sided roof and you repair or replace all four sections at once, that's clearly a new roof, a capital improvement. If you put on a brand new roof which will last ten years, you can write off only one-tenth each year. But suppose only a quarter of it was leaking and you got just that quarter fixed, and the roofing bill said clearly "Roof Repairs, $200." The IRS couldn't get you to capitalize because you didn't need a whole new roof. You took care of only one section needing an emergency repair. Of course if it is an old roof the chances are that next season another section will leak and you can fix that up. It can then be expensed as another repair. If, in the third year you have another leak, you'll expense that. In the fourth year the same. The net result is that in four years you have a brand new roof but you've been able to expense it off right away instead of writing it off over ten years. Remember, if you want write-offs, do repairs and do them piecemeal, not as part of a general remodeling plan—or at least not as part of any plan the IRS can ascertain.

Now let me introduce you to the concept of the tax lottery system. It works like this: The IRS does not audit everybody. It does not even audit all landlords. Often audits are aimed at one specific enforcement problem which the president has thought up in that particular year in order to get a few votes. For example, a directive may come down some year that property owners should get a rough treatment because it is thought that they are expensing too many four-martini business lunches. The IRS will pull your tax return to see if you wrote off a lot of lunches. That year taxmen may not even look at your depreciation schedules because they are interested in only one little area—how many martinis you drank. The agent may say you should have charged off only $500 for lunches and you charged off $1,100. The IRS wants to knock $600 off your expenses. Most taxpayers don't argue because they don't want the agents delving into every single accounting entry. As I told you, accounting is an art, not a science, and the IRS could take you to court over every single expense if it wanted to be nasty. Since court lawyers and accountants are expensive ($100 per hour) even if you win and keep your $600 expenses, it would probably result in a couple of thousand dollars thrown away in legal costs. Not to mention fooling around for months and going to countless meetings and conferences. Generally, if you are audited, give in, settle fast, and keep expenses down. If possible keep the IRS agents out of your hair. If you are argumentative they may start going over everything. But remember, not everyone is audited. The IRS uses the lottery system. If your name is not pulled and three years pass, you're home free. The statute of limitations says that the IRS can question your return for only three years after it's filed. However, if they suspect you of tax evasion, they have up to seven years to charge you with criminal tax frauds.

If you've been audited once for a particular year, they generally don't come back at you for the same year, even if during the first audit they just asked about one very narrow issue (such as the yacht you kept to entertain your tenants). If you gave in on the yacht maybe they will let you keep your ten-year depreciation schedules.

Once you own real estate there are many other gimmicks you can use that are entirely legal. Let me give you one more: Suppose you have a teenage kid who goes to high school. I'm not sure what teenage kids get as an allowance these days, but let's say you give him $100 a month. If you give your kid $100 a month for his albums, gasoline, and baseball uniforms, of course there is no deduction—you don't get any tax benefit. So, why not *hire* your kid instead of just giving him that money? Let him do minor jobs around the property you own. Keep a record of what those duties are: wash the windows, paint the walls, vacuum, clean the yard. Give him $100 a month for that. What can happen here? What if you had your own kids or three or four kids to whom you previously were giving money without getting any tax benefit. Suppose you now *pay* those kids $750 a year? That $750 × 4 kids is now deductible to you as an expense! It's not taxable to the kid, however, because people don't have to pay income taxes if they earn a certain minimum, which as of 1980 was $3,300.

Here's another advantage to owning real estate: If you have a windfall in your non-real estate business (whatever that business may be) there are a few maneuvers to shelter that unexpected income. They are legitimate and at this point perfectly legal and ethical. Owning real estate makes it possible for you to shift income and losses to different years. Suppose you got a $5,000 bonus in December from your particular business. You hadn't planned on that, right? Now you need to generate a $5,000 loss if you want to avoid paying tax on that bonus. One thing you can do is prepay your real estate taxes, insurance premiums or any other expenses (except interest) in connection with real estate. That way you generate a $5,000 loss when it's needed. Another way to do the same thing is to prepay any legal or accounting fees, or almost any expense for that matter. Of course if you don't happen to have the cash you can always borrow to prepay bills. Once you are a real estate owner, lenders realize that we do this sort of thing and are quite accommodating about making loans in December to be paid back the following year. As a result, you shouldn't have any difficulty shifting expenses (or income) back and forth between the years to keep your income tax at zero, regardless of unexpected factors.

A logical question at this point is, "Since you have now exposed all these loopholes to the unwashed masses, don't you think this in itself might cause Congress to clamp down and make it impossible to do in the future what you have done in the past?"

There is that risk, of course, but if any logic or sanity exists in Washington (and I usually doubt there is), they must realize that housing and construction are two of the most vital sections of the economy, right up there with food production and distribution. Farmers get all sorts of subsidies and benefits to encourage them to work long hours at physically difficult and somewhat unpleasant tasks. Likewise, real estate has to get some special encouragement from government if money and effort is to flow into buildings and homes. There are negative factors involved with real estate (look at the chapter on problem tenants!), so there must be something to make it more attractive than Swiss bank accounts, gold, fine art, or antiques. That "something" exists in being left alone and being able to defer taxes. Without the benefits of overflow depreciation and trading up tax free, you can be sure I'd walk away from my holdings tomorrow. I'd let the lending institutions take over my empire. The government could have it all if they wanted it. If the rules were changed, money would flow out of real estate in a flood the likes of which haven't been seen since Noah's days. We'd follow England down the tubes—creating the European situation where there is virtually no new construction except for inefficient public housing erected at government expense. Of course, "government" expense is always taxpayer expense. Congress often enacts British socialistic legislation here almost exactly a decade after it proves to be unworkable in England. This indicates that there may be no logic or sanity in Washington.

The present system of no-government-meddling, plus tax breaks for real estate investors, works. Whole cities could be housed in the projects built by wealthy investors who backed ventures solely for their tax shelter features. The present system of a relatively free economy in real estate works. It delivers reasonably priced dwellings, factories, warehouses, offices, and stores to the people who use them.

The United States is the only country in the world with no housing problem. Housing here is abundant, with an existing housing stock supplying per person double the square footage of other developed countries. Our low costs for finished housing are a marvel to the world. In Denmark, Sweden, France, and England there are ten-year waiting lists for apartments. All but the most expensive housing is built wastefully by governments at substantial cost to the taxpayers. Homes or apartments are simply not available.

In the United States the only problems exist in a growing number of cities where *local* governments have instituted high taxes, rent controls or both. In New York no new residential construction takes place unless it is super-luxurious condos or public slums erected and maintained at enormous taxpayer expense. Some areas in New York look like Dresden, Germany, after the bombings. The strangulation of private real estate in New York has made it the most unliveable city in the world and has played a large part in bankrupting the city. Even *talk* by politicians of the elimination of the tax shelter features from real estate will cause a rapid outflow of capital from this industry just as surely as presently existing tax incentives have caused wealthy people to invest in real estate tax shelters. Since rent control was enacted in San Francisco, not a single new (private) rental apartment house has been built.

But in other areas, I feel that the unhealthy socialistic trends of the past fifty years are finally being reversed. The successful taxpayer revolt in California—led by property owners—reduced real estate taxes by two-thirds. If that can be done nationally, you and I can spend less time working on loopholes, and more time being productive. With income taxes at a maximum of 20% I'd be more than happy to pay my share—wouldn't you?

Until then, let's play by the present rules, take advantage of the laws as they stand, and pay no taxes at all—legally.

CHAPTER 18

1031 Exchanges—Buying and Selling Tax Free

Knowing how to make a tax-free real estate exchange is extremely important. I'm going to tell you what a tax-free trade is, why you should trade, when you should trade, and how you should trade. As a result of this information, instead of selling property and paying up to 65% of your profits in federal and state taxes, you will be able to make deals and save substantial amounts of money. This involves big money that would otherwise have been squandered in taxes. The net result of your mastering the technique of trading up will be to increase your net worth at tremendous speed. This will give you a fast, clear path to financial independence. With financial freedom you gain control over your own destiny.

What we are covering specifically is the use of Internal Revenue Tax Code Section 1031 relating to tax-free, or more accurately, tax-deferred exchanges. After reading this you will be able to mastermind your own tax-free trades without a lawyer or CPA at your side. In addition, you will understand exchanging better than a vast majority of lawyers, accountants, and real estate brokers.

First of all, let's clear up the biggest misunderstanding concerning trades of real property. Most people believe if you own a small property and you want to trade up to a bigger property, you have to find someone with a big property who is willing to take your smaller property in trade. Nothing could be further from the truth. Here is what really happens: You want to trade up from a single-family home you own (as a rental unit) to a bigger property, say a twenty-unit apartment building. The owner of those twenty units doesn't want your single-family house because it is smaller. He wants to trade up himself. In the real world the owner of the large piece of property you want almost always wishes to trade up himself. He will seldom want to sell for cash, and will rarely, if ever, want to trade *down*.

"But," you may say, "you are not talking about trading after all, are you? Because I always thought that when you traded you gave something other than cash in return from the person you traded with." But here is where I will clarify a common misconception about real estate trading. Exchanges or trades under section 1031 of the IRS code are never *really* trades or exchanges of property A for property B. Section 1031 (tax-free) exchanges are simply paper exchanges done solely for tax purposes. 1031 exchanges are a completely legal IRS-approved way of avoiding taxes when you sell property at a profit and immediately invest in other property. What this 1031 exchange really is is a way to "sell" your property without paying any capital gains tax, any ordinary income tax, or any tax at all!

There are three main requirements for such tax-free exchanges. The fourth requirement (an immediate reinvestment of proceeds) has some flexibility. First, there must be like property sold and like property acquired. But "like" property for the IRS has a very special meaning I will explain later. Second, the property you are buying must have a bigger price tag than the property you are selling. Third, the property you are buying must have a bigger mortgage than the property you are selling. And fourth (this is where some flexibility comes in), there should be a *simultaneous* closing of the two deals. But, if you structure the "trade" carefully you can sell now and reinvest several months or even several years later.

The "trading" is all done on paper. There is no real trade. There is just an elaborate fiction to avoid taxes. The section 1031 deal is an artificial method of selling and buying that would never exist but for the tax code. It's a way that you and I can "sell" property by meeting requirements set forth by a certain very important federal law known as section 1031 of the Internal Revenue Code.

If you have ever looked up anything in the tax code, you know the code is indeed code. It is difficult to understand, uses obscure language, and is almost impossible to read. But in contrast to most other sections, 1031 is relatively clear and is only one paragraph long. It says:

> No gain or loss shall be recognized if property held for productive use in trade or business or for investment is exchanged solely for

property of a like kind to be held either for productive use in trade or business or for investment.

Specifically excluded from this section are stock in trade, property held primarily for sale, stocks, bonds, notes, claims against other people, certificates of trust, or other securities.

To have your deal meet the code requirements it is necessary to previously establish an *intent* that the property you own and the properties you are acquiring are for investment, not for a quick resale. Then, all you have to do is adhere to the three main requirements for a 1031 exchange. As I said:

- It must be a like for like exchange.
- The new property must have a bigger price tag.
- The new property must have a bigger mortgage.

The fact that your *intent* in doing a 1031 exchange is solely to avoid taxes cannot be held against you and will not invalidate the tax-free status of your trade. Actually, you could broadcast on national network and place an ad in the *New York Times* saying that your whole, exclusive, and only purpose in doing a section 1031 exchange was to avoid taxes. And, if the IRS heard that announcement and knew your intention, your exchange would *still* be tax free—as long as you followed the exact provisions of section 1031. Under existing federal tax laws, almost any other tax-saving business transaction could be disregarded by the IRS if tax avoidance was your main motivation.

The only reason for doing a 1031 exchange is to take advantage of a legally approved method of avoiding taxes. This section is one of the few of the tax code that have been interpreted in favor of the taxpayer in many court cases. For perhaps the first time in your "tax planning" you do not have to go through elaborate shenanigans to manufacture "evidence" to convince the IRS that what you did was a bona fide business transaction without tax avoidance motives. It is sufficient that your exchange was done for no other purpose than beating the IRS out of taxes.

Normally, in other areas of tax law, if you arrange almost any transaction for the purpose of avoiding taxes, you will achieve the opposite result. The IRS will say "any transaction you did just for tax benefits is not bona fide and we will tax you anyway." But 1031 is different. Just follow the three rules, like for like, bigger price, bigger mortgage, and you are home free—free of taxes, that is. You will notice that section 1031 applies not only to real estate. Before I elaborate on how to use it in real estate, let's take some other examples. First, gold coins and foreign money; second, antique cars. Last, we'll look at real estate.

Suppose in your opinion, Austrian Corona gold coins will go up in value faster than South African Kruger Rand gold coins. You have $1,000 worth of Rands, ten coins that you bought for $100 each. You swap them for $1,000 worth of Coronas, also ten coins. In a few days your prediction comes true, and the Coronas are in fact worth 20% more than the Rands. By trading, you accomplished what amounts to a tax-free sale of your Kruger Rands. You acquired ten Austrian Coronas with ten Rands. Had you paid a capital gains tax on the sale of your Rands, you would have been able to buy only five Coronas. Now that the Rands went up by say 20%, you trade back for twelve Rands. If you had paid taxes you would be down to five and one-half Rands from the ten you started with. Now, let's say you own Swiss francs today but you feel that German marks will go up at a faster rate. You can exchange your Swiss francs for German marks, tax free.

If what you did was a sale instead of an exchange—what would your tax situation look like? Say you bought marks for $10,000. They now have a market value of $20,000. If you sold them for dollars you would have a $10,000 gain and a tax to pay of around 40% of that $10,000 gain. You would *lose* $4,000 of your capital and would be able to spend only $16,000 on German marks. So by *trading* your Swiss francs for German marks you keep your profits and do not have to pay any tax! In effect, you have used your entire $20,000 worth of Swiss francs to get $20,000 of German marks. If the marks go up relative to the francs (which is what you thought they would do), you can trade back and forth indefinitely, and thereby keep increasing your wealth, at least in dollar terms. In real terms, all paper money is depreciating.

Where do you get the money to live on in the meantime? You could borrow dollars against your foreign money—*tax free!*

Next, assume you had an antique 1910 Buick. Why would you want a tax-free exchange? Because you would avoid the capital gains tax that would otherwise be due if you merely sold the car at a big profit, took the money, and then went out to buy another car. So you can do a three-way exchange of the car you own for the one you want to buy—and thus avoid any taxes. As in real estate, the owner of what you want probably doesn't want what you have to trade—so a three-way deal is needed. Let's see how a three-way trade works in real estate.

Real Estate Trades

Now, you will recall that the property eligible for a tax-free exchange had to be property held for productive use in a trade or business or for investment and could not be property held primarily for sale. How do you make sure that the IRS cannot establish that you were holding the property, the gold coins, foreign money, antique cars, or real estate, for sale?

At the outset you should form the required intention with regard to *every* piece of property that you ever buy or ever consider buying. Your intention must be that you are *buying for the long-term*, that is, you *are buying "it" for a long-term investment*. You have no intention of selling. You will not sell. I repeat, you will not ever sell that property. That *must* be your intention if you want to own property that qualifies for trading.

It is necessary and essential that at the time you buy the property you write everyone who might possibly be interested in your intentions, and also everyone who isn't interested, that your *intention* with regard to that specific piece of property is never to sell it! Got that??? Keep carbon copies of those letters. You tell everyone in sight and you even write on your offer form, "this property is being purchased for investment and not for resale." Nobody cares except the IRS and it is they you have to convince that any trading property you own was bought for investment, not stock in trade. It is going to be considered stock in trade if you are willing to sell it at a profit the minute a good offer materializes.

You might consider creating plenty of evidence of your investment intentions by asking a broker you know to write you a letter asking you if your property is for sale. Then you can reply in the most strongly imaginable terms that you are outraged that they would consider offering you mere money for your property. Rant and rave a little: "I would never consider selling my property to you or to anyone else! I bought this for investment purposes and I am not of a mind to sell that property just because somebody offers me a quick profit." Be irate. Be firm!

With five or six file copies of similar answers to inquiries about possible sale, the IRS will be hard put to classify that property as dealer property, because, by their definition, "dealer property" is property which you bought with the intention of reselling to someone else, not as a long-term investment. So, to summarize, it is very important to form the proper intention at the time you buy any property that you are going to hold that property as a long-term investment and you are not going to sell it—unless your circumstances change drastically. You are going to buy that property for investment.

Another reason that is acceptable to the IRS is that you bought the property for the production of income and not for resale. As another example, let us say you bought a building for the purpose of manufacturing rubber tires. You buy a tire factory with the intention of manufacturing tires, not to resell the building at a profit. Now, of course, use in trade or business may be interpreted another way. Your trade or business could and should be owning and operating warehouses or other income property such as apartment buildings or stores. But the important thing is that *if the IRS suspects that you were a (shudder) speculator and just bought to resell, they will hit you with an ordinary income tax and won't let you do a tax-free exchange.* The important thing is to make it very clear to everyone, at every stage of your operations, that you are not in the business of buying property to sell at a profit.

Why? Well, to have that intention—to buy property with the intention of selling it at a profit, and then to reinvest the money—would be stupid. These days *ordinary income* is taxed at up to 50% by the Feds. California state tax for instance adds another 11%. For example if you bought property with the intention of selling it for a quick buck, then you would also have the intention of giving 61% of your profits away to Uncle Sam and your state. (You can adjust the figure to meet *your* state tax.) That would be a pretty stupid intention when the law as expressed in section 1031 gives you the opportunity to dispose of your property in a tax-free exchange, or at 20% capital gains tax rates.

The only motive for doing a 1031 exchange is tax savings, and, as I've said, that is considerable. There is really no other motive. Naturally it would be much easier, even if you wanted to acquire other property,

Why is the IRS like the Catholic Church?

Your lips tell me "NO-NO" BUT THERE'S "YES-YES" IN your eyes!

Both find "sin" in what you were *thinking,* not in what you *did.*

to sell, then to take that money and buy property number 2, the bigger and better property. You wouldn't have to worry about doing all the paperwork required for a 1031 exchange. But, with a big potential tax bite involved, obviously it is better to take the time and take the effort to do a 1031 exchange rather than merely to sell your property, take the proceeds, and invest it in other properties. Why? Because if you do a sale and are taxed at ordinary income tax rates, the federal and state governments could take over 60% of your profits from the sale!

Now you want to know, *when* should I exchange? *When* should I start trying to arrange an exchange under section 1031? The answer is: Any time you find a bigger and better property than the one that you own and it's for sale at a fair price, consider arranging a 1031 exchange.

I have heard some so-called authorities say that you start looking for an exchange only when your depreciation runs out. That may be anywhere from ten to fifteen years after you have acquired the property. Don't tell the IRS, but you should be ready to exchange *one day* after you get the property, just as long as the new deal is better than the one you're getting out of. The prospective trade property must have the magic three factors—1) like for like; 2) bigger price tag; and 3) bigger loan.

Don't wait until depreciation runs out. If you want to be a Tycoon always keep your eyes open for good real estate deals. Be prepared to use the equity in property that you already own as the down payment on property you hope to acquire. Are there any alternatives to a 1031 exchange that you should consider? Of course there are.

If it's possible to make a no-money-down deal for the place you are acquiring and not dispose of the place you already own, then hold on to good investment property. If you are able to acquire property number 2 without trading for a low down payment that you have or can borrow, try to hold on to it. Remember one of the greatest real estate fortunes of all time—that of Vincent Astor—was built on the motto "Never sell the land" if you don't have to. And he formed that intention even before the tax code made it so necessary.

With that, I will show you how a classic 1031 trade works. In the real world, every trade involves at least *three* people. There are never just two people because in the real world there has to be a cash buyer, that is someone who comes into the deal with money and no property to trade. At the other, or upper, end of the trade, there is usually someone who is selling real estate for cash. "He" may be a tax-free entity like a pension fund, foundation, or charity. Or he is cashing in his chips and willing to pay the tax on the sale. More than likely the seller is going to arrange for his own trade up. Getting all these characters together might seem like a tall order, but we are going to see what happens in a typical trade deal —the 1031 exchange that goes on every day between sophisticated large-scale real estate investors, the likes of which you will be within the next three years.

Let's dissect a typical simple tax-free exchange. There are three characters in our drama. We will call you Mr. Dumpy because many years ago you bought "El Dumpo," a little house in the ghetto at a cost of $2,000. Today it is worth $10,000. It brings you $100 a month in rent. You have a potential $8,000 profit or capital gain on the house. If you sold it outright, you would have to pay a capital gain tax on the $8,000 profit you would make. Depending on your tax bracket, that could be up to $3,200 or more.

You have been looking around at various real estate deals and you've found Mr. Classy who owns a $100,000 apartment house of four units in a nice section of Reno, Nevada. He has it up for sale and will take $100,000. Step number 1 is for you to go to Mr. Classy to negotiate price. We will assume that Mr. Classy agrees to sell you his four-plex for the sum of $100,000 payable in cash, within ninety days.

But you write on your offer to Mr. Classy, after you have put in all of the other standard terms: "This acquisition subject to buyer being able to find a buyer for 23 El Dumpo Lane, Oakland, at a price of $10,000 or better and structuring this deal as a tax-free exchange under section 1031 IRC." Now Mr. Classy, if he is not a sophisticated investor, will want to know why you put that sentence in this contract. And then you are going to show him this chapter. You show him that if you are able to close the sale of your house and buy Mr. Classy's house on the same day, and you do all the paperwork just right, then you will not have to pay any tax on the sale.

Mr. Classy, upon learning about exchanges, will think trading is so clever that he will want to do a simultaneous trade of his property so that he can get the same benefits. Actually, in the real world, Mr. Classy and people like him have already arranged for an exchange just like you are doing, except that Mr. Classy is probably buying a $1,000,000 property. The owner of the $1,000,000 property is in turn probably arranging to trade into a $2,000,000 property. And that seller of the $2,000,000 property is moving up to a $10,000,000 shopping center and so on up the line.

In the real world, when you close your first trade you may well find that not only your trade, but also six or seven or eight other trades all in the same chain must close simultaneously with your deal. Now that, of course, involves a lot of fancy footwork. And if you have ever been in any real estate deals at all, you know that even simple deals seldom close on time. So you can just imagine the postponements that will occur with a large number of closings all having to be done on the same day. Some people have conflicting appointments and medical problems. There are spouses who have to be brought in to sign papers, some may be involved in divorce proceedings. It should be obvious that in your typical exchange there are normally all kinds of special problems. Exchanges rarely, if ever, close on the day scheduled.

That is one reason why most real estate brokers do not like trades. When you mention trading to a typical real estate broker, he will do all he can to discourage it. Brokers will lie and tell you that the tax saving really is not significant. They will advise "just sell your property and forget about the fancy complicated trading business." But what these brokers are really saying is that they don't want their commission delayed. Since brokers don't like their commissions to be postponed and they like a deal to close as quickly as it can, that is the real reason they will discourage you from doing a tax-free exchange. Whether you pay zero tax or a half-million capital gains tax is of little concern to a real estate broker. Their commission is the same regardless of your tax liability. Obviously the broker would rather have you do a simple deal and pay a big income tax rather than do what from their point of view is a complicated deal just to save you a great amount of money in taxes. Moral: Don't let anyone talk you out of it. It is your money, your future, and your freedom!

Let's get back to our example. Your first trade will be very simple and very easy to understand. Your first step as an exchanger was to go out and find a bigger property that you wanted to exchange into.

Step number 2 is to *find a cash buyer for your property*. Now that doesn't mean the cash buyer has to have all cash, but he has to be able to raise a down payment plus financing, so that at the close he will come up with a total of $10,000 in cash to be able to cash out Mr. Classy.

Now what do I mean by "cash out" Mr. Classy? Well, look at Mr. Classy's motivation for a minute. He doesn't really want your little dumpy house. If anything, he wants a much bigger and better apartment building than the one he is selling. But for the moment, assume that Classy just wants to cash out. In real life you will find that cashing out is often the motivation of the person with the bigger property. He may want to cash in his chips and retire, or maybe it is an estate sale. But seldom, if ever, does the owner of a bigger property want to trade down into a little dump.

I won't say it never happens, but I have just never seen a "trade down," and I have been involved in a hundred or more trades. As I say, I've never once seen the owner of a bigger property who wants to trade down into a smaller one. The only time something like that happens is with residences where parents formerly had a large family. The kids went off to school or got married. Now they want a smaller house. When we are talking about residences or owner-occupied homes, a whole different set of trading rules apply and we will cover those later. But the point is we are here learning about exchanging *investment* or *income* property. It could be vacant land, held for investment, farms, or factories but not "principal residences."

Getting back to our story of Mr. Classy and Mr. Dumpy and Mr. Cash, Mr. Classy wants to cash out by selling you his four-plex. Mr. Cash wants to buy El Dumpo. You are Mr. Dumpy and you won't sell your property to Mr. Cash just outright because if you did you would have to pay a substantial amount of capital gains tax. So here is what you do. This is how you arrange your exchange:

You go to your favorite escrow company. You tell them that you want them to arrange a tax-free three-way exchange under section 1031 of the Internal Revenue Code. Give them the prices, names, and addresses involved and they will do all the paperwork. As always it is your responsibility to make sure that they don't foul up. So you know how to check on them, this is what the title company should do. Prior to the day set for closing, they should ask you for a deed to El Dumpo. This deed should transfer title to El Dumpo to Mr. Classy. Then they will get a signed deed from Mr. Classy covering El Dumpo, transferring title to Mr. Cash. They will also need a deed from Mr. Classy for his big apartment building transferring title to you, Mr. Dumpy.

When the smoke clears on the day of the closing, this is what happens. Mr. Classy technically (and always technically) "buys" El Dumpo, but it is done with the understanding that he will simultaneously sell it, or deed it, to Mr. Cash. Mr. Cash will deposit in escrow $10,000—part of it may be coming from a mortgage and part of it is his own money—but in any event, $10,000 will be deposited with the title company and that $10,000 will be handed to Mr. Classy in exchange for his deed to the apartment building and the deed to El Dumpo. Now, Mr. Classy has to get one other thing and that's $90,000 so that his total receipts for the day will be $100,000.

Where does he get the $90,000 from? Well, you, Mr. Dumpy, have arranged for a $90,000 loan in connection with buying Mr. Classy's apartment house. Perhaps you got $80,000 from a savings and loan and $10,000 from your mother-in-law or a hard money lender, or even $10,000 from Mr. Classy himself who carried back a second. In any event, Mr. Classy now has the $100,000 he wanted in the first place. Mr. Classy walks away from the deal with money. He does not own El Dumpo. That has been sold out of the trade to Mr. Cash. Chances are, in the real world, that Mr. Classy will have arranged a trade up and his $100,000 will be used as the down payment on a still larger property, but that is no concern of yours.

To summarize, Dumpy, that's you, ends up with title to Classy's $100,000 four-plex. Mr. Cash ends up with the title to, and ownership of, the $10,000 El Dumpo. Mr. Classy walks away with a total of $100,000 in cash or paper he's carried back. As mentioned, more than likely he's arranged his own trade to close the same day. Classy will probably "trade-up" and buy an even bigger and better property, perhaps an eight-plex or sixteen units.

You saw how, for an instant, Mr. Classy did in fact own El Dumpo. He sold it immediately, to Mr. Cash. Now it is very important that in an exchange the person with the big property takes title to the property at the bottom end of the trade. There are no tax consequences to Mr. Classy for having bought and simultaneously sold the dump. He bought it for $10,000 and he sold it for $10,000. Whether he was a dealer or not is irrelevant because there was no profit. He bought and sold at the same price.

You, Mr. Dumpy were the owner of El Dumpo and you now have achieved your objective, which was to use your entire $10,000 equity in that house (assuming there was no mortgage) as if it were cash, as a down payment to buy the four-plex, the bigger building you wanted to go into. You had a $10,000 property free and clear and you used that property, just as if it were cash, to make the down payment on the bigger property you are going to move into. If you had not done it as an exchange there would have been a capital gains tax on the profit resulting from a cash sale of the dump. But no tax at all was due, because you did a 1031 exchange. It's really quite simple, isn't it?

Now that you understand the concept, let's talk in detail about the requirements of a 1031 exchange. First of all, there must be "like property for like property." What does the IRS mean by that? Does it mean you can trade a four-plex only for another apartment building? Not at all. You could have a single-family rental home (not your principal residence) that was worth half a million and you could trade it for an apartment building of twenty units that was also worth any amount more than half a million.

A three-way tax-free trade

MR DUMPY OWNS 'EL DUMPO'   MR CLASSY OWNS THE CLASSY APTS.   MR. CASH HAS $10,000   BANKER HAS $90,000 CASH.

THE BANK PUTS 90,000 IN THE POT
MR. CASH PUTS 10,000 IN THE POT.

MR DUMPY DEEDS EL DUMPO TO MR CLASSY

MR CLASSY DEEDS EL DUMPO TO MR CASH. AT THE SAME TIME HE DEEDS THE CLASSY APTS. TO MR DUMPY

MR CASH OWNS EL DUMPO   MR DUMPY OWNS CLASSY APTS.   MR CLASSY WALKS AWAY WITH $100,000   THE BANK KEEPS AN IOU FOR $90,000

You can trade *any* sort of real estate that is held for investment purposes for any other sort of real estate that is held for investment purposes. A farm for a store. Store for office buildings. Offices for land. Land for homes. Don't let anyone tell you that you can't trade a farm for an apartment building, or an apartment building for a shopping center. Shops can be traded for homes, or homes for farms, or apartments for vacant land—all of that is like-kind property, just so long as it is held for investment purposes *or* for the production of income *or* for use in your trade or business.

What is *not* like for like? Assume you bought vacant land, created a subdivision and then you built twenty homes on it. If you had advertised those twenty homes for sale to whoever came along, then the IRS would say that these homes were your inventory. It would be just like a jeweler's inventory of diamonds. If he made a profit on jewels he'd have to pay ordinary income tax on his profit. More importantly, because it was stock in trade, he could not *trade* that property tax free at all. Therefore, you cannot trade so-called "dealer property" for investment property.

Is there any other kind of unlike property that you might get in trouble with? Certainly there is. Your primary residence is governed by a different set of rules. You cannot trade your primary residence for an

This is what the IRS gets in a 1031 exchange!

The shaft!

apartment building or for another house which you are not going to move into. How can you get around that rule?

Is there a way to trade your primary residence for income property? Well, that's very simple. All you do is move out of your primary residence and rent it out. Once it has been rented out for a reasonable period of time (at least six months), it is no longer your primary residence. It has been transformed into income property. You can then trade it for other income property. *But a residence can be sold for cash tax free and need not be traded under a different tax rule.* Using that option you'd have up to two years to purchase a more costly residence.

What's the next requirement for a tax-free exchange? The first was "like for like." The second one is "bigger price." The place you are trading up to has to have a higher price tag than the place you're getting out of.

Supposing in our example you own a $10,000 dump and you are going to trade but you're going to wind up with a $9,000 dump plus $1,000 cash. That would be called "trading down," and in that case you would realize $1,000 taxable cash. That $1,000 cash would be taxable to you, either as ordinary income or capital gain. Had you traded for a $10,000 deal, you could have worked things out so that there was no tax. The whole purpose of making an exchange in the first place is to avoid any tax.

To review, the place that you are trading into should have a bigger price tag, and common sense should require that it's a bigger and better place than the one you are disposing of. Naturally the place you're trading into (not a tax requirement, but just common sense) should be a better *value* than the place you're getting out of. Obviously if you think you are getting less than fair market value for the place you are getting rid of and you are paying over market value for the place you are getting into, then I can think of no reason to do an exchange. What would the purpose be? Besides tax benefits, always look at basic economics before you exchange or before you do any deal, for that matter. After the exchange is over, you should make more money. You should be getting more cash flow. Cash flow, as you remember, is the net money left over after you pay mortgages, expenses, and real estate taxes. If you would have more cash flow from staying in the old property than from the one you're buying, stop and think it over. The improved cash flow doesn't have to be immediate, but you certainly should have the prospect of making more money (after taxes) out of the new deal than the one you're getting out of.

The final requirement of a tax-free exchange is that the place you're getting into should have a bigger loan on it than the loan on the place you are selling. That's pretty straightforward. In the case of our example, El Dumpo had an $8,000 loan against it. But the place you're getting into is going to have a $90,000 loan against it. No problems there.

What happens if the loan on the new place, for some reason, is smaller? Then you have to take the smaller loan on the new place and subtract it from the larger loan. The net "loan relief" figure that you get constitutes taxable income to you. How do you avoid that problem? You arrange things so that the place you are going to buy has a bigger loan than the place you are selling. You can do it by refinancing the old place before you trade. Simple!

Can you do an exchange like for like, bigger price, and bigger loan and *on the day of the closing* take out a lot of cash? The answer is no. If you do that, there will be tax consequences. You always have to arrange your affairs so that you do not take out any cash on the day of the exchange. There are plenty of other ways to get cash out of an exchange.

You can refinance the old property and take out cash before the deal closes. Remember, when you refinance property you already own, any money you borrow is tax-free money. The fact that you trade up later, as long as you follow the rules (like for like, bigger price, bigger loan), doesn't result in the money you got in an earlier "refi" becoming taxable.

What if you do not refinance? In a proposed trade you meet the three requirements. Like for like, bigger price, bigger loan. You close the deal and trade up into the new building. Assume for the moment you had a very big equity in your original property, so the loan on the new property is less than 80% of the value. For example, you had a $50,000 free and clear duplex and you are using that equity as the down payment on a $100,000 free and clear four-plex. You would have a $50,000 equity in the new four-plex after the deal closed. The way you would get tax-free cash out of that deal is to wait a respectable amount of time (thirty days, anyway) to refinance.

After the deal closed, *then* you'd arrange to refinance the new property with an 80% or an $80,000 loan, thereby raising $30,000 additional tax-free cash. The IRS rule on the subject is that refinancing of the place you end up with cannot have been arranged prior to the exchange date. So, even if it is your intention to refinance, you should not tell anyone your intention nor arrange refinancing until after you have taken the title. Don't send in any loan applications. Don't start that until *after* you close the deal or the IRS might try to tax the refinancing proceeds. The same rule would apply to refinancing the place you are about to get rid of in an exchange. That should be done on a date prior to the date of any of your negotiating or signing papers with the seller of the big property. The IRS rule is, if you take money out of a trade as part of the trade, the money will be taxable.

Refinancing negotiated as part of an exchange can give rise to tax consequences. I will not go into the formula of how it's taxed because I advocate structuring every deal so you don't have to pay any tax at all. You can do that by simply exchanging like for like, paying a bigger price, and taking over a bigger loan. If there is no loan on either property that's OK because you can always *add* cash to close a trade-up without tax consequences to yourself.

Suppose that the only property you have is a single-family residence and you want to do the equivalent of a section 1031 exchange getting yourself a bigger and better residence. Actually, that's covered by a different section of the Internal Revenue Code, section 1034. That section provides you do not have to go through the rigamarole of a simultaneous trade and transfer of title. These complexities are eliminated. All you have to do is sell your residence. Then you have eighteen months to take that money and find another house. The same three rules apply. But with section 1034, like for like means when you sell a primary residence you must buy another primary residence. The new place has to have a bigger price but the loan amounts are irrelevant with residences. As a result, you can come out of the sale of a residence and acquisition of a new one with a lot of cash.

Let's see how it works: Suppose you own a $100,000 house free and clear. You bought it cheap thirty years ago. You now sell your home for $100,000. Now you've got $100,000 cash. Next, within eighteen months, you buy a $101,000 house with a $10,000 cash down payment. Assuming a $10,000 down payment on a $101,000 house, that leaves you with $91,000 cash, tax free, to use for speculating in real estate, or whatever you want to do with it. So you see, section 1034 is actually considerably more liberal than section 1031 because you don't have to do any same-day close, and you can pick up a lot of cash by heavily mortgaging your new home. You can sell, have use of the money while you take eighteen months to look around for a new place. It's twenty-four months if you *build* a new home. The twenty-four months from the sale date applies to the date when you actually physically move into a new property, not when you pay for it. You have to be physically residing in a newly built place twenty-four months from the time you sell the old place. With new construction you can also move into the new place twenty-four months *before* you sell the old one and get the same benefits. If you're over fifty-five, the first $100,000 in capital gain on a residence is tax free, even if you don't purchase another house.

If you want to trade from an expensive residence into income property, you have to move out of the residence, rent it, or at least try to rent it, thereby converting it to income, or investment property. Then, of course, you can do a 1031 exchange by arranging simultaneous closes of escrow, just as we did in our example with Mr. Cash, Mr. Dumpy, and Mr. Classy.

Is there any disadvantage to exchanging? Yes. It's a very minor disadvantage. It results from the rule that you *must* carry forward the depreciated basis of your old property into your new property. Now, that was a big mouthful of words. Let me explain how the accounting works.

In our example, to keep the math simple, assume that the $10,000 dump you bought was on land of little or no value. You bought it ten years ago for $10,000 and over the years, since it was run down rental property, you depreciated it down to zero. So, although your original cost was $10,000, your basis (that's what the IRS people use to describe the net figure you get when you take cost less depreciation over the years) was zero. As you remember, if you bought something for $10,000, depreciated it down to zero, and then sold it for $10,000, you would, for tax purposes, have a $10,000 profit. This is the tax consequence even though your actual profit, since you bought and sold at the same price, was zero. Why would you have a $10,000 "profit"? Because the IRS let you use that depreciation—let's say for ten years, $10,000 a year—to shelter your outside or regular income. They do not let you get away with sheltering your ordinary income for ten years and then sell the property and pay no tax at all. No, they make you recover that depreciation when you sell, giving rise to the accountants' saying, "This year's depreciation is a future year's taxable capital gain."

So, you had a $10,000 property. You depreciated it down to zero. Now you're going to buy a $100,000 property. In an exchange you must now adjust the basis of the new property by taking the depreciation that you have *already taken* on El Dumpo and carrying it forward into the price of the Classy apartments. Now it is really pretty easy to do because in our example you're using that fully depreciated $10,000 property as a down payment, just as if it were $10,000 cash on the new property for $100,000.

Since you've fully depreciated that $10,000 property, what you do is treat the new $100,000 property as if you had already depreciated $10,000 of it. You acquired the $100,000 property in an exchange. You used your fully depreciated $10,000 property as your trade-in. Assuming you have a ten-year useful life expectancy on the new place, you start with a tax *basis* on the new property of only $90,000. You do not get to take depreciation on the full $100,000 price because you are *carrying forward* the used-up depreciation. But now you deduct from the depreciable basis of the new property the $10,000 depreciation you already used up on the trade-in. As a result, you get only $9,000 a year depreciation on the Classy apartments instead of $10,000 per year depreciation.

I hope that teaches you the principle of the "carry-forward of basis." With multiple properties and the various complicated deals we go into these days the actual accounting can get a little hairy. But now that you know the principle, you can probably figure out your carry-forward basis on a simple deal. On your tax return I'd advise you to get a CPA to look your figures over!

In most trades you will be getting a lot more in depreciation deductions after the trade than you were getting before the trade. If the price of the property you are getting into is a lot more than the price of the property you are getting out of, you'll always have plenty of over-flow depreciation. Let me explain how that works.

If you had a $10,000 property, assuming your depreciation hadn't run out and it was being depreciated on a ten-year life, you were getting a $1,000-a-year depreciation allowance. But if you go to a $100,000 property, even if the $10,000 property was fully depreciated, you would get $9,000 a year annual depreciation allowable out of the new property. That means you're exchanging a zero or $1,000 a year depreciation allowance for a $9,000 depreciation allowance. So obviously one advantage of trading up is that you can, without laying out any cash, increase your depreciation deductions drastically. If you own a $10,000 building that had a ten-year life and you were in your ninth year, one of the classic reasons for looking for a trade is to generate new depreciation when your old depreciation schedule is about to run out. You can shelter all your outside salary or professional income with depreciation as more fully explained in the chapter "Pay No Taxes Ever Again—Legally!"

Another reason for trading up is to take your profits out of old deals, tax free, acquire new, larger properties and then raise more cash by refinancing the new property after the close of escrow. You don't pay ordinary income tax or capital gains taxes when you exchange, and of course *borrowed money is never taxable.*

You can also use a trade to get out of three or four small slummy properties into one bigger property. You can consolidate small holdings by trading up into one big project. Just arrange for our Mr. Classy to take title, only for a second, to your three, four, six, or ten dumps. You can get out of slumlording; sell the whole mess at a stroke and move into "Pride of Ownership" deals. Of course you have to prearrange for the sale of your dumps to Mr. Cash buyers. In this way you can exchange a lot of little scattered junk properties into one first-class apartment complex or shopping center.

Another reason you might want to do a trade is to generate a larger scale of operations. In other words, on day 1 you had half-a-dozen single-family homes you were renting out. Because the rental income was marginal you had to do everything yourself: maintenance, repairs, and collecting rent. That took up a lot of your time. But if you could trade those small homes up into a hundred-unit office building, then the cash flow and the rents from that hundred offices will support a full-time manager and a handyman who could run the place without you. You would then become more of an executive and less of a janitor. No more stopped up toilets or unpleasant details.

When you trade up into bigger properties you generate a larger amount of cash flow. There is money for staff, and, of course, larger amounts of borrowing power. In a few years you become a much more important individual to bankers, suppliers, and everybody else when the rents you have coming in are $900,000 a year rather than $9,000.

Some people exchange because they want to change location. For instance, you may think that the property you own in Philadelphia or San Diego is over-valued. Property in Palm Springs, San Antonio, or Costa Rica is, you feel, going to increase in price at a much more rapid rate. Hopefully you will be getting much more appreciation by reinvesting in another location. You can trade out of property in one city and go to another city. Not only that, you can trade US property for non-US property *or* you can trade your foreign property for US property. There are no geographic requirements under section 1031! You can trade into or out of any type of investment property in the world. And, of course, if you trade up at regular intervals you will go from being a small property owner to Tycoon status.

Now that you know the basics of exchanging let me pass on just a couple of warnings so you don't screw up. First of all, there is a good form some folks use called an "exchange agreement." The IRS, when they are giving somebody a real thorough audit, like to review all the papers. If they find a "buy and sell" agreement (an agreement that shows you are buying Mr. Classy's place and you are selling your place to Mr. Cash) they may try to disallow the exchange because they say you didn't do the paperwork properly. But you are home free if Mr. Classy actually took title to El Dumpo. You should have some sort of agreement covering the mechanics. One suggestion follows:

Addendum to Deposit Receipt
Offer to Purchase the Classy Apartments,
Dated June 1, 1981

The Undersigned Mr. Classy does hereby agree to take in trade for the Classy Apartments title to El Dumpo for the sole purpose of effecting a section 1031 tax-deferred exchange for Mr. Dumpy. Mr. Classy agrees to immediately convey title to El Dumpo to Mr. Cash, or such other buyer out-of-trade as may be found. It is understood that this exchange is being made as an accommodation to Mr. Dumpy and shall not result in any additional costs, risks, or liabilities to Mr. Classy. All such costs or risks shall be borne by Mr. Dumpy. In the event Mr. Cash is unable to complete the purchase of El Dumpo by September 1st, 1981, it is agreed that on that date Mr. Dumpy will purchase the Classy Apartments at the price and terms agreed upon in the attached Deposit Receipt.

_____   _____
David Dumpy   **Calvin Classy**

_____   _____
Mrs. Humpty Dumpy   **Mrs. Corrinne Classy**

(All contracts should be adapted to your own deals with the help of a competent attorney.)

The crucial thing in a tax-free exchange is the taking of title to the smaller property by Mr. Classy before it is deeded to the cash buyer. To do it exactly right you should create some sort of exchange agreement, making it obvious to an IRS agent what was done. You need only have a letter that you and Mr. Classy sign showing your intention to do a proper 1031 exchange. You both understand that you are really just selling El Dumpo to a third party and buying the Classy place. Mr. Classy understands that he is just taking title to the dump as a convenience to you, but the IRS (if they want to give you a hard time) will insist upon seeing an exchange agreement. Our sample "Addendum" should do the trick.

Let's assume another problem: For some reason Mr. Classy at the closing doesn't want or isn't able to sign a proper deed to El Dumpo. The most common reason—he is not getting along with his wife. A divorce may be pending. As a result Mrs. Classy won't sign papers for him. Under the law of most states a wife has an automatic interest in any real estate that her husband owns. But if the wife will not sign, or Mr. Classy cannot sign the deed, there's a solution. It is possible for the owners involved to deed all the properties in the trade to a title company as nominee or straw man. The title company then completes the trade and deeds out El Dumpo to Mr. Cash and the Classy apartments to you. This is an alternative way of doing a legal tax-free exchange.

Once again: Both properties in the trade are deeded to a title company. The title company, acting as an agent for Mr. Classy, conveys to

Mr. Cash. Remember, in real estate (or in any other business), wherever there is a problem, there is always a way around it. I certainly hope that my Tycoons never assume that all is lost. If Mrs. Classy refused to sign the trade papers for El Dumpo, you would simply have asked the title company if they know any other way of doing it. They probably would have told you they could take the title as just explained. If they didn't make any useful suggestions, it would be up to you to go to another source for ideas. Never give up until you have exhausted every title company, every lawyer, every accountant, and every trade broker in your city. Get the deal to close—one way or another. It's easy to give up! But Tycoons are a different breed. They always close their deals. When the going gets tough, the tough get going. A cliché, but apt!

Another problem that often comes up is that the chap taking the role of Mr. Classy in our agreement says, "Look, I'll cooperate with you in doing a tax-free exchange. I'll do whatever you want. I also want a real firm deal on my sale so if you're not able to make an exchange I want you to personally guarantee that you will take the property anyway." If that happens, you have a decision to make. Are you willing to take the property even if you do not sell your old place? Can you raise the money to close the deal? I would generally prefer to put into my exchange agreement that if I do not sell El Dumpo to a third party I would deed it to Mr. Classy and buy it back myself within a year at the exchange price. Or as an alternative I might try to get a concession from the seller; he would take back a big enough second mortgage to cover the smaller amount of cash I would have had to make up for if El Dumpo could not be sold. I would also see how much cash I could get out of a refinance of El Dumpo and try to renegotiate either price or terms to fit the realities of my pocketbook.

The best possibility is that you might be able to talk Mr. Classy into really taking title and possession of El Dumpo, especially if you guarantee rents at a certain level satisfactory to Mr. Classy. You can, if you have to, guarantee to manage El Dumpo. You can further guarantee to sell it for him within a year, or whatever time period you both can agree upon. If it can't be sold, you can buy it back yourself.

In case you are ever audited by the IRS and they find out you've used our sample contract, to the effect that if an exchange could not be arranged, you, as buyer, would pay cash and take over the property anyway—the IRS agent may not know his law very well. **The agent might try to disallow the trade** saying there really was not an exchange. "You just wanted to buy his place and sell your place," says the IRS. "All your agreements were buy/sell agreements, not exchange agreements." The

IRS agent may wrongly try to disallow the tax-free exchange. If that happens, you just tell the IRS agent that there was a case in 1935 called the *Mercantile Trust* case. It was a very famous case for exchangers. In that case there was an agreement to exchange with a "sale in lieu" provision just like in our sample form. The deal was approved by the courts as a tax-free exchange! In other words, there was contractual language between the parties in that particular case that if the property was not in fact exchanged the deal would go through anyway and the property would be bought for cash. The IRS tried to say that even though there was an exchange later, the Mr. Dumpy of Mercantile Trust did not really have any intention to do a 1031 exchange. The good old IRS was trying back in 1935 to say that a secret intention to buy rather than trade resulted in a "non–tax-free exchange." But the court said as long as the parties go through the motions required by section 1031 it doesn't really matter what was in their heart of hearts.

There was another interesting twist in 1962 in the *Baird Publishing Co.* case. It involved a delayed exchange. A religious organization wanted to acquire a building that was owned by Baird Publishing Co. A church seems to have owned all the property on the block except Baird's factory and wanted it all for their new church. Baird didn't particularly want to sell his little printing plant until the church agreed to build Baird a brand new building nearby. But they wanted to buy the Baird building immediately. Since Baird didn't want to pay taxes a trade was written up on paper. The deal was to give Baird a new building built to his specifications a little distance from the old one. The exchange contract provided that Baird could stay in the old building rent free until the new one was finished. Only when the new building was finished would Baird move all his publishing equipment over to the new place. So what essentially happened in the Baird case was: The church bought Baird's property on day 1. Considerably later, the new building was completed. Baird moved, and title was then conveyed to Baird. He got his new publishing company building, worth considerably more than the old one. The IRS, as you might imagine, said this was not a simultaneous exchange and disallowed it as a tax-free exchange. When it got to court, the judge decided that even though legal title to the trade-in property passed long before title to the new place passed to Baird, Baird still had the use of the old place rent free and the "equitable" title remained with Baird. In other words, the court felt "real ownership" passed to the church only when Baird finally moved out of El Dumpo and moved into the new building. So they let Baird have a delayed tax-free exchange.

Now, let me tell you how you could possibly use that case to your advantage. You've got a red hot buyer for some property that you own and they want to tie up your property. They want it badly and are willing to pay you a very good price. You think your building is worth only $70,000, but the buyer is willing to give you $100,000. The only problem is that you haven't found a suitable property you want to trade up into. You could, of course, have the buyer build for you. But here is my suggestion how you could structure a variation on the Baird delayed trade to still come within the rule of the *Baird Publishing Co.* case. You sell your property to the new buyer. We will call them the "Church," just to make the example tie in with Baird. You sell your property to Church, but do it on a contract of sale. That is, you give possession, but keep title. Church "agrees to buy" but does not close the deal by taking title. Your keeping title and giving up possession would probably be construed as your keeping a substantial interest in the property just like Baird, who, in his case, gave up title while he kept possession.

I think if you, as seller, kept title to your property and delivered physical possession to the buyer and then had Church put $100,000 cash or an IOU for $100,000 into a title company escrow to be held until you found a suitable trade property, you would have the makings of a good deferred tax-free exchange. You would go out and find the trade property. When you do, whether it is six months later or five years later, it shouldn't matter to the IRS. Once you have found the trade-up property, have the title company use the $100,000 on deposit as the down payment on the place you are buying. Now, very important: *Church should take title to the new property* and a second later convey to you. Simultaneously, you convey a deed to El Dumpo to Church. Both titles change hands at the time instant. It would seem to me that the Baird Rule provides a way for you to take advantage of a situation where you find somebody who really wants your property and will pay a premium price at a time you haven't found "trade-up" property.

Another famous case for traders was the *Starker* case. Up until 1977, every "trader" was going crazy using the so-called Starker Rule. Everybody in the business thought it stood for the proposition that if you found a buyer for your property all you did was sell your property to him, transfer title, and tell that buyer to put the money into an escrow company (not to give it to you). Then you both gave the escrow company instructions that that money could be taken out only to buy suitable exchange property. The new trade-up property would be purchased years later in the name of your buyer who would simultaneously deed it to you, thereby accomplishing a tax-free exchange. That was a pretty good rule while it lasted. But, in the state of Oregon, Judge Solomon, who decided the original *Starker* case, in a different case I call

Starker II came to the conclusion that he had made a mistake. The net result is that many knowledgeable people in real estate felt that the Starker Rule was dead, and title to all properties in a trade should pass simultaneously. But then, a federal appeals court held that Judge Solomon was right the first time, in *Starker I*. The latest case, known as *Starker III*, virtually eliminated capital gains taxes for Tycoons.

The Latest Case on Exchanges

All good real estate Tycoons who attended my lectures know that the single most important real estate/tax case ever decided was the famous *Starker* case, known in the trade as *Starker I*. *Starker I* held that as long as a seller of investment real estate carefully avoided getting cash in hand, the proceeds from a sale of investment property could be held by a third party, and be invested in another investment property at a later date, without any capital gain (or ordinary income) taxes on the deal.

The events giving rise to *Starker I* took place in the mid-1960s. *Starker I* was decided a number of years later. The IRS did not appeal the case, and it was thought to be a final judgment. Later it turned into a long-running soap opera with the IRS bringing a similar action against another member of the Starker family involving the same transaction, and strangely enough the case was heard by the same judge. Even stranger, the same judge (Solomon by name) changed his mind and said his earlier decision would give rise to too much tax avoidance. In a cryptic decision, Solomon seemed to say that a valid, tax-free 1031 exchange required a simultaneous transfer of title.

Almost fifteen years after the facts, a three-judge federal appeals court heard the appeal of *Starker II*, and *reversed* the decision (the second decision, that is) of Judge Solomon.

Thus, now we have as the undisputed law of the land a relatively clear decision I will call *Starker III*. This one gives tax-avoidance enthusiasts an even greater victory than *Starker I*. *Starker III* is nothing short of an amazing triumph against the IRS. Here is what you need to know to have your lawyer or accountant structure a trade. *Starker III* is officially known as *Starker v United States*, 602 F 2d 1341 (1979). The full opinion may be read in any law library. Incidentally, while a victory for all of us, poor Starker had to pay the tax up-front and sue for a refund. After waiting for fifteen years for a decision, he'll get back inflation eroded dollars worth (in real estate values) about 12¢ on the 1966 dollar. With the court costs and lawyers fees, it was hardly a victory for Starker. Of course he will get interest from the IRS—but they'll just be a few more 12¢ dollars.

Here is what the decision said, in my view:

1. You can't sell investment property and reinvest in a residence for yourself. If you do, you must pay the capital gain tax on the sale of the business property. Nothing new there—we all know that a 1031 exchange must involve "like kind" properties.

2. After the smoke clears in a complex 1031 transaction, you must end up with *ownership* of property. If you never get title *or* possession of the new trade-up property, but if you direct title to be transferred to a friend or relative, that will be treated as the equivalent of taking cash and making a gift.

3. The "ownership" you end up with does not necessarily have to be *title*. A *lease* of thirty years or more, a life estate, or a contract of sale will be considered the equivalent of title. The court in *Starker III* was not concerned with who held "bare legal title" to the trade-up property. They looked for who was the "real" owner. It is very nice to have this formerly unclear point straightened out.

4. It is not necessary that the property one sells and the property one ends up with transfer at the same time. In the *Starker* facts, the time between the sale and the purchase of the trade-up property was several *years* . . . The key to keeping the deal *tax free* was *not taking any cash in hand*. In *Starker,* the cash was held in a special trust-type account by the seller—but if the cash had been held by a broker, title company, or any "independent" person with the *intention* of all parties that the funds be used only for purchasing trade-up property, you'd be home free—tax free, that is.

5. The possibility that (if no suitable trade property is located) you can demand and get your cash is not enough to destroy the tax-free nature of the deal. The key is your *intention* that you *prefer* to end up with another investment property and *not* cash. If you do eventually end up with property, the IRS may not challenge the 1031 Exchange on the grounds that you had the right to take out your cash without a trade. Naturally, if you received cash, profits would be taxable in the year received. The trade would be aborted. But no tax would be due until *either* the funds were invested in like-kind property (at which point only the accrued interest would be taxed) *or* until the year that the funds were withdrawn for personal use.

6. If you sell a property for say $100,000 profit and have the proceeds held by a title company or other independent trustee in say a "money market fund" at 12% per annum interest, and three years later you buy a property for $136,000 using all the money in your account, the court says that the interest earned *is not taxable* to you

until it is taken out and/or spent. It *is taxable* as *ordinary income* in the year received or spent, but not before.

7. This *Starker III* decision applies not only to real estate, but to the sale of almost any investment or property used in a trade or business. Trucks are specifically mentioned in the opinion, but there is no reason to suppose that a sale of coins, diamonds, gold bullion, antiques, art works, or *any* investment medium would not be covered. Securities are specifically *excluded*.

What this important decision means is that if you want to get out of a bad real estate deal, any declining investment—or just take advantage of a good offer, you can do so—tax free—by leaving the cash in some sort of trust. You can arrange for the acquisition of trade property at a later date. The mechanics of handling the paperwork probably should be handled by a good lawyer or the legal department of a title company familiar with the *Starker III* case. It also means that unless you have dire need for the cash, you'd be an utter idiot not to arrange for the funds from any sale of assets to go into a special "1031 exchange account" to be drawn out only when you need the money. Creating such an account will defer indefinitely the tax on *any* sale until you pull out the money (under the reasoning of the *Starker III* decision).

Delayed Real Estate Exchange Agreement

Re: *Moonglow Lane*
Exchanger: *Bob Buyer*
Owner: *Sam Seller*
Escrow Agent: *Efficient Title Co.*

I. The undersigned owner is disposing of his interest in the above property in exchange for the above exchanger depositing cash proceeds which represent the exchange value of the property and agreeing to purchase for him with said funds like-kind property that would qualify as a tax-free exchange under section 1031 of the Internal Revenue Code. The said escrow agent will hold the funds in a savings account as trustee, and funds will not be available to owner except as provided herein.

II. It is understood that owner would not make a sale nor close this transaction unless it was a tax-free exchange under section 1031, Internal Revenue Code.

A. The property being disposed of is one which was purchased for investment and is currently being held for the production of income, and not for resale.

B. The exchanger does not now own property which the owner wants to acquire, but the exchanger and owner will agree upon suitable property within 36 months at which time the cash balance in escrow will be used by the exchanger to purchase said property for owner.

C. The cash balance in escrow and the interest thereon shall not be available to owner, until exchanger purchases trade-up property for owner.

D. Title to the property and cash representing exchange value shall be held by the escrow agent as trustee. If no trade property is located within 36 months, then the owner shall have the right to withdraw and the exchanger shall have the right to close out its books by paying all funds in this trustee savings account to owner and conveying it to the order of the exchanger. But until that time, owner shall have no right to the deposit which remains the property of exchanger subject to this agreement. If no trade property is located and exchanger refuses to approve delivery of cash proceeds, owner can recover possession and title to above property. Until such time, owner shall retain equitable title to the property.

E. Owner would not sell the property to exchanger without an exchange agreement valid under 26 U.S.C. Section 1031 of the Internal Revenue Code, and all parties understand that this transaction is an exchange under section 1031. However, exchanger assumes no responsibility whatsoever for any rulings on the taxability or nontaxability of the exchange value herein.

F. Exchanger will take title to the new property that is selected if this is deemed necessary under IRS rules, before the (new) exchange property is transferred to owner, and will fully cooperate in effectuating a tax-exempt exchange for owner.

G. This document shall serve as instructions to the title company to hold all exchange proceeds due owner until suitable trade property is located and proceeds are used to acquire trade property, or until property is reconveyed by buyer to seller.

Date: _____   _____
                                  OWNER

                                  _____
                                  EXCHANGER

As a conclusion, I would have to join in the view that the Starker Rule is not engraved in granite and the IRS wants to see the case law reversed. But the law is a very funny thing and since every case is a little bit different, and the intention of the parties is always a little bit different, who knows? You might fight it out with the IRS and get your transaction ruled to be a valid tax-free exchange. Disputed real estate trades seem to be one of the few areas of the tax law where the taxpayer often prevails against the IRS.

In summary, it is best to follow long-established 1031 exchange procedures and do a *simultaneous exchange* where possible. But if you create something that looks vaguely like a trade, you might as well risk treating it tax-wise as a tax-free exchange. The worst that can happen is that the IRS will disallow it. If your tax-free exchange is disallowed, you may be able to settle the tax they claimed is due for a small percentage on the dollar. If the IRS will not be reasonable, you can fight it out in court where the odds are the court will side with you. In any event, you have the use of the money for half a dozen years until your case is decided.

CHAPTER 19

The Tax Code
Can Make You Rich

This chapter is concerned with avoiding taxes. But for some of us, the immediate problem is *making* enough money so that we can someday be in the enviable position of using all these neat little tricks to keep it from the tax man. In earlier chapters, all I did was talk about ways to make your fortune. You remember that the best way to get rich was to identify a common need or problem. Then, you, as an opportunist, can create an appropriate product or service. All the great fortunes made in the past 10,000 years were amassed by people who could **find a need and fill it.**

As a reader of this book, you must be painfully aware of the great need felt by millions of Americans and citizens of other countries having high tax rates. They want to avoid taxes. Information on how to avoid taxes is a multimillion-dollar business for many companies and individuals. But you don't have to write a book like this or become a certified public accountant to cash in. There is a far better way, and the people who go into that end of the business make far more money than you have ever dreamed of. By the time you finish this book, you will know more about tax avoidance than 99% of the population. That puts you in the unique position of being able to help other people invest their "funny money" or pretax dollars in *tax shelters*.

Have you ever seen an article like the one on the next page? Is there any reason you couldn't be like Klaus Hebben? In this chapter I will show you how to start out with virtually no money—in your own home town! By next December you could be in control of millions of dollars worth of property. **More money will be made in the last quarter of the 20th cen-**

tury by people who set up what I call "super-terranean" investments than in any other form of enterprise!

This is the age of the rapacious thieving government and the only people on the other side may be *you* and me.

Here is the way to not only join, but to *lead* a legal tax revolt in a way that will make you filthy rich.

The Vancouver Sun, Monday, November 5, 1979

Resources attracting German money

CALGARY (CP)—A cosmopolitan crowd of investors has been pouring money into Alberta, lured by its resource industries.

Challenging the U.S dominance as the primary non-Canadian source of venture capital is West Germany, which has a highly attractive tax write-off legislation for investing abroad.

Klaus Hebben, a youthful, self-effacing entrepreneur, is one of the new breed of West German investors.

In the last six years, Hebben has put more than $500 million of German venture capital to work in North America, mostly in junior oil companies in Alberta.

German seed money helped launch, among others, Czar Resources, Ltd., Peyto Oils Ltd., Bonanza Resources Inc., Coseka Resources Ltd., Petromark Minerals Ltd. and Canadian Hunter Exploration Ltd.

Canadian Hunter, which found gas in the Deep Basin of western Alberta in 1977, has been an outstanding success story. Hebben liked the unconventional theories of gas occurrence advanced by Canadian Hunter, so much so that he concluded a string of joint venture deals worth more than $40 million.

Hebben said in an interview that the key to the continued flow of German risk capital is appropriate tax legislation at home, which permits 100% write-off of all exploratory expenses undertaken abroad by investors, who also get tax deferment on their foreign earnings.

The Munich Group, as the chain of corporate entities stretched between the Bavarian capital and North America is known, will be delivering some $100 million of new financing to North America annually, mostly to Western Canadian resource companies.

"There is still some romance to Western Canada as far as the German investor is concerned," Hebben said. Petroleum prospects provide the best bets for a fivefold return German investors are promised over twenty-five years.

Hebben said about 80% of the money will be invested in Canada and the rest in the United States.

In West Germany, the Gesellschaft Zür Exploration Von Erdöl Und Erdgas, commonly known as the Triple E organization, is the vehicle used by Hebben to solicit private capital in search of a tax shelter.

The money of German investors in due course reaches Bluesky Oil and Gas Ltd., main operating company in Canada.

Bluesky in turn concludes joint venture arrangements with Canadian companies in need of outside financing and willing to give up some of the working interest in a project.

Hebben's companies so far have entered into about 200 joint venture deals with Canadian and US partners. German investors in general are "cautious but ready to take reasonable chances," Hebben said.

He said barring negative Canadian legislation and a massive economic upheaval back home, West German investors will continue to enlarge their presence in Canada.

Obviously there is a tremendous need for good tax shelters—investments that make economic sense, and can at the same time take the pretax dollars of people in the higher tax brackets and put them to work generating tax deductions, investment tax credits, and other "paper losses" to help the overburdened productive classes keep a little more of their hard-earned money. At my front-lawn classes in Mill Valley, I noticed that there were always two types of individuals in attendance: the doctors, lawyers, accountants, plumbers, and others who were sick and tired of paying up to 85% of their earnings in taxes, but who simply had no time to spend looking for suitable real estate investments, and the "Young Hungry Hustlers." The people in the first group would have been tickled pink for someone else to do all the work in return for up to half of the profits. They all had had experience with investment groups and tax-shelter syndicates. That experience was almost always abysmal. Over a four-year period, my own surveys (of approximately 3,000 investors) indicated that more than 97% of all "tax-shelter" investments were pure garbage. They never returned the original investment (much less any profit) to the guy who put in the money. That was because most of the people in the tax-shelter business are flakes, phonies, and promoters who know little about investments and even less about the tax code. The world *needs* honest, knowledgeable originators of tax-shelter investments.

The second group at my lectures, the "Young Hungry Hustlers," were usually recent college graduates who were not yet earning enough to worry about their taxes. They had motivation, time, intelligence—but little or no money. It was possible for the Hustlers to make no-money-down deals and many of them owned five or six buildings within a few months after taking my classes. But no-money-down deals were available only on relatively small problematic properties. The Hustlers had to pass up the multimillion-dollar deals even if a small amount of cash was required.

Then the inevitable happened. One of the more creative Hustlers announced that he would like to take investor partners in on deals on this basis: Hustler would find the deal, do all the negotiations, manage the property, and eventually refinance or resell it. The investor would do nothing but look over the deal and the paperwork at the beginning, put up *all* the money, hold title to the property (if desired), and take *all* the tax benefits. When it came time to sell or trade up, profits would be split 50/50 with the investor getting a minimum of 10% annual return on his money before Hustler got anything.

As it turned out, this arrangement turned out to be wonderful for both parties. The Hustler didn't get paid unless he produced, and the investor got a minimum return even if the deal didn't work out too well. In the crazy California market, the investors averaged about 50% per annum returns on their money—and the Hustlers, well, they got an infinite return on no investment at all. Of course, they earned it—they found a good investment and made it work out.

The difference between these deals and the standard real estate syndication was immense. The investment that is packaged by a major investment house is normally the garbage of the real estate market. It may be a good property—but the price is double or triple what experienced real estate people would pay. Further, most real estate syndicators are not compensated "on the come"—or on the contingent fee principle. Typically, little or none of the investor's money finds its way into a syndicated deal. Most of it goes for commissions and advertising. The syndicator is paid "up front," and his profit is already made once the investors are found and the deal is closed. Obviously, there is no incentive to give the investors a good deal. Thus, they get garbage!

In what I am going to call the "mini-partnership" there is a close relationship between the investor and the active partner. Usually there are just the two of them in the deal. With proper buy-out agreements if the active partner does not perform, the investor can kick him out of the deal and owe him little or nothing.

To accomplish their objectives, many of my *Tycoon Class* graduates came to me to draw up a partnership agreement that was fair to both parties. Several partnerships were created. Let me emphasize that my form is for use by beginners on small deals.

Now you may be a plumber making $175,000 per year—in which case you can use this agreement as a model form for a deal with your son-in-law. Or, if you are not wealthy but think you can put deals together, here is a form you can use to give your investor a fair shake. This partnership agreement, with minor variations, can be used for almost all real estate deals, mineral exploration, leasing. It is exempt from state and federal regulation, and the agreement is strictly between the partners. Unless you have a disagreement that can't be resolved and the partnership agreement is shown to an arbitrator or a judge, you and your partner are the only people who ever have to see it.

My suggested form is only a guide, and should be modified to suit the needs and desires of you and your partner.

Most people of substantial wealth have this choice: 1) Pay taxes to a thieving, rapacious government, or 2) Give pretax "soft dollars" to thieving, rapacious promoters of garbage tax shelters.

This agreement may give you a third alternative.

Partnership Agreement

Date: *January 1, 1981*

This agreement is between Irving Investor and Tom Tycoon, hereafter known as "I" and "T." *[Note: Under the laws of most states and the federal government, up to ten investors may be involved with a deal before it is considered a "public offering." Also it may not be shown to over 25 potential investors. This form is intended for use by no more than a pair of Active Investors and a pair of Passive Investors.]*

The above named partners have agreed to acquire a twenty unit apartment building to be owned and operated by them as the T & I Partnership The business address of the partnership shall be Apartment #1, 123 Amen Drive, Salt Lake City, the residence of Tom Tycoon, who as part of this agreement shall receive said apartment rent-free and shall manage said apartment building without further compensation from the partnership, except as here provided.

This agreement shall be effective as of this date which is the date title and possession of the said apartment building passes to the T & I partnership. *[Note: If Tom Tycoon is not a "proven quantity" it is suggested that title to any property acquired be kept in the name of the investor(s) who put up the money.]*

This partnership shall continue for a period of three years unless dissolved by mutual agreement or as otherwise provided herein. Thirty-two months from this date the property will be put up for sale by listing it with *Robert Real Estate Broker* at a price to be set by him.

The parties to this agreement agree to contribute to the business as follows: I will contribute all cash needed to acquire the property. Thereafter, in the event of any negative cash flow, repairs or other contingencies requiring funds, both partners agree to contribute equally; T will contribute *no* initial cash, but as his contribution has located the investment property, negotiated for its acquisition and financing; and by this agreement undertakes to supervise all physical repair work needed to improve the property; to manage and collect rents; and to the best of his ability take over all problems of running this partnership on a day-to-day basis, including the obtaining of suitable 1031 exchange property within the next three years.

For their respective contributions, any cash flow including refinancing proceeds is to be used to first

a. Return in full the original contribution of $25,000 made by I, then

b. Return to I any additional contributions plus a minimum annual return of 10% per annum on any cash invested, then

c. Return to T any cash invested in the deal plus a return of 10% per annum on any outstanding investment, then

d. Any balance to be shared between the parties on an equal basis

e. In the event of losses from any cause, they shall be shared equally.

Books and records of all expenses and receipts shall be kept by T on the Safeguard Account System for Real Estate, by T and shall be available for inspection by I or his designated agent during all business hours.

All funds of the partnership shall be deposited daily at the Desert National Bank of Salt Lake City in a joint account. Withdrawals of over $200 shall require the signatures of both parties.

DISSENTING REMEDY

In the event that either party wishes to dissolve the relationship he may offer to buy out the other at a certain price set by him. Thereafter, the other partner shall have ten days to either accept the offer or pay the other partner the price previously offered to him. Provided however, that if T is making the buy out offer, it must be for at least the amount of I's investment plus 10% per annum. In the event a third-party buyer has materialized and either party does not wish to sell, the partner who wishes to hold agrees to buy out the other party for whatever his share of the resulting profit would have been. The partner selling agrees to convey his interest immediately to the holding partner.

DEATH OR ABANDONMENT

In the event T dies or is absent from the project for more than five continuous days, I shall automatically acquire a 100% interest in said project with no further obligation or debt to T or his estate.

In the event I dies, T may a) complete the project as planned and pay I's share to I's heirs, or, at T's sole option, b) T may buy out the interest of I's estate for the amount invested by I plus 12% per annum return.

COVENANT NOT TO SUE

T covenants not to sue I at any time during the life of this agreement, and T expressly agrees that his maximum damages shall be the amount of his actual investment returned to him.

OTHER ACTIVITIES OF PARTNERS

It is agreed that I is not expected to put in any time or effort running the partnership property, and he is not restricted in any way by this agreement from making othe investments.

T agrees to devote all his spare time to this project and not to undertake the management of any other businesses or real estate ventures without the express written permission of I. In the event I gives such permission for T to engage in other spare-time entrepreneurial activities, it is agreed that I shall have no interest in profits from other ventures. In the event that 123 Amen Drive is fully occupied and is being properly managed, I agrees to give his permission for T to work on other projects.

DEPRECIATION AND TAX BENEFITS

Since I is putting up all the cash, it is agreed that for state and federal income-tax purposes he shall get 100% of the write-offs and tax benefits including any tax credits or depreciation allowances generated by this property.

INSURANCE

It is agreed that T will, prior to the closing hereof, insure the property with a comprehensive fire policy in the face amount of $500,000; procure liability insurance in the amount of $1,000,000 with a waiver of the business risk exclusion, and that title to the property shall not be acquired until such coverage is obtained, in writing.

ARBITRATION

In the event the partners cannot agree, both parties shall submit any dispute to *Albert Arbitrator* and agree that his decision shall bind them as a final judgment in a court of law.

MISCELLANEOUS

The parties agree not to endorse any note nor become surety for any person(s) without the written consent of the other. It is further agreed that any contracts or obligations undertaken by either partner in respect of business other than the 123 Amen Drive property shall in no way bind or obligate the other partner.

In the event that there are more than three vacancies in the property for more than three consecutive months and/or delinquent rents in three units or more during this time period, T agrees to either contribute to the partnership an amount equal to said rents, in cash, or to remove himself from the premises, quit claim the property to I, and renounce any further interest in it to I. *[Note: This paragraph was included to indicate a type of "minimum-performance standard" to be set by I for T to live up to. In the event T does not do his job, I will, for all practical purposes, be able to fire T and terminate T's interest in the property. A quit claim deed should be executed at the time of the agreement to implement this.]*

On Date: _1/1/81_   , the parties have signed this agreement.

Irving Investor   _Tom Tycoon_

[Note: Always use a notary public to acknowledge partnership agreements or any contracts involving real estate.]

Now that you have the agreement and an inkling of what I am talking about, you wonder, "What shall I do with it?"

This is my suggestion: Particularly around year's end, get the *Wall Street Journal, Barron's,* and your local newspapers. You might also want to splurge on a Sunday *New York* and *Los Angeles Times.* You will see dozens of ads for "year-end tax shelters." Respond to all of them. See what they are offering. Let the salesman come out and call on you. Observe his technique, note what is convincing and where he leaves you cold.

A lot of wealthy people go absolutely bananas at year's end and they will "invest" in any garbage that gives them a substantial tax deduction and even a glimmer of hope for an eventual profit.

Your fortune can be made by giving these people a *decent* investment and tax shelter. How do you find the deals? Simply act on what you've learned in this book and read some of the other books listed on the order form in the back of this book, and look at everything that is on the market. There are plenty of deals—far more than you can handle. But the best ones require work and creativity. Money is *easy* to get. There are thousands of investors with money burning a hole in their pockets.

How do you meet the investors?

One way might be to put an ad like this in your local paper:

> **Armchair Investors Wanted!** You are too busy to look for deals. I've got the deals and the expertise to make them earn 50% per year for you. $20,000 minimum investment should give you huge tax loss this year, and substantial cash profit. Call Monteverdi Properties Corp. for full details. No charge or obligation. Phone: 333-444-5555

You could give a free or nominal charge seminar for tax shelter investors at your home or at a local hotel meeting room. You could write all the local certified public accountants about your deals. Believe me when I say that if you have a deal "with a good story," it is as easy as pie to market it. Once you have closed a few deals and made your investors some money, you will have to employ beaters to keep new investors away from you.

In my own case, I seldom took in partners because I just didn't want to be bothered by a bunch of idiots who would always be telling me how to run a business I knew far better than they did. But to my surprise, when I laid the law down to a few investors and said, "If you want in on my deals, you read your semiannual statements and *keep out of my hair*," I was left alone. My agreement (in contrast to the sample provided) was a lot tougher to the investor simply because I knew I could and would average about 100% return per year for the investor—but only if I made the decisions and wasn't bothered by them. Today I still do a few syndications from time to time with minimum investments of $50,000. If you want to be on my list, that's fine. My investors get full disclosure at the beginning, regular reports in between, and a full statement when the deal is sold off or (more often) refinanced and traded up. But I don't want any weak sisters or Willy Worrywarts in deals with me. Those types can be as annoying as fuzzy-thinking-deadbeat-leftist tenants. *You* may have to put up with them at first as a "Hungry Hustler." After you make your investors a good return, you'll be able to pick and choose new investors from a long waiting list. Word will get around that you are "some kind of financial genius."

You personally can make pots and pots of money as a syndicator. The reason is simple. Suppose you find a million-dollar property that you hope to upgrade and sell in a year for $1.3 million. If it takes $100,000 down to make the deal, you get an outside investor to put up the whole $100,000. A year later you sell. The investor gets a 100% return, and you have $100,000 to trade up into another profitable building. Putting together only one big deal a year can make you a multimillionaire without a dime of your own money at risk. The investor loves you because you do all the work and produce better profits than he can on his own. You can soon take all the deals that come along because you have a following of eager moneyed investors. Soon you'll have groups of investors. If you don't take your money out in cash—but trade up to bigger and better deals—your own wealth builds up tax free. You live on tax-free refinancing proceeds like I do. *And that's how you can make millions! Now go out and do it!*

CHAPTER 20

Hints for '82 and Beyond

People not already in the real estate game don't realize the magnitude of the gifts bestowed by dear old Uncle Sam on real estate by Ronald Reagan's Economic Recovery Tax Act. This law takes effect in stages between 1981 and 1985. For real estate investors it provides more than an offset for some of the negative things that have been happening in the industry. Let's look at the bad news first:

More and more states or local municipalities have decided to follow the disastrous example of New York City. Rent control ordinances are springing up nationwide, like mushrooms. The message to you should be very loud, and clear: WATCH OUT! Anyone who would invest in *apartments* had better plan on being hog-tied into a bad scene. Costs and interest will rise with inflation, but rents may be held back to some arbitrary level set by Fuzzy-Thinking Leftist Experts.

• Prices in the "Sunbelt" on all desirable rental properties have reached levels at which the cash-on-cash returns available (in general) are about half of the prime rate. This means that most wealthy investors are buying up the existing income property supply in expectation of higher rents that may not materialize and of course for tax benefits. For the "Tycoon" this means more than ever the bargains take more work to find. You must seek out the "Yuck" property and often fix it up or solve the management problems. If your state allows you to buy property "subject to" existing loans, you should look for assumable loans at old fixed rates of interest. Not only do you not have to qualify, but the lender will be stuck with you for the next twenty or twenty-five years at 9 to 11%. Properties with old fixed-rate loans are going to be off the market by 1984. They are the best deals for '82–'83.

• Direct Government Subsidy Programs to low income renters seem to be slowing down and during the next five years will probably be cut back substantially. If you have a long term lease with a Housing Authority, you are OK—but there will probably not be appropriations for expanded programs. An exception will be very special areas with political clout—near Washington, D.C., for instance.

That's the bad news, now for the goodies!

While the new tax law is not a true "reform," a change in rates allowed for depreciation significantly benefits anyone who goes into a real estate deal after January 1, 1981. The biggest news is that instead of arguing over "useful life" with the IRS you will be allowed to take a *15-year life* on ANY STRUCTURE for depreciation purposes. "Depreciation" is henceforward to be known as the Accelerated Cost Recovery System or ACRS. If you take a straight line 15-year life on real property, if it is sold at any time, the ACRS deduction taken in past years is recovered as a *capital gain*. If an investor wants even bigger deductions in the early years he can take 175% of the 15-year life on property (declining balance) which works out to 11.67% of the value of the structure as a first-year deduction. Obviously if you bought a $100,000 income property with 5% down or $5000, you would get an income tax deduction of $11,670. The IRS under the new rules couldn't give you any argument. Your deal could be made entirely with assumable loan— on which there was no personal liability—and the IRS would still have to give you the deduction because the "at risk" rules do not apply to real estate.

Equipment used in your real estate business, such as your pick-up truck, washers and dryers, snow-blowers can now be "expensed" or written off in the year of purchase up to $5000 per year in '82 and '83, $7500 per year in '84 and '85, and $10,000 per year annually thereafter. It doesn't matter whether you paid cash or "nothing down." For items purchased over the expensing limit, there is a very liberal 6% Investment Tax Credit, plus you can depreciate (Whoops) take "ACRS" over 3 years straight line or accelerated by 150%. If you *lease* equipment so long as the lessor agrees, *you* can take the tax credit and the fast depreciation.

To get maximum tax benefits in '82 and beyond, consider selling all your real property investments and old equipment, and buying different stuff. You get much better tax credits and depreciation on investments or equipment you acquire starting now. (Acquisitions made during 1981 may for the most part use the new ACRS on the 1981 income tax return.) The Congressional purpose of all these apparent giveaways, in case you haven't guessed it, is to get people to come out of hibernation and invest in new plant, equipment and real estate. If enough people respond, we should have an economic boom. My views on *where* to look for bargains in 1982–85 might start with the Deep South. Because of the general "flight to the Sunbelt" I believe that some Northern cities may be oversold. So I'd look for single family houses, condos and commercial properties in my favorite towns of the Frozen North, Baltimore, Philadelphia and Montreal. Stay away from apartment complexes unless the deals are structured so that you can't lose money even in the event of horrific rent controls rolling back rents to 1959 levels. Isolated single family houses or condos are OK because the authorities have a hard time keeping track of them. They can usually be sold (*due* to rent controls which always halt new developments, making old ones more valuable) at a terrific premium to an "owner-user."

For the decade of the 1980's I'd also suggest diversifying away from real estate into other areas. Everyone should have at least one side business to fall back on for cash flow and tax benefits. If you are interested in learning more about non-real estate opportunities I have discovered or am currently working on, send me a stamped, self-addressed envelope with $2 to cover costs and handling, and ask for our small very un-slick "Distributor's Handbook." You can use it to operate any at-home business, but I wrote it up for people interested in dealing in "Tycoon" products. Everyone should have a side business at home. Distributing for AMWAY is very good because you can get most of the consumer goods you need at wholesale prices. I have information on that, too—free.

The new tax laws are designed to get you off your fanny into some productive activity. That is also the purpose of this book. It's my mission in life. You can't get depreciation, tax credits, or any write-offs of your home, personal car or vacation trips as a mere wage-slave employee. But once you start actually investing or being in business for yourself (even if you keep the security blanket of the wage-slave job), you will not only make more money, you'll pay for less taxes. Your life will *work* better. Your wife (or husband) will love you more. You and your kids can travel and work together toward common goals. Take advantage of all the new loopholes (I'd prefer to call them tax incentives). You'll be helping yourself and your country. You'll keep the grabby hands of the IRS out of your pockets, and strike a blow for rugged individualism, Freedom, and Family Solidarity. Now, go out there and do it! Making more money is patriotic.

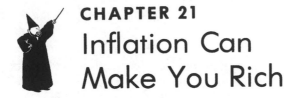

CHAPTER 21

Inflation Can Make You Rich

Everytime I read in the papers that the cost of living has increased again, I am delighted. It makes my day! I jump for joy! Inflation has already made me very rich. Every day inflation gets worse, I do better. You can do the same—if you will think like a Tycoon.

Remember how to make inflation work for you.

Pretend that it's Monday. Pretend that on Tuesday, all salaries, wages, and prices will double by government order. If MacDonald's hamburgers were $1 on Monday, they will be $2 on Tuesday. If houses were $75,000 today, they will be $150,000 tomorrow. And, of course, if your savings account was $10,000, it will still be $10,000 tomorrow—but money will buy only half as much in the way of goods and services. Mortgage payments on your home will still be just exactly what they were* in dollars, but those fixed payments will be only half as burdensome—because your income will double. The national debt will be the same in dollars, but it will have been effectively cut in half.

How about taxes? Income taxes, after a heavy dose of inflation, will take an increasing bite out of your earnings. Huge capital gains are artificially created so the government can take a big chunk of "profits" when you sell. If you are not already in the highest state and federal bracket (currently 50% federal tax, with 11% being a typical state income tax), inflation will put you there. Every wage earner will soon be in the same maximum tax bracket with the super-rich. The old "soak the rich" income tax has become "soak the middle class." Creating inflation is just one of several sneaky ways the government reneges on its debts and increases its tax revenues.

*Variable loans are changing this as of 1981–1983.

242

If you knew that inflation and taxes would devour your savings and 90% of your visible or unsheltered income in twenty-four hours, you'd do something! If you knew that the price of everything was going to double tomorrow, you'd do something about it! Then you'd be acting like a Tycoon.

Tomorrow will be here very soon! Tomorrow may take a few years to arrive, but till then, prices will continue to increase at an increasing rate. Higher percentages of your income *will* be taken by taxes and used to fund socialistic schemes of government. Irresponsible politicians will continue to discover that inflating the money supply by printing more and more money is the least politically objectionable way of raising taxes and government revenue. Thus credit will be expanded. Worthless paper money will continue to be printed. This is inflation. Before you can get rich you must take fairly obvious steps to protect yourself against worthless money and government schemes to tax you into oblivion.

And after you have protected yourself, you can take advantage of inflation and put it to work. Stop and think! Try to think like a Tycoon. What can you do to profit from a doubling of all prices in the next twenty-four hours? How can you profit from higher taxes? Do not read on until you have spent at least ten minutes writing. Make a list of what you can do to reduce government's ability to squeeze taxes out of you. Can you make money *selling* other people tax shelters you create? List at least five ways to increase your real wealth *if* you could be sure that inflation was going to make the price of all things double twenty-four hours from now.

You'd go into debt and buy things, wouldn't you? Be very specific in listing a number of businesses or investments that should do well under the pressures of increasing inflation.

If you know that your taxes will go up drastically, learning how to reduce your taxes should be your first line of defense against inflation.

Let's talk again about reducing taxes:

Who is always raped the worst by taxes?

1. The wage-slave can't afford lawyers and accountants. Unlike an executive or business owner, he has little opportunity to create imaginative deductions or arrange for tax-free distributions or expense-account money to himself.

2. Also squeezed by taxes are owners of savings accounts and receivers of interest who even today must pay up to 61% of "unearned" income to state and federal governments.

Remember who is hurt the worst by inflation. It's the same unlucky people!

1. The wage-slave, whose income usually rises less rapidly than inflation, pays a greater portion of his earnings in taxes each year even though his "real" spending power is dropping.
2. Even more damaged is the investor, who keeps his money in money—for instance, bonds or savings accounts. Investors lose earning power even faster than wage-slaves. Any owner of a bond, bank account, or any monetary instrument must earn over 40% per year to *break even* after inflation and taxes. And, of course no passive investment earns anywhere near that much.

The answer for you thus becomes as simple as pie:

• Don't be a wage-slave!

• Don't keep your money in a bank or its equivalent!

• Invest in income-producing real estate!

Given a time frame of two years instead of twenty-four hours, you should begin a program of acquiring things and/or saleable skills. What *should* you do with your time and money? You'd be a lot better off than a wage-slave if you could make your spending money from tax-sheltered real estate or small businesses that you personally own and operate. During times of inflation, service or cash businesses do very well. Night clubs, hotels, bars, restaurants, entertainment enterprises all do well. Also popular are sporting events, religion, gambling, escapist books, cosmetics, and other self-improvement products. And, of course, there are the professions. As taxes become more and more oppressive, lawyers and accountants become more of a survival necessity.

If your income comes from cash (dealings in stamps or coins, for instance), it becomes harder for IRS agents to nail you if some of that cash does not get properly reported. Of course I always advocate using *legal* tax shelters to *avoid* taxes. Tax *evasion* is illegal and unnecessary. But with taxes hitting 80% and more, survival may someday depend upon how much you can hide from the tax collector. If you can barter your services, you can get many of the things you need tax free.

If you are going to beat inflation and act like a Tycoon, the first step is to make yourself knowledgeable about taxes and thus less tax vulnerable. You must put yourself in a position to generate untaxed benefits or tax-sheltered cash. Virtually any small business or income property investment is a preferred way to beat the wage-slave high-tax trap.

For those who must remain at least part-time wage-slaves, only one major "loophole" exists: real estate. Owners of income property can do their accounting in such a way that taxable income from any outside job or investment can be sheltered or wiped out "on paper" so that no taxes are due. This book is mainly about using real estate to escape taxes and profit from inflation.

Obviously, in times of inflation and confiscatory taxes on *unearned income* those who lend money (owners of savings accounts, mortgages, bondholders, etc.) get a swift kick in the pants. *Borrowers* who have bought income-earning properties or businesses sit on top of the world! One can borrow (without any risk of loss) the entire cost of a building. After making a no-money-down deal, the Tycoon will make money two ways: The real estate will go up in dollar value—due to inflation. The borrowed mortgage money can be paid off with ever-increasing rents. When every other price doubles, rents (if not artificially regulated) will double too. Income increases each year. Tenants who pay $200 per month for a small office will be paying $400 in 3 years. But loan payments, properly negotiated, can remain relatively constant.

If this year you were to buy $1,000,000 worth of real estate with $1,000,000 in borrowed money, and if your income property were to break even during the year, in a year of 20% inflation, at the beginning of year 2, your financial picture would look like this:

Value of building	$1,200,000
Loan due (original cost)	1,000,000
Equity, or net worth	$ 200,000

Naturally, next year's dollars would be worth only 80% of last year's dollars, but the $200,000 increase in your net worth is still worth a real solid $160,000 in constant dollars. Or, to put it another way, $200,000 next year will still buy you $160,000 worth of goodies.

Before being boggled by the thought of owning a million dollars worth of property, remember that an ordinary run-down tract house in a coastal city of California can be worth $150,000. Thus, a million dollars worth of real estate is about seven very ordinary homes. Obtaining this much property in the course of a year is about as difficult as falling off a log. Getting your properties for no money down and making them pay for themselves without any negative cash flow is harder—but it *is* possible—if you know how.

Tycoons know how to do it, and so will you.

I've taught over 15,000 people like you how to think like a Tycoon at my marathon weekend seminars. They cost about $350. Most of my ex-students are now earning more money than they can spend (and paying less taxes). Much of my best material is in this book. Read it carefully. Do half of what I tell you here and you'll be a millionaire in two years!

CHAPTER 22
New Directions

I've taught you how to make a million dollars in two years, and no doubt a substantial portion of my readers (hopefully you among them), will have the stamina to achieve financial independence in the near future. What will you do then? From my life you can see that merely being well-off didn't insure happiness. But as Mae West said, "I've been poor and miserable and I've been rich and miserable, and rich is better." Not that I'm particularly miserable. Things are going rather well lately.

I learned that once you've obtained financial independence, you can do whatever you want. You can move out of undesirable situations to a climate or among people you find more enjoyable. The world is wide open. You can write, teach, or politic. And if you are rich, people listen. You might go back to page one of this book and start doing all those things I told you were a waste of time (before you were rich)—like getting high, buying a terrific car, going around the world. You can be promiscuous or even get drunk until you tire of it. But you will have freedom in a world that permits very very few people to be free. **You can do as you will with all the days of your life.**

You've read through my book now. Perhaps you wonder how I spend my personal time and my freedom: I've avoided the trap of being tied down by business ventures and properties. I hired a bright associate to handle rent collections and administrative details. I'm free to come and go as I please. I give my *Tycoon Class Seminars* twice a year because

246

I enjoy meeting new, interesting, ambitious people. I zip off to Europe, Africa, or Asia several months every year. I explore new investment opportunities or look after old ones. Every deal I make now has to involve those I enjoy working with. Every venture has to have a minimum of aggravation and maximum of fun for me.

Right now I'd like to buy a part of a resort in some friendly tax-haven country like the Cayman Islands, perhaps Hong Kong or Thailand. To be of interest, a deal has to be financially sound, but maximum profit is no longer my primary goal. A pleasant climate, meeting attractive, intelligent people, good food, a government that doesn't hassle me—that's all I ask for in a business venture.

Animals have been eating other animals since the beginning of time. Civilized Americans now consume each other with due process of law: The "poor" majority steals from a productive and harder-working minority. Learning and teaching ways to preserve the products of one's own enterprising—our hard-earned money—has been my most recent project. If you're ambitious and hard-working you will have the same problem. How can you keep what you've worked for from a cynical, rapacious government?

When I am treated unfairly by some petty bureaucrat in the Internal Revenue Service, for instance, I no longer have to cringe and give in to avoid crippling legal expenses. I can fight back. For starters, I can afford to hire the best lawyers. It's unfair that you have to be rich and prominent to have a chance at justice, but that's the way it is. Best of all, like other Tycoons, I have the luxury of having little or no personal contact with the unreasonable I.R.eSSers. I can join and even run for office with the Libertarian Party, whose main goal is the abolition of the income tax. I can fight an unfair and inhuman system with my books and lectures. It is possible for me to render public service by exposing stupidities that need to be exposed.

As you see, I am getting my kicks by solving my problems (and yours), having fun and making money doing it. By the way, there is never an end to *problems* no matter how much money you have. Having "do-it-yourself" projects, preferably projects that will also help other people, filling needs, keeps me truly happy. I am happy and satisfied. I'm no longer looking for any guru to give me a life plan. Nor do I want to be your guru or leader. Life is a do-it-yourself project. I do want to help you be self-sufficient, busy, productive, and adding a bit each day to the collective wealth of the world, and the comfort, pleasure, and *freedom* of everyone in it.

Once you've made it financially, I think you'll become a much better person. You can be generous with your time and money in a way that was not possible before. Self-indulgence in illegal, immoral, or fattening pleasures isn't as much of a thrill as it once was. It's there for the taking. Ho hum! So what do you do for encores? You think about public service. You think about how you can give something back to society. You think about getting your message out to the fuzzy-thinking leftists who want a revolution that will make America an unfree country, a "socialist paradise" where anyone with an original idea goes to jail. So that is where I am starting: In jail. I have been accepted by San Quentin Prison and Pleasanton Federal Prison to give my *Tycoon Classes* to inmates. I won't make a dime, but maybe it will help some former thieves and fuzzy-thinking leftists in the pokey realize that there are other possibilities: The Free Enterprise System, if left alone, can still produce the best products, the best people, and the best society that this world has ever known.

Hopefully you have enjoyed this book and will drop me a note letting me know how you felt about it. How can I improve on later versions? In any event, I hope this book will help you get where you want to be!

In earlier editions of this book I offered to answer any reader questions free of charge. As *Tycoon* became a bestseller, this policy didn't leave me enough time to eat or sleep, much less do any of my own real estate deals. Now with each written question I ask for a donation to my favorite charity, the Free Enterprise Society, preferably cash. You want me to call you about any personal matter, answer a question, or just to chat? A $20 bill gets you five, maybe ten minutes of my time. Put your questions in writing and I'll call you back, collect.

All the best wishes to you,
Bill "Tycoon" Greene

Reading List

You don't make a dime sitting home and reading, but you can't go off half-cocked either. Here's Bill's list of the best books for you to read. The first three are essential. All prices subject to change—due to inflation.

REALTY BLUEBOOK, c/o Bill Greene, P. O. Box 810, Mill Valley, CA 94942. $15.00 includes postage and handling. This fat manual contains loan amortization tables, contract forms, checklists to use when buying property. It summarizes laws affecting real estate and gives tax hints. It is the "Bible" of the real estate world. Very technical material is made simple. We got it for our readers "wholesale." Phone below.

TAX REVOLT, written and published by Bill "Tycoon" Greene, Box 810, Mill Valley, CA 94942. $16 includes postage and handling. Phone orders taken with VISA/Master, (415) 383-8264. A continuation of *Think Like a Tycoon*, this 440-page hardbound book, printed in large type for easy reading shows you how to avoid paying taxes on your hard-earned profits and how to make another two million at a stroke by creating tax-shelter investments for sale to others. Other topics include almost every ploy and scheme known to modern man for avoiding taxes. These involve forming your own church, foreign corporations and trusts, joining the subterranean economy, and developing a severe case of bad breath before your tax audit. In the same humorous style as this book, *Tax Revolt* takes you to the stratospheric world of the international wheeler dealer who teaches San Quentin convicts to be Tycoons while launching a space satellite to broadcast religious programs and collect tax free donations. If you liked this book, you must read *Tax Revolt*.

101 NEW LOOPHOLES is Bill Greene's latest book. Call or write Bill to order it at $6 per copy. This book shows you how to use and profit from the new (1981-1985) tax law.

LANDLORDING, by Leigh Robinson, c/o Bill Greene (as above). $17.00. This book is so good Bill wishes he had written it himself. It is full of entertaining practical knowledge of tools, eviction techniques, and forms. It contains all the practical information you need to manage property effectively. A **must** for any landlord. It's always "sold out" at stores, so we've laid in a supply just for our readers.

HOW TO MAKE MONEY TWENTY FOUR HOURS A DAY, by Elbert Lee. $10. Elbert was one of my students. He took my *Tycoon Techniques,* put them to use, and reportedly made his own million. Then he wrote this great little book. Written from the point of view of a young black man who started off poor, it has lots of valuable information. Order from Bill Greene.

HOW TO BUY DISTRESS PROPERTY by Bill Greene (325 pages, 8½" x 11" manual) $55. If you've ever wondered how *some* people are able to buy wholesale, picking up choice real estate deals for 25¢ on the dollar, this technical manual shows you how. The handbook for Bill's $350 Seminar on California Distress Property, it spells out complex bidding procedures that scare off the general public. It also lists trustees in bankruptcy, tax sales, public administrators, and many other sources maintaining distress sale mailing lists. All states have similar opportunities but this book is California oriented. Order with money back guarantee from Bill Greene.

HOW TO INSPECT A HOUSE, by George Hoffman, Woodward Books, Box 773, Corte Madera, California. Available in bookstores. *Do not order from Bill Greene.* All you will need to know about making an intelligent physical appraisal of real property by an unusually intelligent former local building inspector. Highly recommended!

HOW TO USE LEVERAGE TO MAKE MONEY IN LOCAL REAL ESTATE, by George Bockl, Prentice Hall, Inc., Englewood Cliffs, New Jersey. When you feel yourself running out of steam, this will give you another shot of adrenalin—lots of new ideas. An inspiration from a Milwaukee real estate man who started from scratch to make over a million in real estate. Available at bookstores. Don't order from B. G.

PRACTICAL INTERNATIONAL TAX PLANNING (Former title: *How to Use Foreign Tax Havens*), 1979, by Attorney Marshall J. Langer, The Practicing Law Institute, B. G. McDonald, Book Sales Manager, 810 7th Avenue, New York, NY 10019. $40.00 (includes postage and handling). If you have a high net worth and want to get fancy, this book will provide you with many useful ideas. The author explains concepts used by wealthy individuals and corporations to reduce taxes with "offshore" operations.

HOW TO GET RICH IN REAL ESTATE, by Robert W. Kent, Prentice Hall, Inc., Englewood Cliffs, New Jersey. At most bookstores. This guy thinks that "Aunt Tobys," his nickname for small urban apartments, are the only way to fly, so if three- to twelve-unit buildings in the city are your bag, read this. This book deals with the real estate market in various cities.

SUE THE B★ST★ARDS, by Douglas Matthews, Arbor House, New York. $2.95, out of print. Get it at the public library. An entertaining book about how to use the small claims court. Well worth reading.

HOW I TURNED $1000 INTO THREE MILLION IN REAL ESTATE—IN MY SPARE TIME, by William Nickerson, Simon and Schuster, Oakland, California. $10.95. At your public library or bookstore. Truly one of the books that turned *me* on to making it in real estate. A bit dated now since the days it was a best seller in the '50s.

THE MONOPOLY GAME and DOUBLE YOUR MONEY IN REAL ESTATE EVERY TWO YEARS by Dave Glubetich, c/o Bill Greene. $9.95 each. Written by a northern California realtor who has a lot of common sense. These books are easy, quick reading. As a realtor he spouts the line you'll hear from the best members of his profession. He tells me he is aiming his work toward the average guy with limited horizons. He doesn't mind negative cash flow, book has been a national bestseller.

CRIMINAL TAX FRAUD, by Crowley. $30. Tricks of the trade used by high-priced tax lawyers to keep their clients in the chips and out of the pokey. Despite the high price of this book, for those worried about IRS persecution it is the best investment you'll ever make. It shows how *not to get caught,* the basic rule being "Keep your mouth shut" when the IRS comes to call and don't give them any leads, clues, or ex-lovers to interview. Though written for lawyers, it reads like a novel and is very *funny.* Get it! Also get on the mailing list for the Practicing Law Institute's many seminars and publications on tax shelters, international tax havens, real estate, etc. Write: Mrs. B. G. McDonald, Book Sales, PLI, 810 7th Avenue, New York, NY 10019.

MASTER TAX GUIDE, Commerce Clearing House, 4025 W. Peterson Avenue, Chicago, IL 60646. $7.50. A 500-page "Bible" of federal tax accountants. CCH publishes a number of books, educational cassettes and newsletters, primarily for lawyers and accountants.

WAKE UP THE FINANCIAL GENIUS INSIDE YOU, by Mark O. Haroldson, mail orders to Bill Greene. $10. Short, good, and very inspirational. Easy, worthwhile spare-time reading.

Newsletters and Other Publications

Mark Skousen, Editor, *Personal Finance,* $48 per year (24 issues). From Bill Greene. Aimed at the hard money enthusiast (coins, gold, and Swiss francs), it's far more intelligently written than most of the doomsday-predicting publications. Some ideas could be worth far more than the cost of a subscription. Ideas on real estate tend to be too general or too impractical (Example, Aug. 1979: "Now is the time to invest in single-family homes in Rhodesia/Zimbabwe"). But stuff like that does tend to open your eyes beyond the city limits of your own home town. They are on top of current events and their analysis of trends is penetrating. I'm sure that physicians and dentists go right out and buy what is advertised: diamonds, gold, books on tax avoidance and coin collecting. But these ads are a good way to see how the winds are blowing. The best material on taxes finds its way into the highly recommended sister publication, *Tax Angles* (below).

Mark Skousen, Editor, *Tax Angles,* $24 per year (12 issues). Sample: $2. A truly excellent service and good value for money. It's a 4-page newsletter, and unlike most of them that are 89% B.S., this one often has usable hard info. Order from Bill Greene.

Bill Greene, Editor and Publisher, *Tycoon Newsletter.* At $2 per year this has to be the bargain of the century. The catch is that Bill only puts out a newsletter when he feels there is something important to say. That could be ten times a year or twice. Also, he doesn't want checks. If you want to risk a $2 bill to be on the mailing list, you pays your money and you takes what you gets. But if you order any book, tape, or other product from Bill Greene, you'll get one newsletter free. Box 810, Mill Valley, CA 94942.

Mark O. Haroldsen, Publisher, *Financial Freedom Report,* $36 per year and well worth it. You may subscribe through me, Bill "Tycoon" Greene, Box 810, Mill Valley CA 94941 (Visa or MasterCharge by phone 415-383-8264). This fat monthly magazine is the largest circulation real estate periodical in America. Aimed at the "embryo" Tycoon, it has inspirational success stories, lots of "how-to-do-it" tips, and interesting ads for real estate deals and business gadgets unobtainable elsewhere. Some have said that Haroldsen makes more money talking and writing about it than doing it. They are probably right. But Mark *did* very well in real estate before he turned his interest to writing his best seller *Wake Up the Financial Genius* . . . (see book reviews). He's found a *need,* and he fills it very well. Highly recommended.

A. D. Kessler, Publisher, *Creative Real Estate,* $27 per year, sample issue $2.75 if you mention Bill "Tycoon" Greene; Box 2446, Leucadia, CA 92024. This monthly magazine is aimed at the "Big Shot" Tycoon who already owns a million in property—or the broker who handles very big deals. I get some of my best ideas from this publication. But it's technical and definitely not for the beginner.

David Glubetich, Publisher, *Impact Real Estate Reports,* $99 per year. Very useful material. Not quite for the novice aimed at by Haroldsen, and not as stratospheric as *Creative Real Estate.* Each month he does a different report. Get a sample report for $6 from among these titles: Buying Single-Family Homes, Syndications, Renovating Run-down Properties, or (my favorite) Using Options in Real Estate. If the one you select is out of print, we'll pick out a good one for you.